The Politics of Crisis Management

D0885665

Crisis management has become a defining feature of contemporary governance. In times of crisis, communities and members of organizations expect their leaders to minimize the impact while critics and bureaucratic competitors make use of social media to blame incumbent rulers and their policies. In this extreme environment, policymakers must somehow establish a sense of normality and foster collective learning from the crisis experience. In the new edition of this uniquely comprehensive analysis, the authors examine how strategic leaders deal with the challenges they face, the political risks and opportunities they encounter, the pitfalls they must avoid, and the paths toward reform they may pursue. The book is grounded in decades of collaborative, cross-national, and multidisciplinary case study research and has been updated to include new insights and examples from the last decade. This is an original and important contribution from experts in public policy and international security.

ARJEN BOIN is Professor of Public Institutions and Governance at the Institute of Political Science, Leiden University.

PAUL 'T HART is Professor of Public Administration at the Utrecht School of Governance, which he joined in 2001. Since June 2011 he has also been Associate Dean at the Netherlands School of Government in The Hague, a position he also held between 2002 and 2005.

ERIC STERN is Professor of Political Science at the College of Emergency Preparedness, Homeland Security and Cyber-Security at University at Albany (SUNY) and senior fellow at CRISMART, Swedish Defense University and the Disaster Research Center, University of Delaware.

BENGT SUNDELIUS is Professor of Government at Uppsala University and the Swedish Defence University, and Strategic Advisor to the Director General of the Swedish Civil Contingencies Agency.

The Politics of Crisis Management

Public Leadership under Pressure

Arjen Boin
Universiteit Leiden

Paul 't Hart
Universiteit Utrecht

Eric Stern
University at Albany (SUNY)

Bengt Sundelius
The Swedish Defence University

CAMBRIDGE
UNIVERSITY PRESS

CAMBRIDGE
UNIVERSITY PRESS

University Printing House, Cambridge CB2 8BS, United Kingdom

One Liberty Plaza, 20th Floor, New York, NY 10006, USA

477 Williamstown Road, Port Melbourne, VIC 3207, Australia

314–321, 3rd Floor, Plot 3, Splendor Forum, Jasola District Centre, New Delhi – 110025, India

79 Anson Road, #06–04/06, Singapore 079906

Cambridge University Press is part of the University of Cambridge.

It furthers the University's mission by disseminating knowledge in the pursuit of education, learning, and research at the highest international levels of excellence.

www.cambridge.org
Information on this title: www.cambridge.org/9781107118461

© Arjen Boin, Paul 't Hart, Eric Stern, and Bengt Sundelius 2017

First published 2017
5th printing 2018

Printed in the United Kingdom by Clays, St Ives plc

A catalog record for this publication is available from the British Library.

Library of Congress Cataloging-in-Publication Data
Names: Boin, Arjen, author. | Hart, Paul 't, author. | Stern, Eric, author. | Sundelius, Bengt, author.
Title: The politics of crisis management: public leadership under pressure / Arjen Boin, Universiteit Leiden, Paul 't Hart, Universiteit Utrecht, Eric Stern, the Swedish National Defence College, Bengt Sundelius, the Swedish National Defence University.
Description: Second edition. | New York : Cambridge University Press, 2016. | First edition entered under title.
Identifiers: LCCN 2016023870| ISBN 9781107118461 (Hardback) | ISBN 9781107544253 (Paperback)
Subjects: LCSH: Crisis management in government.
Classification: LCC JF1525.C74 B65 2016 | DDC 352.3– dc23 LC record available at https://lccn.loc.gov/2016023870

ISBN 978-1-107-11846-1 Hardback
ISBN 978-1-107-54425-3 Paperback

Contents

Figures

Tables

Introduction to the Second Edition

The original edition of this book was published in late 2005. Ten years on, the salience of its topic is undiminished. In the past decade, the world has seen many natural catastrophes, industrial accidents, high-profile acts of terrorism, crowd tragedies, cyber scares, infrastructure break-downs, mass shootings, migration flows, and humanitarian emergencies. There is a growing awareness that in an increasingly interconnected world, crises do not stop at borders and can span entire regions or even assume a global scale.

Public expectations of governments and their leaders in times of crisis remain high. Public leaders are expected to be prepared for a wide variety of contingencies; they must "ramp up" their performance when a crisis emerges. At the same time, it is becoming increasingly clear that the tasks of crisis leadership require more than organizing an effective response. Leaders must build and support transboundary collaboration and transnational institutions that can effectively deal with the borderless nature of contemporary crises.

Much has happened over the past decade in the world of crisis man-agement. It is fair to say that crisis management has become a profession, an industry, and a growing community of practice and research. In many governments and corporations, there are now more dedicated roles, high-level bodies, training and exercise programs, conferences, and high-tech command and communication facilities than there were a decade ago. A cross-disciplinary array of researchers, consultants, soft-ware developers, and manufacturers push the trends toward professionalization, propelled by ever-growing demand from both the corporate and the public sectors. This is perhaps what one might expect in the risk societies that the advanced nations have become. Citizens, markets, media, and politicians expect that risk is minimized, threats are mitigated, and crises are effectively combated. Leaders who fail to take this seriously will lose credibility, support or even their job when caught by a crisis.

The response to the first edition of the book neatly dovetails this trend. It has struck a chord, both with students and practitioners. As authors of the book, we were fortunate enough to receive invitations to speak to, train, exercise, and evaluate crisis managers from a wide range of countries and sectors. Even today, the book continues to be widely used in courses worldwide and in several languages. The feedback we have received during the many encounters with practitioners, students, and colleagues has been inspiring. It has become part of the industry. Due to the continuing demand, we owe it to our readers to produce a thoroughly updated edition that takes into account what has happened in the last decade, both in practice (new cases, new phenomena, new challenges) and in the world of crisis research (new concepts, new empirical research, new insights).

The text before you is the outcome of this effort. We have retained the basic structure of the previous version with five strategic challenges of crisis leadership as the backbone and organizing principle. But we have thoroughly updated and revised the substance of our arguments in each of the chapters, reflecting what we hold to be the current state of the art in crisis research. We have also introduced many new case examples.

The rewriting of this book has been a team effort. We are deeply grateful for the help and support of many excellent students and colleagues, too numerous to name here. We single out a few people who have been instrumental. David Schelfhout at Utrecht University helped to mine the post-2005 crisis literature. Lavinia Cadar at Crisisplan provided much-needed editorial support in highly efficient fashion. John Haslam at Cambridge University Press responded positively to our proposal for an update and waited patiently for us to deliver. Margaret Puskar-Pasewicz provided the final copy editing of our manuscript. We thank our colleagues at the Utrecht School of Governance, Leiden University's Institute of Political Science, Crisisplan, the Disaster Research Center at the University of Delaware, and the CRISMART team at the Swedish National Defence University. We thank the Swedish Civil Contingencies Agency (MSB) for financial support.

These colleagues have been part of our "crisis environment" and provide ongoing reminders that we are not alone in this line of inquiry. We have benefited greatly from the progress they have made in their own studies on crisis management over the last decade, and we hope this new edition does justice to their endeavors.

ARJEN BOIN, PAUL 'T HART, ERIC STERN, BENGT SUNDELIUS

December 2015

1 Managing Crises
Five Strategic Leadership Tasks

1.1 Crisis Management and Public Leadership

Governance has increasingly become a matter of crisis management. Crises routinely shatter the peace and order of societies. They arrive as "rude surprises" and "inconvenient truths" wreaking havoc and destroying the legitimacy of public institutions. Natural disasters, the collapse of financial systems, high-tech catastrophes, lone-wolf terrorists, mass revolts, new pandemics, geopolitical powder kegs, and cyber attacks – the list of potential crises is long and growing.

Disruptions of the dominant order are as old as life itself. The Bible can be read as a catalog of the frightening crises that have beset humankind since time immemorial. Most of the world still confronts these "old" crises on a regular basis. But we also see new crises – and new twists on more familiar ones – that define the times we live in: Lehman Brothers and the Euro crisis, Arab Spring and failed states, Fukushima and Deepwater Horizon, Mumbai and Paris, Ebola and ISIS.[1]

In such times of crisis, citizens look to their leaders. The system is out of kilter, and leaders are expected to chart pathways out of the crisis. The public expects them to avert the threat or at least minimize the damage of the crisis at hand. They must explain what went wrong. They must adapt, change or abandon routine ways of operating where needed and create public confidence in the new status quo. They should work toward enhancing community resilience, preparing society for future shocks.[2]

Crises provide real-world "stress tests" to the resilience of political systems and the crisis management capacities of leaders. They play out against a backdrop of public expectations (influenced in part by leaders themselves) that can be very challenging to meet. In some cases, the quality of crisis management makes the difference between life and death, chaos and order, breakdown and resilience. When governments and their leaders respond well to a crisis, the damage is limited. When emerging vulnerabilities and threats are adequately assessed and addressed, some potentially devastating contingencies simply do not happen. When crisis management fails, the impact increases.

Crisis management bears directly on the lives of citizens and the well-being of societies. The notion of "crisis management" as used in this book is shorthand for a set of interrelated and extraordinary governance challenges. Crisis management is effective when a combination of tasks is accomplished: an emerging crisis is swiftly detected, responders understand what is happening, critical decisions are made by the right people, the efforts of responders are orchestrated, government communicates with its citizens, and the aftermath of a crisis is marked by proper accountability procedures and a willingness to collectively learn the lessons of that crisis.

None of these tasks are easy to perform. Information may not be forthcoming and communication is often difficult. The crisis response typically involves many organizations, public and private, preexisting as well as newly emerging, increasingly also beyond national borders. Mass and social media scrutinize and assess the performance of crisis leaders and the impact of crisis response strategies, providing critics with many fora to air their grievances. It is in this atmosphere that governments and their leaders must shape response and recovery operations, communicate with stakeholders, discover what went wrong, account for their actions, initiate steps for improvement, and eventually, seek to (re)establish a sense of normalcy. Crises create extraordinary circumstances for governance.

At the same time, crises provide leaders with extraordinary opportunities to demonstrate their capacity to lead and fulfill aims that would be impossible to achieve under normal circumstances. When a sense of shock, vulnerability, loss, and outrage pervades a community, crisis can produce strong criticism of the existing institutional order and of the policy processes that underpin it. Many crises nurture an appetite for radical change. Astute leaders will not hesitate to exploit this "window of opportunity."[3] As Rahm Emanuel, President Obama's chief of staff during the financial crisis, put it: "you never want a serious crisis to go to waste."[4]

This book is about public leadership in times of crisis. It discusses how presidents and mayors, local politicians and elected administrators, public managers and top civil servants answer to public expectations, or fail to do so, when leadership is needed most. It examines how political, organizational, and community leaders take up this essential and increasingly salient task of contemporary governance. It maps the manifold challenges that leaders face in a crisis and identifies the pitfalls that they face in their efforts to manage crises.

This introductory chapter outlines our perspective on crisis management. We discuss the nature and dynamics of crisis events. We explore their origins. And we outline the strategic tasks of crisis management around which this book revolves.

1.2   The Nature of Crises

The term "crisis" frequently appears in book titles, newspaper headlines, political discourse, and social conversation. It generally refers to an undesirable and unexpected situation: when we talk about crisis, we mean that something bad threatens a person, group, organization, culture, society, or, when we think really big, the world at large. Something must be done, urgently, to make sure that this threat will not materialize.

In academic discourse, a crisis marks a phase of disorder in the development of a person, an organization, a community, an ecosystem, a business sector, or a polity.[5] A personal crisis denotes a period of emotional turmoil or illness, preceded and followed by mental stability or physical repair. An economic crisis refers to a period of severe decline in business activity and profitability, consumer confidence, and overall economic strength. An ecological crisis refers to a changing environment that threatens the survival of a species or population. A political regime crisis refers to a situation in which political elites and institutions are at risk of being replaced by an alternative set of actors and arrangements.

Crises, in other words, are critical junctures in the lives of systems – times at which their ability to function can no longer be taken for granted. We speak of a crisis when people experience (or, as we shall see later in this book, deliberately "frame") such critical junctures as urgent threats that must be addressed as a matter of top priority. In our definition of crisis, a social system – a community, an organization, a policy sector, a country, or an entire region – experiences an urgent threat to its basic structures or fundamental values, which harbors many "unknowns" and appears to require a far-reaching response.[6] This definition has three key components: threat, urgency, and uncertainty. Let us take a closer look at these crisis components.

Crises occur when members of a social system sense that the core values or life-sustaining features of a system have come under *threat*.[7] Think of widely shared values such as safety and security, justice and rule of law, welfare and health, integrity and civil liberties, which are jeopardized or de-prioritized as a result of (looming) violence, public disorder, destruction, erosion, or other forms of adversity. Consider the cascading impacts when critical infrastructures supporting our way of life – such as electricity, gas, water, or communication systems – break down and disrupt lifelines and daily routines for a prolonged time period. The more important the value(s) or structures under threat, the deeper the sense of crisis.

In many crises, it is obvious what is at stake. For instance, when a wildfire threatens the lives and livelihoods of people, many will share the same deeply felt sense of crisis. But it is not always this clear cut. A threat is not always measurable in terms of widespread physical or material damage. For example, acts of terrorism typically hit comparatively few, but instill fear and outrage among many. The death toll may be insignificant in comparison with the insidious threats of daily life (e.g., traffic deaths, air pollution, deadly diseases), but it is the very act of terrorism, the timing, location, and target, that creates a widely shared sense of threat. Many terror attacks are specifically designed to make people worry not only about what has happened to others (somewhere else) but what *might* happen to them.[8]

We only speak of crisis when a salient threat generates a sense of *urgency*. It is important to understand that urgency, like threat, is often a socially constructed rather than an inherent property of a situation. Some serious threats do not pose immediate problems: think of climate change or future pension deficits. A crisis denotes a situation when people experience threats as "clear and present dangers" that must be addressed now rather than later. The perception that time is at a premium is therefore a defining element of crisis: the threat is here, it is real, and it must be dealt with as soon as possible.

Urgency can be experienced quite differently depending on one's proximity to the crisis. Personally threatened individuals will have a more pressing sense of urgency than distant observers. Similar differences can be found within a response network. Urgency is more self-evident and non-negotiable, for instance, at the tactical and operational level of disaster management, riot policing, or counterterrorism: incident commanders sometimes have to make life-or-death decisions within minutes or seconds.[9] Leaders at the strategic level of a disaster response rarely experience the same sense of extreme urgency. They rarely have to make split-second decisions. Their attention is mostly focused on issues that play out over hours, days, or weeks. At both levels, however, urgency is experienced as a compression of time. What normally may be done in months or weeks should now be done in days, hours, or minutes.[10]

Authorities may choose to play up or play down the need for a quick decision. In crisis negotiations, for instance, adversaries use urgency as a strategy: they impose ultimatums or deny the time sensitivity of a problem. Authorities can and do treat time and urgency as a lever to increase or release pressure on their colleagues and adversaries. But adversaries do the same, as they try to coax government into action or seek to delegitimize governmental intentions.

We only speak of a crisis when in addition to perceptions of threat and urgency, there is also a high degree of *uncertainty*. This uncertainty pertains both to the nature and the potential consequences of the threat: what is happening, how did it happen, what's next, how bad will it be? Uncertainty affects the search for solutions: what can we do, what happens if we select this option? Uncertainty typically applies to other factors in the crisis process as well, such as people's initial and emergent responses to the crisis.

Threat, urgency, and uncertainty are not necessarily objective, situational parameters of unsettling events; they also are semantic and strategic levers that actors can pull to influence how we think about such events. Perceptions of the same crisis events will differ among different actors in the system, sometimes even among members of the same crisis response team. Their specific roles, responsibilities, values, interests, expertise, and experiences will lead different actors to articulate and communicate their distinct views. This gives rise to the "politics of crisis management" that forms the heart of this book: in a crisis, leaders and other stakeholders will seek to impose upon their key audiences competing views about the nature and depth of the problems facing the system.

Crisis Typologies

Crises come in many shapes and sizes: man-made and natural, local and international, economic and cultural. Consequently, scholars have devoted considerable effort to developing typologies, and using these to outline approaches to managing different types of crises.[11] None has become dominant; they all serve different purposes. The three key elements of crisis identified above – threat, urgency, uncertainty – help us to understand how crises can differ and how these differences shape distinct challenges for crisis leaders.

When we focus on the threat, we can make a distinction with regard to the *locus* of crisis, in other words, what it hits. Some crises threaten the health and safety of people and their possessions as well as the community's critical infrastructures, its economic viability, and the norms and values that hold it together. These situations are usually referred to in terms of emergencies or disasters (depending on the outcome).[12] But sometimes crises pertain to the ways a community or organization is run. The performance of organizations, or the competence and integrity of key officeholders, threatens the legitimacy of an organization or public institution. We then speak of an institutional crisis.[13] As we will see, the challenges that leaders face are shaped by the nature of the crisis at hand.

We can also make a distinction about *where* the crisis hits. Crises that threaten multiple geographical or policy domains – we call them trans-boundary crises – are much harder to manage than crises that respect the man-made borders that are used to organize administrative and political response capacities. These are usually "cascading" crises: a crisis in one societal subsystem (e.g., geophysical, socio-technical, political, eco-nomic, information, or service supply) causes disruptions in others.[14]

Second, we can make a distinction based on the perceived *urgency* of the threat. The more people agree that a problem needs to be resolved quickly, the higher the crisis level. So-called creeping crises provide leaders with plenty of time to develop solutions, but the lack of urgency typically makes it harder to create the winning coalitions that are needed to push through required policy changes. When there is little time to act, on the other hand, leaders may have more authority to unilaterally impose changes.

Third, we can distinguish crises based on the level of *uncertainty*. U.S. Secretary of Defense Donald Rumsfeld famously suggested that there are "known unknowns" and "unknown unknowns."[15] When it is understood what can and should be done to counter an urgent threat, the crisis falls within the category of known unknowns. For instance, many local gov-ernments are well prepared to deal with threats that periodically recur and are relatively well understood, such as moderate hurricanes, floods, or demonstrations. Contingency plans and well-rehearsed escalation scenarios provide them with standard operating procedures well suited to situations that arise with some sort of regularity. These dangerous events can usually be dealt with through planning, training, exercising, and sufficient allocation of resources.

The hardest crises are marked by unknown unknowns. They surprise in various ways; they are fundamentally ambiguous, even messy. So much happens in such a short time, so many problems appear simultan-eously or in rapid succession, so many people do not know what to think and whom or what to trust, that a generalized sense of uncertainty emerges. These are unique events that defy conventional approaches to planning.[16] It is very difficult to plan in detail for unexpected and unknown events.

These dimensions suggest that crises can prompt different leadership challenges in different phases of the crisis trajectories. Some crises may require the rapid application of plans and professional skills; the leadership challenge is to have good plans and professional responders in place. In this book, we refer to these events in terms of emergencies. The leadership challenge presented by slow-onset, creeping crises is quite different: to detect early what is often hard to spot, grasp its long-term implications, and mobilize momentum for tackling the emerging threat before it passes some critical threshold and becomes a crisis. An institutional crisis brings yet different challenges: leaders will have to shape stakeholder perceptions that underpin the legitimacy (and thus the functioning) of public organizations. A hitherto unknown transboundary threat that unfolds in real time – the ultimate "black swan" – may well bring seemingly impossible challenges for crisis leaders. In this book, we seek to relate how these differences affect and inform the challenges that crisis leaders face.

1.3   The Origins of Crises

If a particular type of crisis were to occur repeatedly, governments could design coping strategies, write plans, and train responders. If governments could understand the causal trajectories of these events, they could even work to prevent them altogether. In fact, governments have prevented many crises over time and are prepared to deal with crises that regularly emerge. Yet, new types of crises continue to emerge, time and again. Why is that?

Theory and research about the causes of crisis have evolved over the years. Linear thinking ("big events must have big causes") has given way to a more subtle perspective that emphasizes the unintended consequences of increased complexity.[17] Crises are now understood as the result of multiple causes, which interact over time to produce threats with devastating potential. In the process leading up to a crisis, seemingly innocent factors can combine and transform into dramatically disruptive forces that threaten the system. These factors are sometimes referred to as pathogens, as they are typically present long before the crisis becomes manifest.[18] Students of natural disaster have noted, for instance, that modern society increases its vulnerability to disaster by building in places where history and technical expertise warn not to build.[19] These are "disasters waiting to happen."

An oft-debated question is whether modern systems have become less or more vulnerable to these critical breakdowns. Contemporary systems typically experience fewer breakdowns, one might argue, as they have become much better equipped to deal with routine failures. Several "modern" features of society – hospitals, computers and telephones, fire trucks and universities, safety regulation, and training – have made some types of crisis that once were rather ubiquitous relatively rare (these crises are pushed back into the emergency box). Others argue that modern society is becoming increasingly vulnerable to breakdowns: when a threat does materialize (say an electrical power outage or a train derailment), the consequences in modern, technology-dependent mass societies can be much bigger than they used to be (lower frequency but higher impact).

The notion that crises are an unwanted by-product of modernity has been popularized by Charles Perrow's theory of disasters in technological systems.[20] This theory recognizes two factors that lie at the heart of both modernization and system vulnerability: complexity and coupling. As socio-technical systems become more complex and increasingly connected (tightly coupled) to other (sub)systems, their vulnerability to disturbances increases exponentially.[21] The more complex a system becomes, the harder it is for anyone to understand it in its entirety. Tight coupling between a system's component parts and those of other systems allows for the rapid proliferation of interactions (and errors) throughout the system. In these complex, tightly coupled systems, we should thus expect periodic failures that have the potential to escalate out of control. Perrow argued that crises and disasters should be viewed as "normal" outcomes of our continuing efforts to make systems increasingly complex and tightly coupled.[22] In this perspective, the very qualities of complex systems that drive modernity also precipitate or exacerbate most, if not all, technological crises.

Perrow's theory finds support in the many empirical analyses of the financial crises that started in 2007. The world of global finance saw remarkable changes in the years leading up to the crisis that enhanced its systemic complexity and created lengthy chains of factors causing its eventual near-collapse.[23] Financial institutions had created a variety of instruments that even the experts did not fully understand. These institutions had become global behemoths, with ties to many industrial, public, and societal sectors. Capital flows occurred in highly complex and tightly coupled systems: billions could be moved in seconds, to and from places few fully grasped. When the sophisticated financial instruments began to malfunction, the global system quickly became unhinged. Unsuspected and unstoppable contagions wreaked havoc everywhere.[24]

The subsequent Euro crisis showed how collaborative arrangements designed to deal with glitches in such systems may actually further increase complexity and tighten interdependencies. As a result, structural vulnerabilities in relatively weak economies can suddenly "explode" and drag down the entire system. This creates a massive set of challenges for the crisis managers of such systems. The Eurozone crisis has exposed just how hard these challenges can be.

Nonlinear dynamics and complexity make an emerging crisis hard to detect. Perrow describes how a relatively minor glitch in a nuclear reactor (Three Mile Island) was misunderstood in the control room. The plant operators initially thought they understood the problem and applied the required technical response. The increased threat baffled the operators (they could not understand why the problem persisted). As they had misinterpreted the warning signal, the response worsened the problem. By again applying the "right" response to the wrong problem, the operators continued to exacerbate the problem. Only after a freshly arrived operator suggested the correct source of the problem did the crisis team manage – just barely – to stave off a disaster.[25]

Complex systems – including social systems such as crowds and online communities – elude straightforward understanding by policymakers who may be formally in charge of them. This creates a situation where growing vulnerabilities go unrecognized and ineffective attempts to deal with seemingly minor disturbances continue. The system thus fuels the lurking crisis.[26] Only a minor trigger is then needed to initiate a destructive cycle of escalation, which may then rapidly spread throughout the system.

Crises can have their roots far away (in a geographical sense) but in a globalized and tightly coupled world they can rapidly snowball, jumping from one system to another, gathering destructive potential along the way. The 2010 and 2011 volcanic ash cloud events are a perfect example of such cascading crises: a volcano eruption over Iceland does little damage locally but within a few days creates havoc in air traffic worldwide, causing enormous economic damage and exposing the limits of existing institutional arrangements in the global air traffic safety system for dealing with such transboundary challenges.[27]

All of this explains why the onset of some of the most notorious crises of our times was completely missed by those in charge. As the crisis process begins to unfold, policy makers do not necessarily see anything out of the ordinary. Everything is still in place, even though hidden interactions eat away at the pillars of the system. It is only when the crisis becomes manifest that policy makers can recognize it for what it is, and even that is a tough task (see further Chapter 2).

Is it really impossible to predict crises? Generally speaking, yes. There is seldom a clear and decisive "moment X" and "factor Y" that can be pinpointed as *the* root of the problem. Quite sophisticated early-warning systems exist in certain areas, such as meteorological and seismic modeling and flood prediction, and some pioneering efforts are under way to develop early-warning models for ethnic and international conflict.[28]

These systems may constitute the best available shot at crisis prediction, but they are far from flawless. They cannot predict exactly when and where a hurricane or flash flood will emerge. Importantly, they only work for what we refer to as emergencies or incidents (the known unknowns); they cannot predict so-called black swans (the unknown unknowns that continue to surprise modern societies everywhere). This is why our book is *not* about prevention or risk management.

1.4   The Challenges of Strategic Crisis Management

Our definition of crisis encompasses a wide variety of critical episodes and junctures. They can be the result of hurricanes and floods, earthquakes and tsunamis, financial meltdowns and surprise attacks, terrorist attacks and hostage takings, environmental threats and exploding factories, infrastructural dramas and organizational decline – unimaginable threats that become real. What these events have in common is that they create a distinctive and sometimes seemingly impossible task environment for leaders: they require urgent decisions while essential information about causes and consequences remains unavailable; they require effective communications to a variety of audiences with widely differing needs, views, and frames of reference. They also require that leaders explain vulnerabilities in existing institutional structures, values, and routines.

A crisis can inflict a major shock on a community, undermining or limiting the very capacities needed to deal with crisis. The job of crisis leadership, then, is to limit the depth and duration of the chaos, bewilderment, helplessness, and anger that this tends to cause, and to mobilize and harness coping capacity from within the community. The set of tasks that leaders must perform in these situations of collective stress together comprise what we refer to as crisis management.

This book captures what public leadership at the strategic level can do to minimize the consequences of – and make the most of the opportunities associated with – crisis. The distinctive contribution we seek to make is to highlight the strategic, political dimensions of crisis leadership: issues of conflict, power, and legitimacy.[29] The adjective "strategic" is important here: this book focuses on leadership that pertains to the *overall direction of crisis responses and the political process surrounding these responses*.

Crises are occasions for public leadership. Citizens whose lives are affected by critical contingencies expect the people in charge to make critical decisions and provide direction even in the most difficult circumstances. So do the journalists who produce the stories that help shape the crisis in the minds of the public. And so do members of parliament, public interest groups, institutional watchdogs, and other voices on the political stage that monitor and influence the behavior of leaders. It does not matter that these expectations may be misplaced, unfair, or illusory. They are real in their political consequences. When events or episodes are widely experienced as a crisis, leadership is expected. If incumbent elites fail to step forward, others might well seize the opportunity to fill the gap.

In studying strategic crisis leadership, we employ a functional rather than a person-centered or relational perspective. We are not interested in personal characteristics (such as intelligence, perseverance, or charisma) that may or may not have an impact on crisis management. Rather, we discuss strategic crisis leadership in terms of five critical tasks.[30] We argue that the performance of these tasks has the potential to affect the crisis outcome.[31]

It does so in at least two ways. First, a well-calibrated and well-organized response to crisis and post-crisis challenges helps to limit the impact of a crisis and facilitate recovery. The sooner that relevant resources reach a disaster site, the more people may be saved. The faster an appropriate technological fix is implemented, the sooner a critical infrastructure may function again. Second, a well-organized and effectively communicated response and recovery helps to repair – or even enhance – public trust in the leadership and the functioning of societal institutions.

These tasks are not exclusively reserved for elected or appointed executive leaders. On the contrary, these tasks are often performed throughout the crisis response network. We assert that anyone holding public office can play a role in the execution of strategic crisis management tasks. Crises can trigger situational leadership: confronted with extreme and fast-paced contingencies, people both inside and outside government take actions, make decisions, and assume authority roles unforeseen by formal plans and regulations. We do believe, however, that the formal leaders carry a special responsibility for making sure that these tasks – which we specify in the following section – are properly addressed and executed (if not by the leaders then by others). They are *strategic* because the effective execution of these tasks sets the course for the response and its outcomes.

This book is thus not so much about operational or tactical crisis response and their distinctive leadership challenges, however important these obviously are in many crisis episodes.[32] That does not mean we will ignore the operational and tactical dimensions of crisis management. To grasp the challenges of strategic crisis leadership, we must at least touch on the more technical aspects of crisis management (e.g., decision tools, communications systems, or the use of tort law).

In this book, we concentrate on *crisis leadership in democratic settings*. The embedded norms and institutional characteristics of liberal democracies constrain the range of responses that public leaders can legitimately consider and implement, and in democracies, political leaders are publicly held to account for their crisis behavior. Many crises could be terminated relatively quickly if governments could simply "write off" certain people, groups, or territories, or when they can take draconian measures to deal with threats, regardless of the human costs or moral implications of their actions. In countries with a free press, rule of law, political opposition, and a solid public accountability structure, this is not possible (and widely seen as deeply undesirable). In a liberal democracy, public leaders must manage a crisis in the context of a delicate political, legal, and moral order that forces them to trade off considerations of effectiveness and efficiency against other embedded values – something leaders of non-democracies do not have to worry about as much.[33]

Exercising crisis leadership in the contemporary context is a tall order. Citizens across the modern world have become at once more fearful and less tolerant of major threats to public health, safety, and prosperity. They have little patience for imperfections, interruptions, and delays in public service delivery. They expect governments to keep them safe, yet they have come to fear glitches and learned to see more of what they fear. As a result, public demand for comprehensive safety and security has become insatiable. In this culture of fear, sometimes referred to as the "risk society," it always becomes a bone of political contention whether the government of the day is really "delivering" safety and security. This becomes a particularly paramount topic when the social order has been clearly compromised by a critical threat.[34]

In liberal democracies, crisis management often is a deeply controversial and intensely political activity. A crisis sets in motion extensive follow-up reporting, investigations by political forums, as well as civil and criminal juridical proceedings. It is not uncommon for public officials and agencies to be singled out as the responsible actors for prevention, preparedness, and responding effectively to the crisis at hand. Many a crisis aftermath turns into a morality play, in which leaders come under severe pressure to atone for past sins. If they refuse to acknowledge their failings, real or not, the crisis will not end (at least not any time soon).[35]

Such is the backdrop against which democratic crisis leadership is to be exercised. We describe in this book what crisis leadership can do to defend and enhance the functioning of societal systems at times when they are under great pressure. Let us now turn to outlining the five key tasks that will help crisis leaders manage a response in an effective and legitimate way.

1.5   The Five Critical Tasks of Strategic Crisis Leadership

We define strategic crisis leadership in terms of five critical tasks:

- *Sense making*: collecting and processing information that will help crisis managers to detect an emerging crisis and understand the significance of what is going on during a crisis.
- *Decision making* and *coordinating*: making critical calls on strategic dilemmas and orchestrating a coherent response to implement those decisions.
- *Meaning making*: offering a situational definition and narrative that is convincing, helpful, and inspiring to citizens and responders.
- *Accounting*: explaining in a public forum what was done to prevent and manage the crisis and why.
- *Learning*: determining the causes of a crisis, assessing the strengths and weaknesses of the responses to it, and undertaking remedial action based on this understanding.

Task 1: Sense Making

It is very difficult to predict crises. But it is possible to detect an emerging crisis in time to shift the course of events in a more favorable direction. Early detection means faster deployment of resources, which, in turn, can save lives. But all too often, escalating crises come as a complete surprise to leaders. It is hard to recognize from vague, ambivalent, and contradictory signals that something out of the ordinary is developing. The critical nature of these developments – and their political implications – is rarely self-evident.

Once a crisis becomes manifest, crisis responders will want to understand what is happening in order to take effective measures to deal with the consequences. They must assess how threatening and urgent the events are, to what or whom, and consider how the situation might develop in the period to come. Leaders must build systems and implement methods that will help appraise the threat and diagnose what the crisis is about. Even if the events that trigger a crisis are highly dramatic, which is not always the case – jet planes hitting skyscrapers, a deadly assault on the editorial offices of a satirical magazine, an explosion at a petrochemical plant – a comprehensive and integrated strategic picture of a complex and dynamic situation never emerges by itself. Signals come from many sources: some loud, some soft, some accurate, some widely off the mark. But how to tell which is which? How are leaders to distill cogent signals from the noise of crisis? How can they make sense of this information?[36]

Task 2: Decision Making and Coordinating

Crises often confront governments and leaders with issues they do not face on a daily basis, for example, the deployment of the military, the use of lethal force, or the radical restriction of civil liberties.[37] The needs and problems triggered by the onset of crisis may be so great that the scarce resources available will have to be prioritized. Crisis decision making is about making hard calls: crisis managers have to weigh policy, political, organizational, ethical, and sometimes personal ramifications, tradeoffs, risks, and opportunities.[38] This is much like politics as usual except that in crisis circumstances the disparities between demand and supply of public resources are much bigger, the situation remains unclear and volatile, and the time to think, consult, and gain acceptance for decisions is highly restricted.

A classic example of crisis decision making is the Cuban Missile Crisis (1963). U.S. President John F. Kennedy was presented with pictures of Soviet missile installations under construction in Cuba. The photos conveyed a geostrategic reality in the making that Kennedy considered unacceptable. But what to do? Each option his advisers presented to him – an air strike, an invasion of Cuba, a naval blockade – would have a momentous impact on Soviet-American relations and possibly on world peace. With time running out and in a cloud of uncertainty about Russian intentions, Kennedy had to make a decision that could lead to nuclear war.

An effective crisis response entails more than making "big" decisions. These decisions must be implemented. The implementation of crisis decisions is usually in the hands of a diffuse network of actors. Getting things done therefore requires horizontal and vertical coordination.[39] Coordination is pivotal to prevent miscommunication, unnecessary overlap, and conflicts between governments, agencies, and actors involved in crisis operations. Even in the Cuban Missile Crisis, often regarded as a triumph of politico-military crisis management, there were serious examples of miscommunication and flawed coordination that could – under slightly different circumstances – have pushed the conflicting parties over the brink.[40]

Getting communities, businesses, and public bureaucracies to work together in times of crisis is a daunting task. Different jurisdictional competencies and different regional and national interests need to be considered. The organizations in a response network may be controlled by different political parties and coalitions. Different professional logics and organizational routines need to be aligned – quickly and seamlessly. Bureau-political "games" may undermine cooperation. In such a context, the question of who is in charge can arouse great passions. We may thus witness the "battle of the Samaritans." This is a well-documented phenomenon in the response to large-scale disasters when governments, agencies, and NGOs push different approaches to and methodologies of disaster response and recovery. As a result, it is difficult to align their actions and avoid spending a surprising amount of energy on maneuvering and squabbling.[41]

In Chapter 3, we explain how difficult it can be for leaders to control the course of crisis events. Events may simply move too fast or the number of players and processes are too numerous for control to be exercised from the top down. We show that being "at the center" of the response is of limited material relevance as crisis responses are shaped in field operations and in networks that lack clearly defined authority relations. Understanding the realities of crisis decision making and coordination thus requires not just focusing on the words and deeds of top leaders but also a thorough understanding of the broader governance context in which a crisis unfolds.[42]

Task 3: Meaning Making

In a crisis, leaders are expected to reduce uncertainty by providing an authoritative account of what is going on, why it is happening, and what needs to be done. When they have made sense of the events and have arrived at some sort of situational appraisal and made strategic policy choices, leaders must get others to accept their definition of the situation. They must impute meaning to the unfolding crisis in such a way that their efforts to manage it are enhanced. If they do not, or if they do not succeed at it, their decisions will not be understood or respected. If other actors in the crisis succeed in dominating the meaning-making process, the ability of incumbent leaders to decide and maneuver is severely constrained.

To this end, leaders are challenged to present a compelling story that describes what the crisis is about: what is at stake, what are its causes, what can be done.[43] The story should be factually correct, offer actionable advice, show empathy, and instill confidence in the crisis response. Whatever one might think about his subsequent policies, there is no disputing that President George W. Bush was highly effective in shaping the public perception of the September 11 attacks.[44]

Leaders are not always this effective. Four years after 9/11, that same President Bush appeared largely ineffective in shaping the public's understanding of what had happened in New Orleans after Hurricane Katrina.[45] After the March 2004 train bombings in Madrid, the Spanish Prime Minister José María Aznar hastily – and unconvincingly – framed the attack as yet another atrocity committed by the regional separatists of the Basque Liberation Front, a long-standing terrorist organisation that had tried to assassinate him some years earlier. That frame was challenged very effectively by an assertive and media-savvy opposition, which – as it turned out through police investigation – convincingly claimed that instead of being hit again by Basque separatists Spain was in fact receiving "pay back" from Al Qaeda for Aznar's staunch support of the U.S. invasion of Iraq. A few days after the attack, an outraged electorate voted Aznar's party out of power.[46]

Leaders are not the only ones trying to frame the crisis. News organizations use many different sources and angles in their frenetic attempts at fact-finding and interpretation. Social media provide new fora for expressing support, criticism, and outrage – for better and worse providing leaders with instant feedback regarding elite and public reactions to crisis response and communication. Among this cacophony of voices and sentiments, leaders must seek to achieve and maintain some degree of influence over the images of the crisis that circulate in the public domain. Their messages coincide and compete with those of other parties, who hold other positions and interests, who are likely to espouse various alternative definitions of the situation, and who advocate different courses of action. Censoring them is hardly a viable option in a democracy. Crises have truly become "framing contests" during which the credibility and authority of public officeholders and institutions hangs in the balance.[47]

In Chapter 4, we examine the meaning-making process in times of crisis. We argue that leadership credibility enhances the quality of crisis messaging and increases the likelihood of political survival after the crisis. We also make the point that leaders cannot depend on their pre-crisis credibility. They must excel in public and political crisis communication in these critical periods if they want to be heard, believed, and followed.

Task 4: Accounting

Governments – at least democratic ones – cannot afford to stay in crisis mode indefinitely. A sense of normalcy will have to return sooner or later, even though a complete return to the status quo as it existed before the onset of crisis may be impossible (and is often undesirable). The system of governance – its rules, its organizations, its power-holders – has to be (re)stabilized; it must regain the necessary legitimacy to perform its usual functions. Leaders cannot bring this about by unilateral decree, even if they possess the formal mandate to initiate and terminate crises in a legal sense (by declaring a state of disaster or by invoking martial law). Formal gestures can follow but never lead the mood of a community. Rendering account of what happened, and why, is a crucial task in a democracy. When done well, it can facilitate closure. Failure may prolong the crisis.

In Chapter 5, we argue that publicly investigating and rendering account of a crisis is an essential but delicate act of moving from crisis to a new normalcy. The burden of proof in accountability discussions lies with executive leaders: in a context of loss, grief, anger, bewilderment, they must establish beyond doubt that they cannot be held responsible for the occurrence or escalation of a crisis. They must show that they did the best they could, given the circumstances. Crisis-induced accountability processes can easily degenerate into "blame games" with a focus on identifying and punishing culprits and thus transforming and prolonging a crisis rather than ending it.[48] The challenge for leaders is to cope with the politics of crisis accountability without resorting to undignified and potentially self-defeating defensive tactics of blame avoidance that serve only to prolong the crisis by transforming it into a political confrontation at knife's edge.

Task 5: Learning

The fifth strategic crisis leadership task is learning. Every crisis can be thought of as a source of potential lessons for contingency planning, organizational reform, policy adaptation, and training for future crises. One would expect all of those involved to study these lessons and feed them back into organizational practices, policies, and laws.

It is often thought that crises present excellent *opportunities* to clean up and start anew. In this mode of reasoning, crises expose systems that are stuck, rusty, rigid, outdated, or otherwise inadequate. This provides momentum for repudiating and replacing them, or at least for more than incremental adjustments and innovations within them. That opportunity must be seized. Barack Obama quickly became a charismatic candidate for the U.S. presidency because his message of "change" resonated so strongly against the backdrop of the faltering Bush administration, undermined as it was by the triple crises of the war in Iraq, the hurricane Katrina fiasco, and the breakdown of the financial system.

Reforms after crises are easy to announce but hard to enact and sustain.[49] There are many cognitive and institutional barriers to learning.[50] This may result in dominant, but not necessarily accurate, lessons that become part of collective memory and a source of historical analogies for future leaders.[51] In Chapter 6, we argue that the political imperatives of crisis management are fundamentally at odds with the institutional preconditions for effective learning from crises. Their actions during and after a crisis can make the difference between a system that learns and one that does not.

At the end of this study, in Chapter 7, we offer some lessons of our own. We move from our primarily descriptive and interpretive aims and discourse into a more prescriptive mode. We present lessons for crisis leadership conveying the practical implications of our central claims. Together, these lessons constitute an agenda for improving public leadership in crises that we hope will reach, inspire, and provoke those who govern us.

Notes

1 The costs of natural and manufactured disasters continue to grow, while scenarios of future crises promise more mayhem (Clarke, 2005). Comfort et al. (2010); Helsloot et al. (2012); Dror (2014). See also http://reports.weforum.org/global-risks-2015/ (accessed July 6, 2015).
2 Comfort, Boin and Demchak (2010).
3 Kingdon (1995).
4 www.wsj.com/articles/SB122721278056345271 (accessed July 6, 2015).
5 Almond, Flanagan, and Mundt (1973); Linz and Stepan (1978); Tilly and Stinchcombe (1997).
6 Rosenthal, Charles, and 't Hart (1989, 10). See also Rosenthal, Boin, and Comfort (2001); Stern (2003); James et al. (2011); Drennan et al. (2014).
7 A threat does not have to materialize before it becomes widely seen as one. The often-cited Thomas Theorem teaches us that it is the perception that makes a threat real in its consequences. Thomas and Thomas (1928).
8 In fact, experts on terrorism label such acts as "performance violence" choreographed for maximum psychological and symbolic impact. Juergensemeyer (2003). See also Stern (2011).
9 Flin (1996); Klein (1999).
10 Boin and Renaud (2013); Fleisher (2013).
11 Pauchant and Mitroff (1992); Rosenthal and Kouzmin (1997); Gundel (2005).
12 The use of the term "disaster" usually does presuppose damage, death, and destruction. See Boin (2005) and, more broadly, Perry and Quarantelli

(2005) for a discussion of the differences between emergencies, disasters, and crises.

13 For an analysis of institutional crises, see Boin and 't Hart (2000); Alink, Boin and 't Hart (2001).

14 Galaz et al. (2011); Fortress (2014).

15 http://archive.defense.gov/Transcripts/Transcript.aspx?TranscriptID=2636 (accessed June 10, 2015).

16 Clarke (2005).

17 Bernstein et al. (2000); Buchanan (2000); Gilpin and Murphy (2008).

18 Reason (1990).

19 Steinberg (2000).

20 Perrow (1984).

21 Turner (1978); Perrow (1994).

22 Cf. Beck (1992).

23 For an excellent introduction, see Eichengreen (2002). See also Sorkin (2010), Blinder (2013); Zahariadis (2014).

24 www.gpo.gov/fdsys/pkg/GPO-FCIC/pdf/GPO-FCIC.pdf   (accessed   June 10, 2015).

25 Perrow (1984, 15–31).

26 Rijpma (1997) argues that redundancy – an often-prescribed tool to help prevent incidents – may actually help cause them.

27 On the concept of cascading crises and their leadership challenges, see Galaz et al. (2011); on the ash cloud crises, Parker (2014); on transboundary crisis management, Boin, Ekengren, and Rhinard (2013).

28 Linwood (2014). On the prediction of "social tipping points," popular since Gladwell's (2000) bestseller launched the concept, see Grimm and Schneider (2011).

29 Developed further in 't Hart (1993). See also Edelman (1977); Linz and Stepan (1978).

30 Pioneering works in this tradition include Barnard (1938); Selznick (1957); Wilson (1989).

31 There is a large field of leadership studies in which the relation between personal characteristics and task fulfillment receives ample attention. For an overview focused on political and public sector leadership, see 't Hart (2014).

32 Some of this ground is covered in Dubrin (2013).

33 The public commotion and subsequent political pressures on the Chinese government to "come clean" with regard to the extent of the SARS outbreak of 2003 or the causes and consequences of the deadly 2011 Wenzhou bullet train crash illustrates that even authoritarian regimes cannot escape crisis-fueled demands for accountability. See Branigan (2011); Olsson and Xue (2012).

34 Beck (1992); Boutelier (2004); Furedi (2005); Klein (2007).

35 Hearit (2006); Kuipers and 't Hart (2014).

36 Weick (1988); Weick and Sutcliffe (2007).

37 See Brecher (1980) on decision making during international crises.

38 Janis (1989); Moore (1998); Crandall et al. (2011); Svedin et al. (2011).

39 Boin and 't Hart (2012).

40 Sagan (1993).
41 Comfort (1989).
42 Stern (2009).
43 Coombs (2007); Coombs and Holladay (2009).
44 Mackiewicz (2008); Reese and Lewis (2009).
45 Littlefield and Quenette (2007); Boin et al. (2010).
46 Olmeda (2008).
47 Boin et al. (2008; 2009). See also Kaplan (2008); Hajer (2009); Jenkin et al. (2011); Ullmer et al. (2015).
48 Kuipers and 't Hart (2014). Although much more pronounced today, the tendency to search for culprits following the occurrence of disaster and crisis is age-old – see Drabek and Quarantelli (1967); Douglas (1992); Hood (2011); and the broader perspective of Tilly (2008).
49 Patashnik (2008).
50 Stern (1997a); Birkland (2006); Smith and Elliott (2007); Boin et al. (2008); Deverell (2009); Pidgeon (2010).
51 Brändström et al. (2004).

2 Sense Making
Grasping Crises as They Unfold

2.1   What the Hell Is Going On?

On the morning of September 11, 2001, U.S. President George W. Bush was listening to a group of children reading at a Sarasota, FL elementary school when he learned about the second plane crashing into the World Trade Center. He stayed in the classroom for several minutes, ostensibly listening to the reading. But the cameras captured the look of shock on his face as the president tried to make sense of the news that the country had come under attack.

The 9/11 terrorist strike took Bush, his country, and the rest of the world by complete surprise. As the drama unfolded live on television screens across the globe, people found themselves watching in disbelief: "This cannot be happening." This sense of collective stress soon gave rise to pressing questions: how could this have happened and why did the authorities not see it coming?[1]

Making sense of an unfolding crisis – from its roots to its "hot" phase and its aftermath – is a core challenge of crisis management. If intelligence agencies recognize an emerging threat early on, they can try to prevent it from materializing. If crisis managers quickly and fully understand the causes, characteristics, and consequences of an unfolding crisis, they are more likely to mitigate its impact. The sense-making task thus has two components: *detection* (of emerging threats and vulnerabilities) and *understanding* (of an unfolding crisis). In this chapter – and this is our *key question* – we ask what factors affect the effectiveness of sense making before and during crises.

Detecting an impending threat before it escalates into a full-blown crisis can be extremely hard. Whether it is a prison riot or a terrorist act, a natural disaster, an international conflict, an environmental contingency, or an economic crisis – authorities rarely see them coming. Yet, hindsight knowledge always seems to reveal that there were strong indications of growing risks or outright warnings that somehow went unnoticed or failed to prompt remedial action. This is not because of some inherent incompetence of policymakers and organizations. In this chapter – and this is our first *core claim* – we argue that many types of impending crises are very difficult to recognize in advance.

Understanding the course of an already unfolding crisis is equally pivotal, and not much easier. The difference between triumph and tragedy in crisis response hinges on the ability to produce, share, and, when necessary, revise accurate assessments of highly unusual, ambiguous, and dynamic situations.[2] Our second *core claim* is somewhat more optimistic: we argue that it is possible to grasp the dynamics of a crisis once it becomes manifest and unfolds. But it is also easy to get it wrong, as many studies of crisis management show.

We begin in Section 2.2 by identifying the barriers to crisis detection. In Section 2.3, we explain why some crisis leaders quickly understand what is going on, whereas others experience great difficulties in reading a crisis as it develops. In Section 2.4, we discuss some promising practices that may help improve both the detection and understanding of emerging crises and disasters.

2.2   Barriers to Crisis Detection

Some people actually do see crises coming. That is what we learn after each crisis, when an earlier warning is typically unearthed. Accusations of incompetence and deliberate denial follow swiftly. At the same time, experts routinely predict all sorts of crises that never materialize (just think of acid rain, Y2K, and Peak Oil). Political psychologist Philip Tetlock asked 284 academic experts to predict threats and crises of the future. He gathered a total of 28,000 predictions. Years later, he checked what had become of their predictions. His group of experts had not performed better than the average citizen would have done, particularly with regard to longer-range (three to five years) forecasts.[3]

Tetlock's research underlines a finding of many related research projects: humans have pervasive shortcomings when it comes to making sense of ill-structured problems and black swan events, and those shortcomings can at best only partially be remedied or compensated for by smart organizing. Whereas experienced crisis managers may well understand situations that they experienced before, it is extremely difficult to predict how novel events with many unknown unknowns will develop.[4]

But the ill-structured nature of events is not the only possible barrier to our recognition and understanding of emerging threats. Organizational factors often hamper our capacity to make sense of crises. And even if there is adequate organizational capacity to reach a clear understanding of an emerging threat, political factors may stand in the way of a shared awareness that a crisis is coming. We will now discuss of these three factors in more detail.

The Nature of Crisis Development

To understand why crises continue to surprise us, it is useful to draw an analogy between crises and diseases.[5] A disease is rooted in a vulnerable state of the body, which may be exacerbated by hereditary factors or the result of unhealthy behavior. The incubation phase sets in when pathogens proliferate and make themselves at home. When their number reaches a certain threshold, the pathogens overtake the body's defense system. The disease is now manifest and the battle for recovery, or survival, begins.

A crisis follows a similar pattern of development. As we explained in Chapter 1, the driving mechanisms of crisis are often concealed by the characteristics of the modern systems in which they emerge. The more complex a system is, the harder it is to understand. In a complex system, destructive interactions between components are therefore hard to detect.

The tight coupling between components within a system allows for a rapid proliferation of destructive interactions throughout the system. In recent years, we have seen that modern systems are increasingly being coupled with other systems.[6] These ties reach across geographic, jurisdictional, and professional boundaries. Modern society is a system of systems, tightly coupled and impossible to fully comprehend.

Timely crisis recognition, then, depends crucially on both the capacity of individuals operating (parts of) these systems and the organizational designs for early crisis detection. Timely recognition, in other words, hinges on the capacity of organizations to collect, share, and interpret information. The research findings are quite sobering, as we will see below. Most individuals and organizations are ill equipped to detect impending crises. Many public organizations lack so-called reliability experts: professionals with a well-developed antenna for detecting latent safety and security threats.[7]

Organizational Barriers

In hindsight, we can often observe that organizations struck by crisis were unable to detect the impending threat. Studies have revealed several key reasons why organizations (and, by implication, governments) fail to generate, interpret, and share information that is essential for effective crisis recognition.

The first reason is that many organizations – public and private – do not spend a great deal of time and resources on the detection of potential crises. Aside from a relatively limited number of specialized safety and security organizations, most public agencies define effectiveness in terms of conditions to be *sought* rather than in terms of conditions to be *avoided*. They seek to achieve certain politically articulated goals (make the trains run on time; provide housing for the poor; bring literacy up to 100 percent; strengthen industrial competitiveness; put a man on the moon). They rarely formulate goals in terms of "things to avoid."

Organizations scan their environment and seek feedback on the goals they must achieve and the day-to-day risks they have learned to recognize.[8] Most organizations do not look for information that may suggest that the world is about to assume a state they wish to avoid. They were never designed to detect low probability contingencies, let alone crises in the making.[9] Their information and performance management systems are designed to provide standardized feedback on goal achievement. These drive the search for data and reinforce the preferred image of the organization as a rational entity.[10]

This preoccupation with achievement rather than avoidance has implications for the capacity to detect crises. The detection of crisis would require the collection of data on aberrant, hitherto unknown events and patterns that may develop into a threat. But in most modern organizations there is little room for the kind of intuition and "gut feeling" that may facilitate coincidental detection of emerging threats.[11] There is no room for seemingly intuitive or randomized scans of the environment to see whether there is "something out there." To compound the problem, in their drive to become efficient, public organizations have increasingly adopted business solutions and eliminated the seemingly dispensable boundary-spanning agents that once were the informal antennas of government.[12]

Some organizations may even create a false sense of security by normalizing the threats they face. They use the language of risk analysis: describing the possible (known) causes of crises, mapping the pathways toward failure, and assigning probability and impact estimates to each scenario. If the aggregate risk (probability × impact) is deemed small enough, it becomes acceptable. The normalization of risk may thus give rise to the notion that "it won't happen around here." It is then easy to forget that risks – however small – can and do materialize. But when so-called black swans do emerge, it may take a long time to recognize them.[13]

This normalization tendency can assume absurd proportions in disaster preparation plans. Lee Clarke describes a variety of "fantasy documents," in which authorities promise that all will be well, come

Armageddon.[14] Clarke offers the fascinating example of the U.S. postal service, which had detailed plans to ensure mail delivery following an all-out nuclear war. Such unbridled optimism may actually escalate risk by giving policy makers a false sense of their coping capacities.

A second reason is that the very procedures of deductive reasoning and bureaucratic interaction that help detect the development of known risks may also create blinders for recognizing unknown risks. By creating a strongly developed framework that facilitates the rapid detection of certain types of threats and hazards, the unforeseen and unimagined crises are left to chance detections. But a rational-scientific way of sense making for such chance detections does not allow for "unscientific" reasoning with regard to crisis recognition. In an organization that works hard to detect known risks before they manifest and cause trouble, early signals of impending novel crises may be simply put aside.

These factors feature prominently in the analysis of NASA and the explosion of the *Challenger* (1986).[15] NASA had developed an elaborate safety system that ran on engineering logic: every decision with regard to every aspect of space shuttle safety was based on facts, rational thinking, tests, experience, and engineering science.[16] When engineers of subcontractor Thiokol feared that the forecasted cold in the night before the January 29, 1986 launch would undermine the resilience of a crucial part (the O-rings), they recommended a delay. Knowing that NASA required hard proof rather than gut feeling, the Thiokol engineers hastily put together a rationale for delay, stating that no launch should take place as long as the temperature did not rise above 53°F. The NASA counterparts not only found the rationale flimsily argued (Thiokol engineers agreed), but they pointed out that the rationale contradicted earlier rationales (a cardinal sin in engineering). NASA administrators were "appalled" by the Thiokol recommendation and decided to press ahead with the launch. The O-rings failed and the *Challenger* disintegrated within ninety seconds after takeoff.

This example underlines Barry Turner's argument that many of the clues needed to detect a crisis in the making can usually be found somewhere within the organizations that are responsible for preventing that emerging threat.[17] But the pieces of the crisis puzzle are not put together before it is too late. Even when a more composite threat picture emerges in the organization, it does not always make it to the top-level policy makers. Nor are these policy makers always interested in listening to and acting upon warnings that lack certainty and specificity.

The problem also occurs between organizations. Useful data are usually scattered across various organizations that operate at various levels of government (or outside the governmental realm). The data must be interpreted, compressed, and transmitted to the right organizations (those who need it). But those who possess the data do not always understand who may need it. People in organizations rarely agree on what the data are telling them and what they mean for the organization or domain(s) for which they bear responsibility.

A timely assessment demands a certain critical mass of competent people who share cogent ideas about what is important and what is not. Many large-scale organizations – certainly in the public sector – lack a common frame that specifies vulnerabilities and prescribes a way of recognizing their development. There are good reasons why complex organizations harbor different subcultures, but the result is the collective blind spots that post-crisis inquiries so often unearth. High-quality intelligence – data about the environment that have been integrated into a coherent story – is therefore often a scarce resource in complex organizations.[18]

Interorganizational politics and rivalry create additional barriers.[19] A shared interpretation and assessment of available data is informed by bureaucratic pulling and hauling within and between public agencies: different values and a variety of group interests come into play. Where one stands depends on where one sits. A certain degree of bureaucratic politics is usually quite healthy for an organization. It is, after all, excessive homogeneity and conformity among policy makers that make it hard to interpret data in a new light, which is often necessary if one is to detect and appraise newly emerging threats.[20] However, unrestrained intraorganizational strife and too little meaningful communication ultimately produce a similarly debilitating effect: information and analysis are no longer treated as representations of some external reality but are primarily seen as bargaining chips. As a result, information gets filtered, watered down, distorted, polished, or suppressed for reasons wholly unrelated to the situation at hand.[21]

Poor information sharing in crisis situations may also be the result of the deliberate compartmentalization of information for security reasons. Sensitive issues are often handled on a so-called need-to-know basis. This makes good sense from a security perspective – the fewer people who are in the know, the fewer who can leak to the press, to political (or bureaucratic) rivals, or to foreign governments. In practice, however, it is often difficult to figure out who "needs to know" what and why.

Different organizational interests, which in turn are based on values, missions, considerations of turf and autonomy, and the marching orders of political masters, undermine the interaction and cooperation on routine issues; the high-stakes context of potential crisis does not necessarily improve things. Some organizations may elect to divorce themselves from an impending threat as they fear that their actions will invite blame and will make the organization vulnerable to long-dragging accountability processes. Other organizations may seek to define the problem at hand in such a way that the organization will actually benefit from the crisis. The chances of a collectively shared assessment thus remain rather low.

Regulatory agencies, which are presumably designed to look for risks and vulnerabilities in the industries they oversee, may be expected to compensate for these pathologies. But regulatory agencies typically require organizations to look for accidents that have happened before (the known unknowns). They may not fully understand the complex technologies and their risks in the organizations that these agencies oversee. Some regulatory agencies are convinced by commercially expedient, reassuring myths concerning the state of risk prevention and mitigation in particular systems.[22] As one example, all these factors were identified as critical factors in explaining how the 2010 BP Deepwater Horizon offshore platform oil spill in the Gulf of Mexico could have occurred.[23]

The Social and Political Construction of Threat Perception

We have thus far treated crises as if they were concrete threat entities lurking in the background that must be recognized before they can be eliminated. But crises are to a considerable degree – in some cases entirely – subjectively constructed threats: before we can speak of a crisis, a considerable number of players must agree that a threat exists and must be dealt with urgently.[24] The process by which a group, organization, or society develops a consensus on crisis is quite opaque. Some seemingly obvious (certainly in hindsight) threats are completely ignored, whereas other in retrospect seemingly minor threats can hold a society in a tight grip for a surprisingly long period of time.

One month after a powerful earthquake off the Japanese coast caused a tsunami that killed thousands and set in motion a disastrous chain of events at the Fukushima Daichi nuclear power plant, the *Guardian* newspaper reported as follows:

The crippled nuclear power plant at Fukushima in Japan might have survived last month's natural disaster had the government not put faith in a flawed earthquake prediction system, a leading scientist has claimed. The Japanese authorities publish annual "hazard maps" to highlight parts of the country deemed at risk from major earthquakes, but there is no reliable scientific basis for the technique, the researcher said. Had the government considered global tremor activity and historical tsunami records instead, they would have appreciated the risk of a magnitude nine earthquake in the area and designed the Fukushima power plant to withstand such an event, said Robert Geller at the University of Tokyo.[25]

A prime reason why governments fail to act on warnings is that most warnings do not speak for themselves. Only when governmental leaders define a situation as a major threat will remedial action be undertaken. This process of recognition may take too much time; some threats never get recognized at all before they materialize. For example, it took Western governments many years before they appreciated the magnitude of the AIDS epidemic.[26]

The reality is that *there is no natural correspondence between objective and subjective threats*. A pivotal manifestation of this discrepancy is *risk inoculation*. Communities and organizations may not appreciate the real risks they run, and therefore not be motivated to invest appropriately in risk prevention, mitigation, and preparedness. Public perceptions of risk can be manipulated by lack of transparency or purposeful framing on the part of risk-producing or risk-regulating entities. On the community side, a collective illusion of invulnerability ("it won't happen here") can take hold after years of incident-free living, leading people to conclude that existing risk regimes must be sufficient whereas in reality they have been largely untested or have unobtrusively eroded.

The Fukushima disaster provides strong echoes of precisely this phenomenon: all too cozy regulator-industry relations in the "nuclear village," local populations living near and partly depending on the power plant, a cultural illusion of Japanese superiority in all matters techno-logical and therefore nuclear, and a collective denial of the reality that the national energy strategy had become hostage to a technology that is fundamentally high-risk and never fully tamable. The general risks of the technology were amplified and exacerbated by the characteristics of those natural hazards – such as earthquakes and tsunamis – that are typical of Japan. Structures *seemed* to be in place, and responsibilities for risk management, preparedness, and response were allocated across a wide range of government authorities. But many of these approaches to risk assessment and planning proved to be exercises in wishful thinking.

Research on public policy making offers another convincing explan-ation for the skewed nature of threat perceptions: many issues (including warnings of impending crises) never make it to the decision-making agenda of political and bureaucratic leaders.[27] One of the most important factors working against crisis recognition is the limited time available to policy makers and public leaders for considering, debating, and deciding upon policy issues. The policy agenda is overcrowded with issues that await decision making. Advocates on all of these issues have fought a hard battle to make it to the top of the agenda; they all claim "their" issue is pivotal and requires urgent attention. But policy makers cannot even consider, let alone act on many of them. Given the fundamental scarcity of attention, policy makers gravitate toward where the most noise is made. In other words: short-term "burning issues" keep more long-term, creeping threats from the policy agenda. Everyone may agree that some looming threat is a potential crisis in the making, but in a world of mediatized politics, trending topics, and quick feedback loops, the urgent drives out the important.

Sometimes it is blunt hardball politics that keeps future threats off the agenda. Organized interests opposed to government regulation of particular risks may form a blocking coalition that uses its leverage to engage in the politics of agenda denial. There are many ways to do so: funding research that argues the problem is negligible; reframing the issue as one of choice, freedom, and rights rather than of danger, risk, and responsibility; attacking the arguments and the motives of advocates for proactive tackling of the issue.[28] In the United States, for instance, it has proven tremendously difficult to agree on the importance of climate change as Republicans, operating in conjunction with a small group of scientists, have worked to undermine the claim that human behavior has caused climate change.

Some crises are not acted upon because the stakeholders involved cannot attract attention to their plight. They fail to frame the issue of their concern in such terms that others understand and share the nature of the threat, sense the urgency, and act accordingly. Think of the Ebola outbreak in Liberia: the NGO Doctors without Borders had warned about the impending epidemic, but their warnings were only a weak signal from the point of view of the governments in the region and the World Health Organization.[29] It was not until the epidemic had reached densely populated urban areas, crossed national boundaries, and induced mass casualties that the issue was framed as a global security threat.

A final barrier to crisis recognition may be the institutional setting in which an emerging crisis is to be recognized. Certain practices, indeed some parts of the modern way of life, have become so ingrained and taken for granted that they effectively blind us to certain threats and make it virtually impossible to deal with them. In a society that depends on fossil fuels, it is surprisingly difficult to gain attention for the rapid depletion of resources. Should leaders be surprised when our economies run into crisis as a result of high oil prices or our energy sectors as a result of low ones? Should anybody be surprised when two passenger planes collide in the choked airways above our mega cities? Can policy makers claim ignorance when a fireworks factory explodes in the middle of a city? Or when a city in a hurricane zone floods?

In sum, much must happen before a significant number of people agree on the status of a problem; much more must happen before they agree that a certain event warrants the crisis label. Whether it is a coalition of the unwilling or the deaf and blind, many emerging threats are simply ignored. This depressing fact becomes most apparent when we consider the range of permanent crises that have actually happened. They are "out there" for all to see: domestic violence; honor killings; the systematic exploitation of women and kids in the sex industry; crime-ridden urban ghettos; sloppy management of high-risk technologies; mass migration flows; endemic corruption – the list of "unrecognized" crises is long.[30]

It appears that impending crises stand a chance to be recognized in time if they are understood as immediate threats to the modern way of living. In democracies, this means that citizens must be mobilized. It appears that only radical primers – presented in the form of powerful drama and emotive symbols – can impress upon a significant majority of people that a threat exists to their way of life.[31] Events must be linked to core values. Statistics rarely succeed to make a case of their own. Problems must be "packaged" if public leaders and their organizations are to recognize growing threats and impending crises before it is too late. Resourceful "claim makers" can influence the political processing of pivotal studies or occasional incidents.[32] This explains why some "non-events" – think of the Y2K crisis or the Peak Oil argument – can skyrocket to the top of the agenda: skillful "framers" translate their issue into a language everyone understands. Moreover, they present a convincing analysis of causes that logically imply and privilege certain solutions.[33]

When a crisis has materialized and has become acute, the nature of the sense-making challenge changes dramatically. But the predicament for leaders does not become any easier, as our analysis below will show.

2.3   Barriers to Understanding an Unfolding Crisis

Once a crisis becomes manifest, crisis managers typically engage in an energetic – if not frantic – search for information as they seek to understand the causes, characteristics, and consequences of the emerging threat.[34] As soon as the undivided attention and vast resources of government have been brought to bear on the crisis, a huge quantity of raw data and processed "intelligence" is generated. In a parallel sphere, the same happens on social media. Without mechanisms for coping with this flow of data, policy makers can easily become paralyzed or indiscriminately attentive to particular items of information, which may unduly affect their judgments. Here we discuss why policy makers often find it hard to make sense of the bewildering flow of data that they receive during a crisis.

We should emphasize again the particular and distinct nature of the information process during the acute stage of a crisis. There are fundamental uncertainties about the nature of the threat, contextual parameters, the efficacy of alternative courses of action, and the reactions of key actors, stakeholders, and other constituencies. These uncertainties are compounded by the shifting aspects of a crisis: the nature of the threat may change and problems cascade rapidly.[35] The Fukushima disaster again provides an example, combining elements of a natural disaster (tsunami, floods), nuclear disaster, infrastructural crisis (widespread electricity failures), political crisis (acute legitimacy problem for the national government), and a transnational health scare.

In a crisis, the pace of events typically undermines the effectiveness of even simple communications. After a natural disaster, for instance, communications with the disaster site may be significantly degraded or even cut off. In fast-moving situations (such as acts of terrorism or riots in urban settings) in which people experience an urgent need to communicate with those who are important to them, cell phone networks may be overwhelmed. At the same time, rumors abound on social media. The consequence of lacking or ambiguous information is continuing uncertainty, which, in turn, causes deep frustrations among policymakers who are desperately trying to find out what is happening. In response, they may resort to acting upon media impressions rather than their internal lines of communication.

A telling example emerges from the chaotic days after Hurricane Katrina struck New Orleans. Rumors of mayhem and violence began to circulate and were amplified by news reporters, who could not venture into the city to verify the rumors. National media reported widespread looting, rapes, and shooting at rescue helicopters (all of these rumors would later prove unfounded). The governor of Louisiana, Kathleen Blanco, issued an emotional warning that rioters would be shot. The result was immediate: many drivers of trucks and buses refused to enter the city, thus delaying the response. When the armed forces arrived, their demeanor was one of entering a besieged city (rather than a flooded city with tired and hungry victims).[36]

If accurate information is actually available at the operational level, the complexity of the information chain connecting the strategic level to the operational level typically impedes high-paced sense making. The sheer size of modern organizations and the number of people they employ means it requires a concerted effort to bring data together.[37] This takes time. When multiple organizations are involved in the sense-making process, skilled people are needed to understand what crisis managers need to know and how the information should be delivered. The inherent gap between the world of first responders and strategic policymakers can easily make critical information disappear "in translation."[38] Crucial bits of intelligence get lost in the steady stream of briefings, memos, phone calls, emails, news reports, tweets, and text messages.

Two sets of factors make it hard for most policymakers to get a grip on this irregular information flow and gain a quick and accurate understanding of a crisis. Crisis-related uncertainties and pressures may generate levels of stress that undermine their cognitive capacity and emotional equanimity in making sense of even straightforward information. Furthermore, the lack of organizational means to compensate for these cognitive limitations can make things worse. We discuss these factors next.

Dealing with Uncertainty Under Pressure

While the human mind is capable of great intellectual feats, it is beset with limitations when it comes to analyzing and understanding complex and volatile situations that are marked by uncertainty.[39] When individuals are bombarded with all sorts of information that may or may not be relevant, the stream threatens to overwhelm their capacity to absorb it all. The challenge is to selectively monitor the environment and "tune out" much of the incoming data in order to preserve the capacity to attend to the most pressing issues at any given time. That is very difficult, even for the most experienced and perceptive of crisis managers.

How do people make sense of uncertainty in high-pressure conditions? A half century of cognitive research supports the view that experience – mentally coded into what psychologists call a system of stored representations – is the basis for sense making, in everyday life as well as in extreme situations. People use encoded experience: they take a scrap of information (a cue, as cognitive psychologists call it) and weave a scenario around it, using their experience and expectations as mental yarn. Human brains collect, organize, store, and recall information by making use of packaging and organizing devices, which are generically called cognitive structures. These cognitive structures – alternatively referred to by researchers as schemas, scripts, analogies, metaphors, or stories – enable people to draw upon encoded and selectively recalled experience to interpret the present and prepare for the future. They thus tend to be attentive to a certain set of issues while ignoring others. What is on one's mind, the content of the cognitive agenda at any given time, heavily affects the way a person monitors and sorts signals from the environment, and how they interpret them.

In addition to their memory, people's expectations are highly significant. Under conditions of ambiguity, humans tend to see what they expect to occur.[40] These expectations may also flow from historical analogies.[41] For example, in the absence of hard information, some decision makers and observers of the Oklahoma City bombing (in April 1995) initially operated from the assumption that Islamic fundamentalist terrorists were responsible. Why was this the case? First of all, an unhelpful analogy was at work: the first World Trade Center bombing in 1993, which was the work of such a group, was still fresh in the mind.[42] Second, domestic groups were not expected to conduct operations on this scale on U.S. soil. As it turned out, these assumptions and expectations proved incorrect – the culprits were American citizens associated with an extremist "militia" organization. A very similar pattern emerged in Norway in the immediate wake of the July 22 attacks by Anders Behring Breivik where it was initially assumed by many that the attack on the Cabinet Offices was probably linked to the Middle East and there was resistance to the notion that the worst terrorist attack in Norwegian history could have been mounted by an ethnic Norwegian.[43] There is a clear pitfall associated with applying the presumed lessons of one crisis to another: crises might *look* similar, but they are unique by definition (see also Chapter 6).[44]

In the face of numerous, complex, and mutually contradictory cues, people tend to use mental heuristics to facilitate classification, interpretation, and judgment of information. Laboratory research has detailed many different patterns by which people overemphasize some bits of information, and ignore or underestimate others. These cognitive short cuts introduce biases in situational assessments.

These heuristics are most often applied without an individual being aware of them. Nobel prize winner Daniel Kahneman offers a simple way to grasp how the brain works, by making a distinction between a "System I" and a "System II." Think of System I as the product of evolution, rooted in the earliest human experiences. This system provides a continuous stream of cues that guide quick but subconscious decision making. This makes a decision process very efficient, as one does not have to approach each and every decision moment afresh. System I produces the heuristics mentioned above.

System II is our rational modus, which allows us to correct for the more unfortunate inclinations offered by System I. If we take our time and engage System II, we can understand that some inclinations may not be wise or efficient; rational thinking will help us to build a better plan. In routine situations, most people are pretty good in activating System II when it matters most. But System II is not always sharp and tires easily. Importantly, System II – our correction for biases – tends to malfunction under conditions of pressure and stress.[45] Also, given that

System I processes are often subconscious, the decision maker may be unaware of the extent to which the effortful and careful deliberations they believe constitute their response are in fact shaped by rapid reactions occurring milliseconds after an environmental stimulus is received.[46]

Cognitive Limitations Imposed by Stress

Stress can distort but also enhance situational assessments in many ways. We speak of stress when the task load of an individual or collective exceeds the individual or joint capacity to fulfill that task load.[47] In a crisis, policymakers often find that they do not have the means – cognitive or otherwise – to deal with the situation. Urgent threats to key societal values and interests raise the stakes for the responsible political leaders, sometimes up to the point of affecting their personal self-esteem and sense of identity.[48]

Stress need not necessarily degrade performance: a little stress may actually help policymakers to focus on their task. There is eu-stress (helpful) and dis-stress (impairing). The relationship between *levels* of stress and most people's performance takes the form of an inverted "U." Absence of stress is associated with lower motivation and performance, moderate (eu-)stress with high performance (due to heightened vigilance and motivation). But high levels of (dis-)stress are associated with sense-making performance.[49]

The *type* of stress a crisis induces or exacerbates in a leader also matters. Different kinds of stress may have rather different psychological consequences. Stress deriving from overload and lack of time has different psychological consequences than stress deriving from value trade-offs, fear of loss, internal dissent, or external conflict. The latter are likely to be more emotionally charged – adding to the emotional component of stress dynamics.[50] A combination of these stress types – likely in crisis – will have serious consequences for the performance of decision makers.[51]

Based on experimental, historical, and field studies, researchers have identified a wide range of specific stress effects. For example, when significantly distressed, individuals are increasingly likely to:

- focus on the short term, to the neglect of longer-term considerations;
- take excessive risks;
- fall back on and rigidly cling to old and deeply rooted behavioral patterns;
- narrow and deepen their span of attention, scrutinizing "central" issues while neglecting "peripheral" ones;
- rely on stereotypes or lapse into fantasies;
- be more easily irritable.[52]

Irving Janis made a useful distinction between cognitive, affiliative, and egocentric sense-making heuristics that decision makers resort to when operating under stress.[53] Cognitive heuristics and biases are the parsimonious but dangerously simplistic ways of making sense of complex situations that facilitate the making of quick, straightforward choices. These choices can then be bolstered by a highly selective treatment of any subsequent information that reaches decision makers. In extreme cases, crisis managers will actively seek out information that seems to corroborate their choices, and ignore or obfuscate information that contains negative feedback about these choices.

Affiliative rules refer to modes of sense making where "policy makers are likely to seek a solution that will avert threats to important values in a way that will not adversely affect their relationships with any "important people" within the organization, especially those to whom they are accountable, and that will not be opposed by subordinates who are expected to implement the new policy decision."[54] Behavioral tendencies of this kind include the propensity to favor conservative options that don't rock the boat and the "preserve harmony rule" that may give rise to the rigid concurrence-seeking in group-level sense making that has become known as groupthink.

Egocentric rules of thumb satisfy strong personal motives. Emotive rules are directed toward satisfying strong emotional needs. Such motives include the need for power and control, or a desire for personal aggrandizement. In many instances these motives are essentially efforts to compensate for deep-seated feelings of insecurity and incompetence. Leaders with a very high need for power and control are likely to harden under stress and take hawkish positions in conflicts.

That said, a total collapse of a decision maker's sense-making ability is probably quite rare.[55] Research suggests that there is probably a large set of fairly adaptive responses between the optimum high point of the curve (moderate stress) and the collapse of performance at high stress levels. Kahneman's dual-process model offers a way forward in understanding the role of emotions. It implies that as stress increases beyond a moderate level while tackling complex tasks, System II resources become depleted. The affective System I then reenters decision making as a supplement, providing simpler, faster decision strategies. System I acts as a crutch that bolsters the sagging System II and prevents decision makers from collapsing in a paroxysm of panic or paralysis. Processing is "mindless," automatic, and heuristic-driven at low levels of stress, "mindful" and comprehensive at moderate levels, and returns to a partially heuristic-driven state under high stress. The dual systems bolster one another at high levels of stress, preventing total collapse of decision performance.

Some leaders do better than others at compartmentalizing stress: they isolate stress arising in one domain and prevent it from contaminating others.[56] President Bill Clinton, for example, demonstrated a remarkable capacity to compartmentalize stress and maintain composure in his public performances and focus during the Monica Lewinsky scandal. President Richard Nixon, however, was unable to cope with the stress when he found himself confronted simultaneously with a critical phase in the Watergate scandal and the 1973 Middle East war. He consumed large quantities of alcohol and behaved in such an erratic manner that his aides limited his ability to launch a nuclear strike.[57] The New Orleans police chief, Eddie Compass, succumbed to stress during the immediate aftermath of Hurricane Katrina (2005). He broke down in public and became a source of rumors suggesting that horrible things were going on in the Superdome ("they're raping babies").[58]

Experience appears to be one important factor in determining how people cope with stress: seasoned experts are usually far more effective at maintaining performance under pressure than novices.[59] Some people remain cool and stay clearheaded under pressure – think of veteran military officers, journalists, and fire and police commanders, for instance. Senior politicians and bureaucrats are generally veterans too – veterans of countless political and bureaucratic battles during their rise to power. Those who make it all the way to the top in competitive political-administrative systems tend to have relatively well-developed mechanisms for coping with stress.

Organizational Factors

Organizational factors generate further challenges to creating an accurate and a shared picture of the situation. A response network typically brings together many organizations. People within these organizations tend to perceive the world differently. This is an inevitable by-product of differences in tasks, jurisdictions, professions, geographical location, and experience. Moreover, various organizations are often drawn into the crisis at different moments in its development: first responders are there immediately, whereas policy organizations come into play later.[60] Different organizations focus on different aspects of the situation and assess information differently. They draw upon different analogies and metaphors, make different inferences and prognoses, and see different interests at stake – each from their own organizational vantage points. These different data sets, vantage points, and professional perspectives can make it hard to arrive at a common understanding. Furthermore, it may be difficult to recognize what pieces of information crossing one's desk might be critical to others or to the overall success of the effort.

We should not be blind to the fact that information is a critical resource in the politics of organizational cooperation and competition. To put it euphemistically, sharing information with others is not necessarily an organization's first concern or reflex when something extraordinary has happened. Furthermore, since information is a key currency of power, officials can receive information based on strategic considerations of interorganizational and intergovernmental politics rather than operational necessities. It can be provided as a reward or as a favor; it can be withheld as punishment or to neutralize a potential adversary.[61]

The absence of effective organizational methods and procedures that facilitate rapid sense making at strategic levels is yet another factor. In our experience, many organizations lack methodology and capacity to sort, share, and understand information coming in from multiple sources speedily and accurately. Few organizations – public or private – have effective mechanisms for high-pressure sense making in place – particularly agencies that are somewhat removed from the traditional emergency management and security services clusters.

To be sure, operators (firefighter, police officer) are usually well trained to jointly analyze available information. But policy makers are not so well trained and usually much less experienced in the realm of crisis management. Most politicians and bureaucrats, however hectic their everyday life may be, rarely have to gauge unfamiliar situations under extreme pressure. Their normal modes of situation assessment and policy deliberation are easily overwhelmed by the bewildering pace, ambiguity, and complexity of crisis.

When senior policy makers are confronted with a stream of operational data – often couched in operational language that is easily misunderstood – they tend to fall back on everyday routines. The typical reaction is to create various "filtering groups," which inevitably delays the information process (and rarely makes it more effective). The result is chaos: critical information floats through the bureaucracy, its ascendance depending on randomness rather than structure.

2.4   Effective Sense Making

Thus far we have painted a somewhat bleak picture of sense making during crises. There is, however, a more optimistic side to the story. Some researchers point to the capacity of experienced crisis managers to read crisis situations. In some organizations that deal with risky technologies, specialized control room staff and practices have proven highly successful in detecting and understanding unfolding crises. Some organizations have created a proactive culture of "looking for problems" in their environment, even during ostensibly "routine" periods, and in addition they have developed an interplay between operators and managers that allows accelerated, decentralized sense making when operational conditions become turbulent and dangerous.[62] Finally, there is the promise of social media and "big data," which some argue will revolutionize sense making in crisis situations. Below we elaborate on these more optimistic observations.

Mental Slides

A growing body of research demonstrates that notwithstanding inherent cognitive and emotional constraints, experienced incident commanders are often capable of a rapid – sometimes nearly instant – yet fairly accurate understanding of unfolding crisis events. They rarely arrive at these rapid situational assessments through an explicit conscious process of deliberation, as researchers of many stripes and colors were long wont to assume.[63] Instead, they rely on mechanisms that look and feel like intuition.[64]

Senior commanders have usually developed a rich store of experience and a repertoire of tactics on which they draw when confronting a critical incident. The minds of these crisis commanders work like a mental version of a mechanical slide carousel containing snapshots of a wide variety of contingencies that they have encountered or learned about. When they find themselves in a threat situation, this is immediately compared with their stored experiences. This mental slide carousel quickly revolves until an adequate match is found. Each slide contains not only an image of the situation but also a recipe for action. Once the specific type of situation is identified, the commander *knows* what to do. In order to double check that the tactic in question is appropriate for this situation, the commander may perform a quick mental simulation to make sure that there isn't some contextual factor that might prevent the tactic from producing the desired outcome.

This mode of information processing, though not infallible, enables competent and efficient performance under difficult, dynamic conditions and peak workloads. It provides experienced commander with a version of a System I that is grounded in reflected experience rather than in brain reflexes and emotional needs. Clearly, this system works best when the new contingency closely resembles at least one of the experiences captured on the commander's mental slides. If the situation is radically different – an unknown unknown – from those stored in memory, however, stored experience may give rise to fundamentally flawed assessments that feel right.

A key question is to what extent one can transfer these practices from the realm of operations to the world of strategy and policy. One possible difference between these two types of leadership settings is the time frames involved.[65] Political and public service leaders are only occasionally called upon to make crucial decisions with just a few moments' notice. They usually have much more time for consultation; strategic situational assessments at the strategic level more often emerge in a matter of hours and days, not minutes and seconds. This creates a somewhat greater potential for leaders to interact with advisers and draw upon a wider range of organizational information resources than field commanders typically have at their disposal.

However, critical-incident commanders probably have more opportunities than policy makers to practice sense making under extreme conditions. Big-city fire commanders, for example, have a chance to practice their diagnostic skills relatively frequently.[66] By contrast, most top-level policy makers do not see real crises of the magnitude we are emphasizing in this book all that often. Most enter office as crisis management novices and may well remain so unless they experience one or several major cases during their tenure. Moreover, the potential variety of crises senior leaders might have to deal with is much larger than that of the average incident commander. This means that they are unlikely to build up sense-making skills through extensive experience, let alone the rich set of "mental slides" that commanders can turn to.

Command Rooms

Drawing on their extensive, long-term research on organizations that successfully weathered several deep crises, Emery Roe and Paul Schulman found that performance reliability depends to a large degree on a small cadre of professionals working in the command room.[67] In nuclear power plants, electricity companies, and air traffic control operations, these command room professionals appear to have an uncanny ability to sense when something might go wrong and understand what is happening when something does go wrong.

Experience was an obvious factor of importance. In addition, extensive in-house training programs prepared them for the job of real-time operations. Importantly, these operators shared a clear awareness of the core events that must be precluded from happening. They were under no illusion that they were in control and understood how vulnerable their core technologies were and how limited the options; they were always busily engaged in developing options and strategies to deal with disturbances. When necessary, these operators reinvented new procedures and new lines of cooperation to replace hierarchical practices of information sharing that were dominant in "normal" times.

High Reliability Organizations

One step up from having proactive and resilient control room staff are organizations that have a more broadly developed and culturally rooted capacity to grasp crisis dynamics.[68] These so-called high reliability organizations (HROs) typically work in fast-paced and potentially deadly environments – think of military, police, and rescue service organizations – but they also exist in high-risk technology environments (nuclear power, petrochemical plants, air traffic control systems). These HROs have developed routines for using provisional information to create a provisional situational assessment and remember that it is just that: provisional. They resist tendencies to adopt and cling to an interpretation based on limited information and hasty analysis. They force themselves to continuously probe their situational assessments – identifying indicators that can be monitored to sound warning bells should the initial assessment be off the mark. As new information becomes available, assessments are updated or even abandoned if the balance of available evidence begins pointing in a different direction.[69] Information is shared broadly and on the basis of a holistic awareness of how one's own role is related to the overall system and an understanding of the information needs of others. Such "heedful" information sharing contributes to organizational vigilance.

The secret of their success lies in three characteristics: safety awareness, decentralization, and training.[70] HROs have created a culture of awareness: employees consider safety the overriding concern in everything they do. They expect emergencies to happen. They look for them because employees know they are expected to do that – even when it comes at the cost of task efficiency. A high degree of decentralization empowers employees to act upon their intuition: when they suspect "something is brewing," they can take it "upstairs" in the knowledge that their surveillance will be noted and appreciated. Managers defer to operator expertise when the situation calls for it. These organizations do not expect employees to rely on their intuition alone (even though leaders of these organizations understand the importance of expert intuition); employees are constantly trained to look for glitches and troubling signs of escalation.

The Promise of Social Media and Big Data

The rise of social media has raised hopes and expectations among practitioners that these new communication tools will enable enhanced sense making in crisis.[71] Social media are now routinely used to warn people about impending crises and disasters; they are also used to offer advice. In addition, they are increasingly being used to *collect* information that otherwise would not be available. There are tools that help decision makers "mine" the data generated by users who are communicating about an unfolding event. For instance, by studying keywords or geolocations, a picture of the situation may emerge that would otherwise be invisible. At the same time, we should note that social media generate more ambiguous information and are instrumental in propagating rumors.[72]

The ubiquitous use of social media – like other information and communications technology practices in our societies – generates big data, which has fed the idea that the analysis of that data will uncover hitherto hidden patterns and inscrutable causal pathways. In theory, this should allow policy makers to discover crises in their earliest stages. While this may well work for "known" and well-structured crises relatively conducive to data analysis and computer modeling, such as floods, hurricanes, and epidemics, we should note that big data is unlikely to foresee the unknown unknowns. Particularly now that we have oceans of data at our fingertips in real time, one needs to know what to look for – or else face the prospect of drowning in the data. Once a crisis is on, big data can be a big help. But whether big data can also help us spot latent vulnerabilities and unfolding incubation of disaster is an open question.

2.5   The Ubiquity of Surprise

A close reading of many crisis cases reveals what in hindsight looks suspiciously like flashing warning lights that should have alerted authorities of things to come. Investigative reporters and blue-ribbon commissions have unearthed an abundance of lavishly detailed pre-warnings, fueling a thriving industry of conspiracy theories.[73] Pearl Harbor, the space shuttle explosions, the 9/11 attacks, the Boston Marathon bombings, Hurricane Katrina, and the financial crisis – these are but a handful of crucial events that in hindsight appeared not quite so inevitable as they were felt to be at the moment of arrival.

Paradoxically, it is the characteristics of modernization that prevent organizations from detecting impending crises.[74] The hidden interaction between small incidents and failed interventions can drive a containable incident toward critical threshold levels. As we showed in this chapter, detecting escalating crises before they strike can thus be surprisingly difficult.

Policy makers at the top of public organizations and governments do not have the luxury of forming impressions about crises after the fact, as commentators and academics do. They live in a world full of uncertainty and ambiguity where at any given time numerous contingencies can materialize and have a profound effect on their domain of responsibility. Recognizing an impending crisis from the sea of possible contingencies is what they and their systems are expected to do. But separating the signals from the noise has always been a tall order, and the mere availability of more data and information-processing algorithms does not necessarily compensate for the unprecedented levels of uncertainty that come with crises.

Once a crisis becomes manifest, policy makers must make sense of the unfolding events in order to limit the damage they may cause. Policy makers do not have perfect, complete, and uncontested information about the potentially escalating challenges facing them. Rather, they begin with a preliminary and provisional picture of what is happening, and, equally importantly, what it all means. Any actions taken or foregone will derive in large measure from the nature and quality of the situational assessments that emerge from the flow of activity prior to the recognition of the crisis.[75]

Crisis managers need to decide which signals to heed, which to ignore, and how to make sense of a threat that has already materialized and that calls for an immediate response. They can only make these decisions on the basis of incomplete, often contradictory information and advice from sources within and outside their own organizations.[76]

In this chapter, we have demonstrated how delicate and vulnerable this process is. We have shown how many organizational features and practices obscure rather than detect threats, and how this accelerates rather than mitigates the development of crises. But the news is not all bad. We have also shown that policy makers and organizations can be successful in maintaining a fungible capacity for reality-testing in even the most difficult circumstances. We must assume that information pathologies will continue to produce rude surprises that will challenge response capacities.[77] At the same time, we know that an organization can improve its sense-making capacities. This is crucially important for an effective and legitimate response. In the next chapter, we turn to these challenges of crisis response.

Notes

1 Or as Queen Elizabeth asked the panelists at a conference on the economic crisis sponsored by the London School of Economics: "Why did nobody notice it?" www.telegraph.co.uk/news/uknews/theroyalfamily/3386353/The-Queen-asks-why-no-one-saw-the-credit-crunch-coming.html (accessed July 10, 2015). In its final report, the National Commission on Terrorist Attacks (in the remainder of this book we will refer to this as the 9/11 Commission) phrased the question slightly differently ("How did this happen?") and added the equally pressing question "And how can we avoid such tragedy again?" (2004: xv). We will return to the latter question in Chapter 6.
2 Cf. Weick (1995: 61).
3 In their book *Superforecasting*, Tetlock and Gardner (2015) found that accountability, training, and narrowing the temporal scope of forecasts can help improve forecasting performance somewhat. See also Tetlock (2005).
4 Klein (2009); Kahneman (2011).
5 This analogy is developed in the work of Turner (1978); Reason (1990).
6 Ansell, Boin, and Keller (2010).
7 Some theories of safety (known under the label of high-reliability theory) see these reliability experts as pivotal safeguards against accidents and crises. Roe and Schulman (2008).
8 Cyert et al. (1963); Simon (1976).
9 Leveson (1995); Weick, Sutcliffe, and Obstfeld (1999); Weick and Sutcliffe (2007).
10 Feldman and March (1981; 1988).
11 Vaughan (1996); March (2010).
12 This drive for efficiency is documented and discussed in the literature on new public management. See, e.g., Pollitt and Bouckaert (2011).
13 Clarke (2005); Taleb (2007).
14 Clarke (1999).
15 We rely here on Vaughan's (1996) extensive analysis.
16 For an enlightening discussion on the engineering mind, see Petroski (1992).
17 Turner and Pidgeon (1997).
18 Cf. Wilensky (1967); Kam (1988); March (1988) and (2010). For instance, communicating within and across organizations is often a problem in itself. Presenting information in such a way that the receiving party understands it, agrees with the content, and appreciates the urgency is difficult (especially when the receiving end is outside the organization). See Parker and Stern (2002; 2005) for additional factors and perspectives.
19 A good discussion of these factors can be found in Wilson (1989).
20 On groupthink, see Janis (1982); 't Hart (1994). In 2004, both American and British reports evaluating the run-up to the Anglo-American invasion of Iraq

mentioned groupthink within the relevant intelligence agencies and inner-circle policymaking groups to be a major contributing cause of the distorted threat assessment regarding Iraq's possession of weapons of mass destruction. See the reports of the Committee of Privy Counselors (2004) and the Senate Intelligence Committee (2004).

21 Preston and 't Hart (1999: 54–58).

22 Vaughan (1996).

23 National Commission on the BP Deepwater Horizon Oil Spill and Offshore Drilling (2011).

24 Edelman (1964; 1971); Bovens and 't Hart (1996).

25 www.theguardian.com/science/2011/apr/13/flawed-earthquake-predictions-fukushima (accessed June 10, 2015).

26 Shilts (1987); Perrow and Guillen (1990).

27 In this field of studies, several schools exist (see Sabatier [1999] for an overview). Here we selectively describe a set of common factors that work against high agenda status. Cf. Parker and Stern (2002).

28 Cobb and Ross (1997).

29 Sondorp et al. (2011).

30 The work of Erikson (1976, 1994) is of special relevance.

31 Think of My Lai and the emergence of film material exposing torture in the American-run prisons in Iraq.

32 Stallings (1995); Cobb and Primo (2003).

33 The Y2K crisis played out in the years leading up to the Millennium (2000). It was widely thought that most of the software in place would not be ready to deal with the year change from 1999 to 2000. Thanks to (or in spite of) widespread efforts to fix software, nothing happened. The Peak Oil thesis holds that the world is running out of oil soon. The thesis reached its highest popularity in the years before the "shale gas revolution" which rendered the oil problem moot. See Goode and Ben-Yehuda (1994) on the similar dynamics of moral panics.

34 Brecher (1993).

35 Rosenthal, Boin, and Bos (2001).

36 This story is best told by Douglas Brinkley (2006).

37 Turner (1978).

38 Boin and Renaud (2013).

39 Jervis (1976: 203–5); Nisbett and Ross (1980: 15–16); Devine, Hamilton, and Ostrom (1994: 3–4).

40 Jervis (1976: 144–54); Weick (1995).

41 Janis and Mann (1977: 15); Neustadt and May (1986); Dyson and Preston (2003).

42 Cf. Brändström et al. (2004).

43 Agrell (2013).

44 Early yet still authoritative statements in this regard include Hermann (1972); Brecher (1979a).

45 For a more detailed application of System I and II logic to crisis sense making, see Dyson and 't Hart (2013).

46 Dijksterhuis and Arts (2010); Kahneman (2011).

47 Stress has been conceptualized in a number of ways. We adopt this definition, which originates in the influential work of Lazarus (1966) and Janis and Mann (1977).

48 Several decades of research have taught us much about the ways in which various types of behavior driven by motivated biases – such as denial, wishful thinking, betrayal, and value conflict – can influence problem framing and decision making. See Jervis (1976); Lebow (1981: 101–19); David (1993: 23); Vandenbroucke (1993: 164–6); Lebow and Stein (1994: 115–17); Parker and Stern (2002).

49 Individuals are thought to have somewhat differently shaped stress curves, in keeping with the notion that some individuals cope better with stress than others. More recent research has begun to question the inverted U-curve interpretation. See further Dyson and 't Hart (2013).

50 Janis and Mann (1977); Lebow and Stein (1994: 331–8).

51 Weick (1995: 103–4).

52 Hermann (1979); Holsti (1979); Post (1991); Weick (1995); Flin (1996: 97–139); Coates (2012). Some researchers argue that the early stress literature has systematically misunderstood the relationship between stress and performance errors. Klein (2001), e.g., has argued that the more important effects of stressors such as extreme time pressure, noise, and ambiguity are that stressors (a) interfere with information gathering and (b) disrupt the ability to recall necessary information and distract decision makers' attention from critical tasks.

53 Janis (1989).

54 Janis (1989: 45).

55 George (1986: 531).

56 It is therefore important to establish empirically to what extent crisis pressures affect the various actors, and what level of stress this actually generates in each of them, as far as can be judged from their recorded behavior. This research strategy was advocated (but not always adhered to) by Brecher (1979b). The best checklist of stress indicators in policy makers dealing with crises can be found in Hermann (1979). An exemplary effort along the lines suggested here is Lindgren (2003).

57 Haldeman and Ambrose (1994).

58 See Spike Lee's documentary *When the Levees Broke* (HBO Films).

59 Klein (2001) has clearly described the capacity of experienced and well-trained practitioners to cope with extreme situations.

60 Rosenthal et al. (1989: 437). Boin and Renaud (2013).

61 Vertzberger (1990).

62 Weick and Sutcliffe (2007).

63 Psychologists' understanding of decision making under stress has changed greatly during the last decade. Social and organizational psychologists have increasingly left the laboratory behind to engage in close observation, interviewing, and case reconstructions of the behavior of skilled practitioners acting in real-world settings. The ways in which commanders at the operational level – fire, police, military – make life-and-death decisions under pressure have come under particular scrutiny. See Flin (1996) and Klein (2001).

64 Klein (2001); Kahneman and Klein (2009); Kahneman (2011).

65 Compare with Simon's (1981) discussion on the importance of time. See also Boin and Renaud (2013) on the differences between the operational and strategic world.

66 Of course, incident commanders can and do run into incidents that are qualitatively and quantitatively different from those for which they have trained and prepared. The experience of the New York City Fire and Police Departments on September 11, 2001 is a case in point. The results of the McKinsey and Company studies commissioned after the attacks show that these organizations were not prepared for a contingency of this magnitude and had great difficulty in organizing an effective response. By contrast, the Mayor's office of emergency management and the Mayor himself adapted quickly and effectively to this challenging situation. See Wachtendorf (2004).

67 Roe and Schulman (2008).

68 Rochlin (1996); Weick and Sutcliffe (2007); Hopkins (2009).

69 Weick, Sutcliffe, and Obstfeld (1999).

70 We derive these factors from the research on high reliability organizations. See Rochlin (1996); Weick and Sutcliffe (2007).

71 Wendling et al. (2013); MacFarlane and Leigh (2014).

72 Meijer and Thaens (2013).

73 The heat waves in Chicago (1995) and France (2003) provide telling examples of the stealth nature of many crises. See Klinenberg (2002) and Lagadec (2004) for analyses of these cases.

74 Turner (1978); Mitroff and Pauchant (1990); Pauchant and Mitroff (1992); Perrow (1999); Seeger et al. (2003).

75 This observation does not rule out the possibility of serendipity – sometimes a shot in the dark hits the mark. Once in a while, action based on inaccurate understanding turns out to have beneficial consequences in crisis as in everyday life. Unlike ordinary people, public policy makers can ill afford to bet on luck.

76 See Stern (2009) for a prescriptive framework that can help leaders to enhance their sense-making skills.

77 Dror (2014).

3 Decision Making and Coordinating
Shaping the Crisis Response

3.1 The Myth of Top-Down Command and Control

In March 2011, U.S. President Barack Obama presided over five national security meetings at the White House to go over plans for a military operation designed to kill the country's nemesis, Osama Bin-Laden. A few weeks later, Obama gave the final order to strike. In the secure Situation Room deep within the White House, Obama and his most trusted aides watched the operation unfold in "real time" as U.S. Special Forces stormed the terror chief's compound in Pakistan. A photograph released by U.S. officials captured the drama as the group watched the world's most wanted terrorist finally meet his end.

On July 7, 2005, the morning rush hour in London formed the backdrop for a series of suicide attacks. Four suicide bombers detonated one charge each, killing fifty-two people and injuring more than 700. Hundreds of rescue workers were engaged in the response. With the underground closed down and roads gridlocked, authorities faced a dilemma. The traffic situation affected the mobility of the rescue services as well as of citizens trying to get home from work. As long as the public transportation systems remained down, chaos would prevail in the city streets. But if there were more bombs placed on buses or trains, the consequences of a premature restart could be dire indeed.[1]

These very different examples of high-stakes decision making illustrate a classic notion of executive leadership: making the critical call when it matters most. Both successes and failures of crisis management are often related to such monumental decisions. This notion of crises as "occasions for decision making" is a dominant one in the scholarly literature on crisis management.[2] How leaders make such high-impact decisions in turbulent circumstances has – for good reasons – been considered pivotal by generations of crisis researchers.

Many studies of crisis management report an "upward" shift in decision making: the authority to make critical decisions is adjusted to the scale of the crisis. When a crisis strikes areas that extend over multiple administrative jurisdictions, responsibility for coordinating government responses typically shifts to regional, national, or, for some types of crises, transnational levels of authority.[3] The same goes for crises that are local in geographical terms but whose depth and complexity exceed the coping capacity of local authorities.[4]

The image of the command room, the devilish dilemma, and the decisive leader plays to the widespread expectation that leaders must govern in times of crisis. Yet, this emphasis on top-level policy makers can obscure other, equally critical, performances by other players in other positions. Public leaders do, of course, make highly consequential decisions during a crisis. But so do other, perhaps less visible lower levels of governmental officials and nongovernmental actors. The global trend with regard to managing disasters, for example, is to recognize the limitations of government capabilities and focus on the challenge of mobilizing the whole society in a coordinated fashion bringing public, private, and nonprofit actors together in an effective partnership for response and recovery.[5]

Crisis responses are shaped not just by decisions but also by the *implementation* of those decisions. This brings us to one of the most persistent challenges of crisis leadership: the shaping and coordination of response networks. Many organizations and groups are typically involved in the implementation of crisis decisions. An efficient and legitimate response depends on the orchestration of their actions. It is often assumed that their actions need to be coordinated in a top-down fashion for the response to be coherent and effective, though this is not always the case. We will argue that crisis leadership has a role to play in orchestrating the response, but it works differently than many people think.

The *key question* of this chapter asks how leaders make strategic, response-shaping decisions and what they can do to achieve a coordinated response. Our *core claim* is that crisis responses take shape not just through strategic decision making from the top down; they also depend on the quality of decision making and coordination throughout the response network(s). How coordination is achieved is therefore critically important.

We first look at how individual leaders and high-level groups function as units of strategic decision making under conditions of crisis. Then we describe three alternative modes of shaping crisis responses: non-decision making, decentralization of decision authority, and improvisation by field commanders and units. In the final sections of the chapter, we focus on crisis coordination.

3.2   Crisis Leaders as Decision Makers

In the course of crises, moments may arrive when fateful choices about the government's course of action have to be made.

At the Fukushima Daiichi Nuclear Power Station, workers fought desperately to stabilize the plants and to halt the release of radioactive materials that could contaminate a wide swath of northeastern Japan. Meanwhile, in the Cabinet building, the prime minister and his closest advisers struggled to understand the situation and to issue effective orders that would protect the people. In the heat of the crisis, this small group of politicians and technical experts became directly involved with managing the on-site response at Fukushima Daiichi, ignoring the typical chain of command and the division of responsibilities among ministries. ... With each minister's subordinates standing by for orders, a total of more than 100 people were crowded into the Emergency Control Center. In neighboring rooms, a large contingent of lower-level staff assembled. Altogether, the scene at the Emergency Control Center resembled the clamorous trading floor of an old stock exchange. There was too much to do all at once. Chief Cabinet Secretary Edano was communicating with local governments in earthquake-stricken areas, but was simultaneously grappling with the issue of how to return millions of commuters from Tokyo to their suburban homes when none of the trains were running. And then the tsunami hit.[6]

When such crises emerge, many will look to government leaders to make the call. A leader may seek and obtain counsel from professional advisers, political associates, spouses, friends, and academic experts. But in the end, it is the leader who must decide. It is not easy to make such calls because:

- they are highly consequential: key values and interests of communities are at stake and the price of both "right" and "wrong" decisions can be high – in social, political, economic, and human terms;
- they are likely to contain genuine dilemmas that can be resolved only through trade-off choices, or "tragic choices," where all of the options have low chances of success or will have major negative (side-)effects;
- they may be called upon to make choices that place others in harm's way or reallocate scarce and critical resources;
- they come with major uncertainties about the nature of the issues, the likelihood of future developments, and the possible impact of various policy options.

This combination of characteristics puts leaders in a difficult spot: everybody is looking to them for strategic direction, yet the very characteristics of crises – threat, urgency, uncertainty, collective stress – make it difficult to provide leadership. In making critical decisions that shape the direction of crisis responses, leaders have to somehow discount the uncertainties, overcome any anxieties they may feel, control their impulses, and commit the government's resources to a course of action that they can only hope is both effective and appropriate in the prevailing political and operational context.

Leaders vary greatly in their crisis decision-making propensities, as a brief comparison of some U.S. presidents illustrates. Some leaders tell themselves that making tough calls is part of their job. They accept that they can get it wrong sometimes. President Harry S. Truman was a clear example of this. Preston observes that "Truman's decisiveness has become legendary, as has his willingness to make tough policy decisions regardless of the political consequences. ... The sign that stood upon his desk in the Oval Office bore the inscription 'The Bucks Stops Here!' and throughout his presidency, Truman recognized this most fundamental aspect of his job."[7]

Likewise, president George H. W. Bush, often criticized for lacking a grand policy vision, tended to grow during crisis, when critical decisions had to be made on urgent, complex matters: "Bush's style was to proceed cautiously, yet be willing to act boldly. ... Close associates describe Bush as the 'quintessential man of the moment' who rarely dealt with problems unless they were forced upon him, yet who tended to be a brilliant crisis manager."[8] Bush's son, President George W. Bush, wore his nickname 'the Decider' as a badge of honor (he composed his presidential memoir around what he saw as the key decisions during his two terms in office). Yet the calls he made during some crises were highly controversial. They arguably led to some of the country's most damaging policy fiascos, including the relentless pursuit of an invasion of Iraq and his administration's controversial response to Hurricane Katrina.[9]

Other leaders are less comfortable with making decisions under pressure. Their personality and style may predispose them to consider all sides of a problem and therefore insist upon extensive analysis, multiple sources of advice, and extensive deliberation with and among advisers before making a decision. Yet other leaders experience crisis decision making as an excruciating predicament. They dread the idea that their decisions may disappoint or even damage others; some are afraid to fail and some become paralyzed by the need to make a choice in the face of conflicting advice.

In some cases, crisis leaders may seek to dissociate themselves as much as possible from managing the crisis response. Confronted with the overwhelming pressures of crisis, they may question whether they and their organizations will be able to cope effectively. When they feel the chances for success are slight, they may seek to escape personal responsibility for potentially fateful government choices and policies.

This produces what we might call "strategic evasion": trying to fly under the radar and continuing to insist that the main responsibility for crisis response lies with other agencies or levels of government.

Again, U.S. presidents provide good examples. Belying his public image (and self-image) as a take-no-prisoners hardliner, Richard Nixon actually found it very difficult to make "big" decisions. Particularly when they concerned himself and his key associates, he experienced them as epic tests of his wit, will, and wisdom that he would spend a lot of energy avoiding, and when that was no longer possible, he would withdraw (sometimes for days) into his inner recesses before making the dreaded call.

President Jimmy Carter succumbed to the cumulative pressures brought upon him by the second world oil crisis, the Soviet invasion of Afghanistan, and the Iranian hostage crisis. These complex and dynamic events shattered key components of his worldview. Perhaps more importantly, the Iranian hostage crisis wore him down psychologically. A micromanager by inclination, he met with his innermost advisers almost every day at breakfast for over a year to discuss the crisis. Eventually, the frustrating lack of progress, the increasingly bitter disagreements between his state department and national security staff advisers, the failure of the military rescue operation, and the increasingly public humiliation of his presidency which the hostage crisis elicited, got to him and negatively affected his decision-making performance.[10]

The voracious reader, ideas man, and debater Bill Clinton had been considered "constitutionally incapable of decisiveness" even as Governor of Arkansas.[11] Procrastination became the default approach to many of the issues he faced as president, particularly in his first term. In crises, Clinton acted as a "delegator-observer," creating room for time-consuming and often inconclusive debates between advisers and agencies.[12]

There are occasions when leaders believe that a decision simply has to be made – and fast.[13] But fast decisions are not necessarily good decisions. In one comprehensive meta-analysis of U.S. presidential decision making during international crises, the quality of crisis decision making was "low" in seven and "medium" in four out of nineteen cases studied.[14] These mixed results are mirrored by many in-depth case studies.[15] Some government leaders defy the sense of urgency and take some time to decide, so that they can reflect and really weigh the values and interests at stake and the desirability and feasibility of the options put before them – even in a crisis. And some government leaders have a better feel for the distinction between strategic and operational decisions, realizing that they should focus on the former, and not resort to top-down micromanagement of the latter.

3.3   Crisis Teams and Group Dynamics

Chief executives are not the only or even the most influential shapers of crisis responses. For one, they need and seek advice. Even in times of crisis, they operate within collective decision-making structures – formal and informal ones. Governance by committee – cabinets, executive boards, project groups, and other "top teams" – does not come to an end once a crisis is perceived or declared. But the nature, authority, and decision rules of those committees may change quite dramatically. Most crisis contingency plans provide for collegial bodies to gather, decide, and coordinate crisis responses. Many leaders form "war cabinets" – small, informal inner circles of key players and confidantes – when they face major crises. Such groups vary in composition, size, and other relevant characteristics, even within the course of a single crisis.[16] They become the critical nodes of what often are vast and highly complex multiorganizational and intergovernmental networks that come into being in response to crises.[17]

Clearly, "top teams" have their virtues in assuring high-performance under turbulent conditions.[18] But they also have potential weaknesses.[19] In the high-pressure, high-consequence context of crises, the potential advantages of groups – increased intellectual and cognitive capacity (following the conventional wisdom that two know more than one) – are easily offset by pathological group dynamics. Understanding crisis decision making therefore requires understanding the group dynamics that may affect decision making.

The main problem, borne out by historical and laboratory studies alike, is that individuals in groups often do not share and use information effectively in advising leaders or reaching collective decisions. Two extreme forms of group behavior impede the quality of group deliberation and choice: conflict and conformity. Some groups fall apart under crisis pressure. In other groups, loyalty to the leader and the preservation of unity eclipse group members' critical faculties and better judgment: "criticism, dissent, and mutual recrimination literally must wait until the crisis is over."[20]

Both extremes typically produce underperformance: too much conflict will paralyze the decision-making process and too much conformity lowers the likelihood that voices will be raised against rash responses and blunt adventurism of the group leader(s). The possibility for extremes is enhanced by the high degree of informality that characterizes the interaction within crisis groups: procedural rules and institutional safeguards that stabilize regular modes of policymaking tend to disappear, especially when turbulent conditions last for some time. While this may stimulate innovative and creative practices, it also leaves groups exposed to a number of vulnerabilities. These include the following.

Ad-hocery and new-group syndrome – The members of top-level coordination groups or crisis teams can be unfamiliar with what is expected of them and the rules of the game that apply. Especially in settings where crises are rare occurrences, chances are high that top executives have little crisis experience and crisis exercises have been few, far between, and not particularly demanding. Moreover, some crises hit at an impossible hour when not all of the regular officeholders are available or just after a new government has been formed or a major cabinet reshuffle has taken place. When this happens, the people gathering around the top table will not always be familiar with one another and with their respective crisis management roles and responsibilities, let alone have experience of working together as a group.

This makes such groups vulnerable to "new-group syndrome," which occurs when

group members are uncertain about their roles and status and thus are concerned about the possibility of being made a scapegoat. . . . Hence they are likely to avoid expressing opinions that are different from those proposed by the leader or other powerful persons in the group, to avoid conflict by failing to criticize one another's ideas, and even to agree overtly with other people's suggestions while disagreeing covertly.[21]

These behaviors may partly be a product of what has been called "false cohesion" grounded in group members' motivations to maintain their position within the inner circle of power and prestige. New-group syndrome can be counteracted by the group leader intervening actively in order to set roles, norms, and ground rules that suspend extra-group status considerations and encourage broad and forthright participation from the very start.

Conformity pressures and groupthink – Laboring under intense pressure and in relative isolation from "life as usual" in the world outside, crisis teams can become more to their members than functional units for deliberation or political arenas for managing internal conflict. They can become "sanctuaries" for a leader and his associates: a place of refuge from the pressures of crisis politics and the dilemmas of crisis management responsibility. An intimate and shielded environment helps them to reduce the anxiety and stress that many of them experience during a crisis.

Such collective stress reduction comes at the price of a diminished capacity for reality-testing.[22] Premature and excessive concurrence seeking among group members – a phenomenon known as groupthink – has been put forward as an explanation of policy fiascos and mismanaged crises. Members of groups affected by groupthink fall prey to groundless but infectious optimism about their ability to see through a crisis successfully. Members who do not share this "illusion of invulnerability" will feel constrained to speak frankly about any doubts and misgivings they may have about the course of action preferred by the group and/or its leaders.[23]

Centrifugality and politicking – At the other end of the spectrum, crises may give rise to intense conflict within decision-making groups. The high-stakes, high-pressure environment of crises can exacerbate preexisting interpersonal, ideological, or bureaucratic tensions between group members. When this happens, crisis decision-making units become battle-grounds, where strategic behavior is the norm.[24] Group members will, for example, use their information and expertise as a weapon or shield in their internecine struggles rather than help the group as a whole reach sensible decisions. Rumors, leaks, silences, and misrepresentations are part and parcel of this process, as are attempts to form or break up cliques within the group. There will be fierce competition for the leader's ear and attempts to destroy the credibility of competitors for the leader's attention. And when members of these politicized crisis groups begin to lose confidence that a successful resolution of the crisis can be achieved, they will focus on saving themselves rather than keeping the group afloat.[25]

Formal procedures and functional requirements usually govern the constitution of crisis teams. In reality, many considerations enter the picture, which may foster imbalances or incorporate conflict into the group process. A leader's personal needs, sentiments, and calculations typically affect who is in and who is out of the loop during a crisis. Many leaders surround themselves with trusted and liked sources of information and advice. Agencies that traditionally are low in the bureaucratic pecking order may simply be overlooked or ignored regardless of their potential importance to the crisis response. The "non-favored" and "forgotten" actors and agencies are thus precluded from airing their perspectives and sharing their information and expertise in the top-level group. Although shutting down difference and dissent in a task group is a very bad idea, particularly when it has to make high-stakes decisions, leaders or other group members sometimes deliberately attempt to "rig" the composition of the inner circle or the process by which the group operates to gain acceptance for their preferred courses of action and deny proponents of competing views a platform.[26]

This creates a double bind for leaders. Arnold Meltsner put it well when he argued that:

> there is a delicate balance between the need for the ruler to be strong-minded [in responding to a crisis] and the need for openness in presenting problems and receiving advice. What is required is a ruler who appears to the external world to be in charge but who, within the inner circle, has created norms of equality to promote discussion, dissent, and multiple perspectives.[27]

Even in the best of circumstances, however, the shadow of hierarchy is always present in groups, even if their formal authority structure is not all that hierarchical: some group members will second-guess the leader's preferences and tell them what they think they will want to hear, or at least avoid telling them what they think they do not want to know.[28]

3.4 Crisis Responses on the Ground

Conventional wisdom dictates that government leaders and top teams make strategic decisions and coordinate government action when crises occur. They are expected to put aside parochial interests and ongoing squabbles – they must act in concert. It would be a mistake, however, to assume that leaders and central governments are always "in control" of the crisis response process.[29] Many pivotal crisis decisions are not and should not be made by heads of government, chief executives, or the official crisis strategy group. Instead they emerge from the world beyond and below.[30] The crisis response in modern society is best characterized in terms of distributed authority and network processes. This is not necessarily counterproductive. A well-structured delegation of decision-making authority can make for a more timely, effective, and legitimate response.[31]

Non-Decision Making

In concentrating on "strategic decisions" and "coordinated responses," we may forget that the course of crises is shaped by circumstance as well as by choice: so-called non-decisions may determine the course of events just as much as deliberate policy decisions. Different forms of non-decision making during crises can be discerned: (1) decisions that are not implemented; (2) decisions not to decide; (3) decisions not to act. These produce responses that are tardy, or prevent action from being taken altogether. Such paralysis is usually blamed on human errors or information system pathologies, but in many instances there are cultural and political dynamics at play within and between the organizations involved.[32]

Consider the 1985 Heysel Stadium soccer disaster in Brussels. The crisis began when fighting broke out between rival groups of British and Italian fans before the start of the 1985 European Football Cup final between Juventus and Liverpool. British hooligans attacked the Italian crowd in the adjacent section of the stands, triggering panic among the Italians locked up in their section. When a stadium wall collapsed under the pressure of bodies seeking to get out, a stampede ensued resulting in thirty-nine deaths and 450 wounded.[33] As the crisis unfolded, several crucial non-decisions shaped the response.

Decisions not implemented – No consistent strategies were devised to manage the flood of telephone calls received at the stadium from anxious friends and relatives of spectators in the Italian section, who, along with millions of viewers all over the world, had witnessed the disaster live on television. In addition, no strategy was formulated for handling the press. The informal group of authorities, assembling in the stadium's VIP lounge, never considered the idea of terminating television coverage of the match.[34]

Decisions not to decide – The Belgian Minister for the Interior watched the match at his Brussels apartment. He assessed that the authorities on the ground were in a better position to judge what should be done, so chose not to involve himself. He did not go to the site of the disaster (a decision for which he was greatly criticized afterwards).

Decisions not to act – The third type of non-decision occurred when judicial authorities were summoned to the stadium immediately after the disaster. Upon arrival, the public prosecutor and the Belgian Minister for Justice conferred with police commanders. The immediate issue was whether or not to make arrests on the spot. Given the lack of police manpower and the operational complications of apprehending individuals in an aggressive crowd, they reluctantly decided on a policy of containment rather than prosecution. This decision not to act became the center of public controversy in the days after the disaster.

Decentralization

Well before September 11, 2001, the Federal Aviation Agency (FAA) and the North American Aerospace Defense Command (NORAD) had developed a procedure for collaboration in the event of a hijacking. Before the FAA could ask NORAD to take down a civil aircraft, "multiple levels of notification and approval at the highest levels of government" were required.[35] In the 9/11 crisis, there was no time to follow protocol, as the FAA's Boston Center – which was tracking American Flight 11 (headed for the World Trade Center's North Tower) – realized. The Boston

Center did not follow the protocol and contacted the military directly, asking for F-15s. After asking whether this was "real-world or exercise," two F-15 aircraft scrambled. As the 9/11 Commission notes: "The air defense of America began with this call."

Minutes before American Flight 11 hit the North Tower, United Flight 175 turned course toward the South Tower. This change went unnoticed, as the flight controller responsible for United 175 was still looking for American Flight 11, which had just crashed. When the controller realized he had a second problem on his hands, a colleague tried to notify the regional managers. They refused to be disturbed, as they were in a meeting discussing the first crash. Meanwhile, American 77 disappeared from the radar of the Indianapolis Center. Unaware of the other hijackings, the controller feared a crash and began to look for clues. This is what happened in the next half hour:

Indianapolis Center never saw Flight 77 turn around. By the time it reappeared in primary radar coverage, controllers had either stopped looking for the aircraft because they thought it had crashed or were looking toward the west [the flight was headed for Los Angeles]. Although the Command Center learned Flight 77 was missing, neither it nor the FAA headquarters issued an all-points bulletin to surrounding centers to search for primary radar targets. American 77 traveled undetected for 36 minutes on a course due east for Washington, DC.[36]

This example demonstrates both the ways in which highly centralized procedures can slow a critical response and the ways in which initiative by lower-level officials can fill the vacuum and help keep the response on track. The logic of centralization enjoys its largest appeal when crisis response plans are made; in other words, when there is not a "live" crisis to deal with. Armed with knowledge of the past – the Cold War scenarios imagined threatening planes coming in from across the ocean – efficient protocols are formulated that invest crisis leaders with the means and authority to deal with the impending threat. But in the immediate hours following the 9/11 attacks, it was a lower-level official who decided to shut down U.S. airspace and force the immediate landing of thousands of airplanes.[37]

Betting on centralization in times of crisis can be a potential liability. The crisis that actually happens always differs from the envisioned ones on which formal crisis management structures are predicated. Protocols may turn out to be time consuming. Channels of centralization may lead to powerless or incapable agencies, bypassing and effectively neutralizing those that are actually capable of making a difference. As Weick observes:

The danger in centralization and contraction of authority is that there may be a reduction in the level of competence directed at the problem. . . . The person in authority is not necessarily the most competent person to deal with a crisis, so a contraction of authority leads either to less action or more confusion.[38]

Centralization of crisis responses has been known to produce policies that are experienced by the staff "on the ground" as insufficient, ineffective, or even counterproductive.[39] Students of disaster management have long argued that centralized modes of responding to distributed and fast-moving threats are a prime source of problems. They recommend decentralization as an unavoidable necessity during crisis response.[40] In some organizations and governments, awareness of centralization's downsides has led to preplanned, formalized decentralization of authority for certain vital areas of crisis response. For example, during the Cold War era, authority to launch nuclear counter strikes in case of a "decapitating" first strike against American centers of political and military decision making was delegated to submarine commanders.[41]

As noted in Chapter 2, high reliability organizations have adopted decentralization as a defining characteristic of their safety culture. In these organizations, command structures for crisis are built on the premise that only those decisions that cannot be taken on the spot will rise to the top where crisis leaders reside.[42] There is evidence from studies of U.S. firms during the post-2008 recession that those who switched to more decentralized modes of decision making weathered the storms much better, as they were more agile and could act quicker to deal with local manifestations of the crisis and craft tailor-made response strategies.[43]

Top leaders and national policy makers, particularly in highly dynamic and technically complex crises, are usually better off relying on and supporting local authorities, expert agencies, and skillful operators rather than "taking charge" (micromanaging) of operational issues themselves. In a system that is guided by widely shared central values, decentralization of decision-making authority is not a risk but an asset to the system's response capacity. It helps leaders to conserve their energy for making the truly strategic calls that no one below can or should make.

Improvisation

Crises have the nasty habit of rendering the best-laid plans and their planned authority structures irrelevant. At New York City's Ground Zero, the entire emergency command center was wiped out by the 9/11 attacks and there was no planned fallback facility for that eventuality; improvisation was the only way to regain oversight and enable strategic decisions to be made in a more centralized fashion.

When uncertainty leads to bewilderment, the crisis response will not resemble a neatly delineated process of strategic decision making and operational execution. Professionals will try to do the best they can do given the circumstances; crisis leaders can only try to facilitate and orchestrate. Consider the 2010 Chilean mine disaster, when thirty-three miners were trapped underground for weeks. The Chileans ended up rescuing their trapped miners through bold and effective improvisation enabled by effective leadership that both empowered and directed that improvisation. As Rashid, Edmonson, and Leonard put it in their study of the response:

> During times of uncertainty, leaders must enlist a diverse group of highly skilled people but ask them to leave behind preconceived notions and prepackaged solutions. Those specialists need to understand that no matter how experienced they might be, they have never before faced the challenge at hand. The group needs to explore, experiment, and invent together, and to integrate deep knowledge and ideas – not just apply them. People have to work in fluid, shifting arrangements, rotating in and out of teams as the demands of the situation evolve.[44]

But it would be overly optimistic to think all responses are this effective. Despite the contemporary rhetoric about the need for "agility" and "resilience" in government, many governments and public agencies are not geared up for improvisation (and decentralization) in their strategic decision making. A critical question in this regard is when improvisation is most likely to work.

Improvisation is most easily achieved when professionals are confronted with known unknowns.[45] We can find the kind of mental preparedness and cultural climate required for effective and legitimate improvisation in organizations – emergency services and other pockets of public operational response capacity – that routinely deal with similar types of incidents.[46] This account of the medical response to the 2011 Boston Marathon bombings is illustrative:

> The response by medical personnel, both at the site of the blast and in the hospitals, was handled nearly completely without central direction. Emergency medical teams and physicians at the scene, following preestablished protocols and improvising as necessary, were largely self-directed in caring for the injured. Doctors and nurses with relevant skills converged on emergency rooms without having to be called. As ambulances delivered patients to hospitals, groups of clinicians self-organized into trauma teams. In one emergency room, people who were not needed to provide direct care realized that there was a congestion problem. They organized themselves in a side room from which they could be called as their particular skills were needed. Several emergency room "incident commanders" commented that they had to give few instructions. One said:

"Everybody spontaneously knew their dance moves." Mass casualty training and drills provided a structure for action within which improvisation to meet special problems was possible.[47]

Some administrative traditions and organizational cultures are particularly conducive to improvisation. They value pragmatism and provide a license to middle managers to "ask forgiveness rather than permission" (as the cliché holds) when they feel circumstances require them to exercise judgment and try unconventional approaches instead of following rules and precedents. In other words, they enable seamless "culture-switching" between routine and crisis conditions.[48]

Other administrative traditions and organizational cultures (those found in many large bureaucracies) constrain or actively discourage the effective use of improvisation.[49] Public bureaucracies are designed to deal in an effective and responsible way with a certain category of social problems, to categorize clients and deliver services in standardized ways – in the interest of efficiency and fairness. These organizations typically attempt to minimize uncertainty for their employees, which allows them to structure their activities and embed best practices.[50] They lack the language and the cultural DNA required to switch gears; they rely on formal rules rather than professional judgment, and on following orders rather than improvisation.

This creates a paradox: when managers and employees in public organizations realize that a crisis demands the organization to improvise, they will look to rules and precedents to guide the required behavior. There is a solution to this apparent paradox: rules can be set up to facilitate a *switch* to improvisation under certain specified circumstances[51]. This can only work when managers have been trained to recognize (and empowered to switch their modus operandi) when available repertoires no longer suffice to deal with the crisis at hand and when sticking to existing routines creates delay and dysfunction in response. Such a switch to "crisis improvisation mode" makes it possible to expedite decisions, cut red tape, improve flexibility, and enable drawing upon extra resources within certain legal limits.

3.5   Crisis Coordination: Challenges, Forms, and Fault Lines[52]

Even when leaders make well-informed decisions that define a clear course of action, they still face the challenge of making sure that their decisions materialize. Leaders depend on organizations – both inside and outside their immediate jurisdiction – to execute their decisions. As most crises typically involve multiple organizations, leaders rely on some level of coordination between these organizations. However, the characteristics of crisis, particularly the early stages of an acute emergency, make central coordination of operations elusive. Smooth cooperation is not easy when the cause of the crisis is unknown, communication is impaired, the damage untold, and the potential consequences of one's actions can only be imagined.

Coordination pertains to the collaboration between response partners.[53] It is helpful to make a conceptual distinction between crisis coordination as *process* (the orchestration of activities) and as *outcome* (concerted action by collaborating actors).[54] The latter definition is about observed collaboration ("the partners were working together in coordinated fashion"). Collaboration, in this sense, may be not much more than the timely sharing of information, but it can also involve far-reaching integration of operations in pursuit of defined strategic objectives – such as "desired national outcomes" – via joint command centers, joint task forces, joint-field offices, or other institutionalized coordination mechanisms. We can also define coordination in terms of a managerial activity, a form of orchestration ("the government tried to coordinate the actions of all those involved"). In this perspective, crisis coordination is about *organizing and safeguarding collaborative processes within networks of actors involved in crisis response and/or recovery*.

The interesting question is why in some cases high levels of collaboration are being achieved (the oft-praised immediate response to the 2005 London bombings) while in others the fabric of "joined-up" governance falls apart at the seams (as happened during the 2005 response to Hurricane Katrina). The field of disaster studies has paid particular attention to this question. Effective cooperation under conditions of crisis is unlikely to emerge by itself.

Planning is by no means a sufficient mechanism for bringing crisis collaboration about.[55] Most governments have in place formal structures of crisis coordination. Such structures (and the processes they enable) may or may not be relevant to what actually happens in the interorganizational and intergovernmental space when a major contingency actually occurs. Many contingency plans, and the coordination structures envisaged within them, can be characterized as "fantasy documents," based on blatantly unrealistic – more often than not overly optimistic – premises.[56] Other plans may be substantively sound but end up as dead letter, as they are ill-disseminated or lack grounding in the relevant executives' mind-sets and organizational cultures.

How can leaders facilitate or impose collaboration between actors within as well as outside government – many of which do not regularly collaborate, or even interact, in day-to-day governance processes? How can they cut across different levels of government? In the event of transboundary crises, how can they establish cross-national and supranational interfaces and platforms?[57] To assess how effective crisis collaboration can be achieved through some form of orchestration, we recognize two dimensions of this issue: *vertical* and *horizontal* coordination.

Vertical coordination is about the relations between actors that stand in some form of (formal or de facto) hierarchical relationship to one another: agency heads or boards and executives of regional offices or niche departments; central agencies and line departments; national and subnational levels of government. In theory, any differences between them can be resolved by a ruling from the center. But in practice, much of the action in crisis response can and will be shaped by actors operating at considerable geographical and mental distance from the core executive, in networks of interdependent stakeholders where no one can be said to be "in charge."[58] Horizontal coordination is about the division of labor between organizations that are not in any hierarchical relationship to one another. Collaboration is a coincidental or negotiated outcome. It can take the shape of lateral platforms and processes of exchange, or the provision of facilitation and direction by a superordinate authority. In democracies, it is rarely, if ever, the result of orders emanating from the executive.

Vertical Coordination: Negotiating Authority

In most systems, vertical coordination is organized around what we may call the "principle of disaster subsidiarity." Crisis preparedness plans (and the legal frameworks undergirding them in many countries) have traditionally been built around the premise that a crisis is best managed by first responders who are located near the geographical location of impact or technical experts who know most about a certain threat. When local authorities cannot cope, they request assistance from higher authorities. While this looks good on paper and tends to work well in crisis simulations, this arrangement does not always work as smoothly as envisioned when a real crisis strikes.

A key issue in vertical coordination is the *upscaling dilemma*: when should higher authorities step in and what, exactly, does "stepping in" entail? Who decides when the moment has come? Shifting crisis management authority up widens the gap between decision makers and the scene. It often necessitates new relations between central authorities and local responders. It may create resentment among local authorities and victims. It is, in short, a delicate decision that prompts the question whether the coordination problem that is solved really is worse than the one that is being created. While the principle of disaster subsidiarity works fine on paper, the reality of crisis tends to demonstrate underlying fault lines. We recognize three types of fault lines, which occur frequently in crisis situations.

Formal fault lines – Detailed divisions of labor for particular types of crisis often prove unsuitable for the network of required actors that must be assembled to deal with the crisis at hand. Crises tend to create unique challenges, which cannot always be foreseen. Few crisis or disaster plans survive contact with reality.[59] This is particularly true for transboundary crises, which spill over geographical and functional borders. Fast-moving crises with multiple "ground zeroes" – think of the H1N1 pandemic, the crisis of sexual abuse discovered in many national congregations of the Roman Catholic Church, the global financial crisis, or IS's recruitment of young Jihadists throughout the West – require different coordination modes than localized ones, such as an industrial explosion or a prison riot.

The nature of the system in question does, of course, matter. In unitary states we may expect vertical coordination to work faster and smoother than in federal states where lines of authority may be more contested. In unitary systems, there tend to be formal arrangements that enable political executives to concentrate formal decision-making authority by some sort of legal mechanism (usually a type of emergency declaration). In federal systems, this is not so easy. Even in times of crisis, it is hard if not impossible, to concentrate decision-making powers into the executive office. Take, for instance, the difficulties experienced by European leaders and EU institutions in the management of the Euro-zone crisis: the question "who is in charge?" cannot be answered unequivocally. The EU's monetary governance arrangements are simply too complex.[60] The more salient question thus becomes: who might have the informal authority necessary to perform the leadership work of crisis coordination: to convene, to set agendas, to frame joint approaches, to employ a calculated mix of hard and soft power required to herd the many cats without whom a concerted approach cannot occur?

Cultural fault lines – It is often assumed that a crisis or disaster should remove all barriers to cooperation that may exist between hierarchically related actors. In reality, crises tend to reinforce preexisting forms of distrust. In systems where local communities regard central (or higher) authorities with distrust, we may therefore expect problems with vertical coordination – efforts to coordinate will be perceived as ill-disguised designs to "take over." Local resilience is celebrated and central "handouts" are viewed with suspicion. In some areas of the United States, for instance, widespread distrust of "the feds" does not enable smooth coordination between local and federal authorities (Hurricane Katrina being a case in point). A history of successful cooperation between different levels of government, on the other hand, may be expected to smooth cooperation.[61] In regions or nations that are repeatedly beset by similar crises, interorganizational and intergovernmental coordination patterns may become institutionalized in networks, whose composition and rules of interaction evolve as part of an emerging crisis management subculture. Likewise, at the community level, so-called disaster subcultures exist in towns or regions that are frequently exposed to natural disasters.[62]

Political fault lines – Who is in charge matters. Some leaders may be tempted to use vertical coordination as a tool to assume power or to avoid responsibility. U.S. presidents understand that issuing a disaster declaration is a symbolically powerful act with few negative side effects; presidential opponents understand that as well.[63] After Hurricane Andrew struck Florida in the summer of 1992, and a few months before the election, the (Democratic) governor of Florida was reportedly slow to request federal assistance as he did not want to enhance the standing of President Bush (a Republican) in the eyes of Floridians. In a similar vein, it has been reported that Governor Blanco was less than eager to bail out Mayor Nagin of New Orleans – even though they were both Democrats, Nagin had supported Blanco's Republican opponent Bobby Jindal in the previous elections. After Hurricane Sandy, the Republican governor of New Jersey, Chris Christie, worked closely with President Obama (to the dismay of many fellow Republicans). These reports, accurate or not, illustrate the often-made observation that crises are opportunities to demonstrate leadership. They are also potential pitfalls for leaders who do not understand the political nature of crisis management.

The acid test for crisis leaders trying to establish vertical coordination comes at ground level: do organizations actually align their behavior and exchange pivotal operational information? When intergovernmental and bureaucratic politics pervade the crisis response process, the chances are slim for a central decision-making center to impose itself on the squabbling factions. Under these conditions, the center runs a good chance of becoming an arena in which the various stakeholders promote different approaches and priorities with regard to what should be done. The typical result is large disparities between the compromise decisions reached in crisis centers and the actual conduct of crisis operations within and between different executive agencies and field managers.

Horizontal Coordination: Matching Function to Place

Crises and disasters come in a great variety of forms posing potentially different demands upon the responding communities and governments. They therefore trigger the involvement of a great number of different organizations representing different "technologies" of crisis response, whose roles and ways of working need to be aligned. The Anthrax crisis, which held the U.S. in its grip during the immediate aftermath of the 9/11 attacks, provides an illuminating example of an emergent network in response to an unimagined threat. Many different organizations that did not routinely work together now had to forge cooperation: hospitals, intelligence organizations, police, specialized army units with knowledge of Anthrax, the U.S. postal service, and all the organizations that received white powder letters.

An elementary challenge for those seeking to achieve a coordinated response is what disaster researchers refer to as the *matching of place and function*.[64] Public organizations are traditionally designed to perform a specific function (e.g., garbage collection, train service, medical care, punishment, and so forth). These organizations perform their function in a given geographic area, under specified conditions. Crises challenge these organizational designs because they rarely fall exactly within the boundaries of predefined policy areas.

Crisis coordination can be further complicated by what is known in the disaster literature as the problem of mass convergence (or mass assault): citizens try to make their way to the scene while government officials rush to be involved in the policy response to the crisis. At the community level, people may have different motives for doing so – varying from concern about the safety of loved ones and genuine altruistic instincts to plain sensationalism – but the effects are the same: roads clog up, which slows the mobilization of emergency responders; much-needed emergency responders must keep "disaster tourists" at bay; communication and physical interaction between responders is hindered. At the elite level, executives and agencies may likewise be driven by a combination of altruistic and opportunistic motives in seeking – or seeking to avoid – involvement in the crisis response effort. Even within the corridors of executive power, a form of "mass assault" may occur, which requires careful management of access, involvement and coordination to achieve a measured and coherent set of government utterances and initiatives.

To be sure, citizen self-organization and spontaneous volunteering are often critical to an effective response, especially in the early phases of a large-scale disaster.[65] Social media has made it easier for citizens to

Table 3.1 *Types of Organizations in Disaster Response Processes*

Tasks	*Regular*	*Non-regular*
Structure		
Existing	Type 1: Established (e.g., police, fire, ambulance services)	Type 2: Extending (e.g., housing, family, social services, tax, schools)
New	Type 3: Expanding (e.g., Red Cross, Salvation Army)	Type 4: Emerging (e.g., recovery authorities, disaster victims' organizations)

organize themselves. At the same time, the efforts of citizens must be aligned with incoming professionals. That is no easy task, if only because incoming first responders may not really be "first" on the scene and earn little respect when they ignore or even dismiss the often heroic efforts of those who rushed to the scene to offer their help.[66]

The variety of groups and organizations that can become involved in crisis responses is well captured in the classic typology of organizational responses to disaster proposed by Russell Dynes.[67] It rests on two pivotal dimensions: Is an organization's involvement in a crisis or disaster part of that organization's core tasks or not? Do the organization's response operations occur within its preexisting structure or does the organization need to adapt its structure or size? Combined, these dimensions produce a four-fold typology (see Table 3.1). Each cell harbors a cluster of organizations with similar characteristics and crisis response predicaments.

Type 1 Established organizations typically constitute the first-line response to an unfolding acute emergency. They often make a real "life and death" difference through the speed, scope, and effectiveness of their response, which, in turn, depends on the quality of their internal communications and the training of their first responders. These organizations have high public visibility and usually enjoy strong public support. They consider themselves to be at the heart of crisis management, and they typically spend a considerable part of their resources on crisis planning, preparation, and training. They tend to be less sensitized to the wider policy and political ramifications that crises might have.

Type 2 Extending organizations play a crucial role in the secondary response to a crisis, that is, dealing with the economic, social, and psychological impacts of crises and disasters. Disaster response is not necessarily part of their core business, though it typically is covered within their broader mandates. Their level of involvement in crisis planning is fairly limited. They are usually part of "the bureaucracy" that citizens experience on a day-to-day basis. The public standing they enjoy prior to the crisis may vary considerably but more often than not is considerably lower than that of the established emergency services. Extending organizations face the challenge of having to switch from sequential processing of individual cases to high-speed, parallel processing of large numbers of cases, and from well-structured, predictable cases to unusual, unregulated cases. This requires improvisation and departures from standard operating procedures. A typical example is the housing authority of a large city that must suddenly relocate a large number of victims who lost their homes due to a flood or explosion or the sudden influx of refugees that require the mobilization of many agencies and volunteers.

Type 3 Expanding organizations are typically human services organizations within and outside government that have crisis management as a key (though not core) component of their mission. In these organizations, the majority of their personnel are routinely committed to tasks other than crisis management (they remain "dormant"). Volunteer-dominated expanding organizations such as the Red Cross perform support roles for the established organizations but may also provide public services in their own right. Their performance stands or falls with their ability to maintain "surge capacity," both quantitatively and qualitatively.

Type 4 Emerging organizations are literally born during, or in the wake of, crises and disasters. They emerge spontaneously and unexpectedly, in reaction to hitherto unplanned needs or perceived deficiencies of the existing response efforts (i.e., victims' groups, recovery networks). Their mandates tend to be ambiguous, their authority structures unclear, and their processes unstructured. They "land" and try to "add value" in an already densely populated organizational space. This is known to create tensions with some of the preexisting organizations. In response to the Katrina disaster, an emergent network of business organizations arose to coordinate responses of the private sector. That collaboration of private and public actors has subsequently been institutionalized in Business Emergency Operations Centers at both state and national levels, which can be activated in times of crisis.[68]

When the organizations in a response network do not work well together, the strategic level must try to induce collaboration through horizontal coordination. There are many problems that may emerge. Horizontal cooperation between responding parties is, for instance, easily undermined by both technical and cultural communication problems. Organizations may entertain different notions of the meaning and necessity of coordination. Emergency workers, for instance, generally understand the need for cooperation but may vehemently disagree on the ways by which other "nonprofessional" organizations try to achieve it. Military organizations prefer hierarchical coordination, whereas medical teams are more likely to resist coordination efforts from above. The variety of interpretations with regard to the necessity and meaning of crisis coordination increases significantly with the increasing complexity of the crisis.

We can organize these tensions by identifying some natural fault lines that can play out in the horizontal coordination arenas, thus undermining the effectiveness of the response network.

"Professionals" versus "amateurs" – The well-trained first responders – often eager to show that they are ready – may be shocked or dismayed (or both) with the perceived lack of speed and experience that "bureaucrats" from Type 2 organizations can display during a crisis. While first responders have their "feet in the mud," they see how the "bureaucrats" fail to "ramp up" to high-speed, high-volume people processing requirements. They wonder aloud how the "do-gooders" of Type 3 organizations can deliver ("we will have to find something for them to do"). The "bureaucrats," in turn, will try to explain that their organizations were doing the best that they can given the impossible tasks at hand. The volunteers of Type 3 organizations are astounded to learn that their contributions are not being valued.

Operational versus strategic perspectives – In the thick of crisis, first responders tend to be solely and urgently concerned with the safety and survival of (potential) victims. This is their mission, it is what they train to do, what makes them tick. This operational perspective, and the total lack of concern with the long term (the here and now is the only thing that matters), conflicts easily (and often rapidly) with the perspective that Type 2 organizations bring to the scene. Other values – fairness and accountability, for example – enter the decision-making arena. Conflicting values can give rise to vehement disagreements that play out on-site, fueling already existing misperceptions about underlying motivations. For instance, the search and rescue dimension of disasters tends to lose importance quickly, making the other organization types more relevant and important. This can lead to frustration among first responders, which feeds mounting disrespect ("we have done our job, why can't you do yours?"). The operational fixation and apparent blindness to the bigger policy picture and long-term considerations beyond the incident at hand tend to confound members of the other organizational types.

On-site versus wider perspectives – Members of Type 3 organizations typically enter the response network from the "outside." They are volunteers who rushed to the scene, leaving behind families and jobs ("we're here to help"). Appreciation for these volunteers may not last long ("nobody here asked you to help"). When outside organizations establish themselves in the arena and claim authority, locals may resist. They may not immediately recognize the competence, ability, or legitimacy of these incoming organizations. This perception can be further strengthened if Type 3 organizations play to their funders, sticking to an action repertoire that is in line with their mandate and refusing to take on additional tasks. Or worse, when Type 3 organizations start fighting each other for "turf," performing in the lights of TV cameras. Type 3 organizations will argue that without funding they cannot help.

The clash of elites – The political and organizational elites that operate in a crisis response network add a critical ingredient to the mix. In the ideal-typical scenario, they will seek to resolve emerging tensions and steer their organizations toward enhanced and flexible collaboration to manage the crisis at hand. But leaders may recognize unsuspected opportunities in a crisis (we will elaborate on the idea of crisis exploitation in following chapters). If it serves their organizational or personal purposes, leaders have been known to initiate strategies and actions that not necessarily work toward a coordinated response. Moreover, in small systems where leaders know each other well, a crisis can easily rekindle simmering tensions between elites. The orchestration of a large-scale response network thus inevitably entails the "handling" of other leaders.

We do not mean to suggest that coordination problems will always play out along these fault lines. We do suggest that leaders, who will be held responsible for coordination failures, should consider these types of fault lines and the roles they play in causing some perennial crisis coordination problems.

3.6   Nurturing Crisis Coordination

The act of coordination, at heart, is a political activity: to create orderly interaction within and among organizations requires delicate choices about power, responsibility, rules of conduct, and division of labor.[69] The core challenge of coordination as a form of administrative politics is rather simple: public institutions tend to be recalcitrant.[70] They are not mere tools and well-oiled machines, in which all employees know what to do, when to do it, and actually do what is expected of them. They have their internal complexities and externally may insist on standing their ground and defending their parochial interests. They are not automatically inclined to fall in line with the pursuit of the presumably superordinate goal of achieving a coordinated crisis response.

For some public agencies, the opportunity to act during a real crisis as opposed to the perennial dress rehearsals constitutes a litmus test for their rationale and capability. Being invisible or looking ineffective during a major emergency can threaten the future of specialized agencies such as civil defense organizations, special police and fire units, and medical emergency teams. When push comes to shove they will have strategic motives to either seek or shun prominent involvement in crisis-management processes. Blame avoidance and "bureaucratic politics" are never far from the mind-set of core executives as they envisage the allocation of crisis management authority, resources, and responsibilities among different parts of the executive, and as they design platforms and procedures governing the interaction between them.

From the political leader's point of view, the time it takes to get the multiorganizational machinery up and running may be disturbing (if not unacceptable) in the face of intense media pressure and public arousal. Past collaboration failures may further increase the temptation for leaders to intervene early. There may also be pressure for higher author-ities to interfere in order to maintain relative organizational integrity in asymmetric collaborative settings. For these reasons, crisis management is conducive to tensions between executive politics and collaborative gov-ernance. Much is at stake politically; if the (collaborative) crisis response is inadequate or does not live up to public expectations, political leaders may suffer the consequences. Leaders, not networks, will be held accountable in the wake of crisis.[71] At times, these political incentives may end up on a collision course with the cornerstones of effective collaboration in crisis: voluntarism, autonomy, adaptation, improvisation, and learning.

And yet some crisis management operations display a remarkable degree of order: crisis centers emerge, information is pooled, resources are allocated, cooperation and improvisation prevail. The local response to the 9/11 attacks and the European response to the 2004 Boxing Day tsunami offer important examples.[72] Such effective coordination does not come about because leaders impose it from the top down or from the center out. Rather it emerges through a system of informal channels, behavioral norms, and agreements.[73]

Coordination is most likely to emerge from crisis-induced chaos when crisis leaders nurture the right conditions for it.[74] One such condition is that actors should be motivated to acknowledge their mutual interde-pendence and begin to share information. Mutual trust is, of course, slow to grow and easy to lose – and many factors affect the trustworthiness of existing or emerging organizational practices.[75] It suffices here to note that the *absence* of trustworthiness is a rather certain way to nip an evolving coordination process in the bud.

The rapid emergence of a coordinated response can give rise to what we call the paradox of effective coordination. When the initial structuring of information, communication, and command flows is perceived as successful, the emerging coordination structure is endowed with legitimacy. This, in turn, firmly establishes the initial structuring. In no time, there is only one way to manage the crisis at hand. This "instant institutionalization" may be beneficial in the early crisis management phase, but the more beneficial it is, the more established the crisis management structure becomes. This may close the crisis decision-making arena off from other actors, which, in turn, can undermine long-term coordination.

Alan Barton describes the result of this paradoxical effect as the "bureaucratization of altruism."[76] In time, the threat of crisis evaporates and attention is focused on a return to normalcy, damage compensation, victim assistance, and lesson drawing. These functions of crisis management typically introduce other institutional actors than the ones involved in the early crisis management phases. Yet it may be hard for these new actors to become involved in a crisis network that has built up a good track record. The shift from immediate concerns to long-term concerns then sets the stage for bureaucratic infighting, distorted information flows, and a breakdown of crisis management effectiveness. To prevent this, wise and flexible management of inclusion and interaction in collaborative response networks is required.[77]

The formalization of coordination – when emerging collaboration becomes subject of standing rules and routines – is a matter of timing. The initial phase of crisis coordination can do without rules, but successive phases require a few key rules that facilitate the interaction between the various actors and structure information flows. In the absence of these rules, the fragile state of evolved coordination can easily collapse under the pressure of multiple actors and politicization of interorganizational and intergovernmental relations. Top-level leaders can play a key part in this process by making crucial decisions, keeping the decision-making process on track, guarding the quality of the decision-making process, and acting as the "external face" of the crisis management operation. Likewise, leaders of the various organizations involved in the coordination process can facilitate or hinder coordination efforts by conveying to their rank and file a cooperative attitude toward other organizations in the crisis response process.

3.7   Deciding and Coordinating: Conclusions

A persistent myth holds that top-level crisis leaders provide the key to a successful crisis response. This conception of crisis management emphasizes planning, command, and control: the plan gives rise to effective coordination and leaders manage the coordinated network from their crisis centers.

In reality, the quality of crisis response has less to do with planning and top-level control. Most effective crisis response operations are characterized by a remarkable degree of improvisation at various levels of government. A truly effective crisis response cannot be forced: it is to a large extent the result of a naturally evolving process of alignment of professionals. This process cannot be managed in linear, step-by-step, and comprehensive fashion from a single crisis command and coordination center. There are simply too many hurdles that separate a leadership decision from its timely execution in the field.

When the response is perceived to fail, there is usually a call for more coordination and stronger leadership. The result can easily be more plans, which emphasize further centralization of authority: bureaucratic pyramids and bureaucratic czars are called upon to forge coordination where it is not forthcoming spontaneously. Increasingly detailed plans based on the last big crisis will likely limit room for improvisation and undermine emergent collaboration. This pattern is a classic example of a post-crisis learning failure – a topic we will revisit in Chapter 6.

Leaders are important – not only as all-powerful "deciders" but rather as designers, facilitators, and guardians of an institutional arrangement that produces effective decision making and coordination processes at all levels. We do not suggest that leaders should simply rely on the innovative capacity of people and organizations to "emerge" in the wake of a crisis. Leaders must provide strategic direction as needed, actively monitor the response, and identify the decisions that are critical to the quality of that response. They should invest in building trusted relationships across organizations, jurisdictions, and communities that are "at risk" of crisis and help them to develop the social capital and trust that are so crucial in facilitating the emergent, informal, fast, and inclusive coordination processes needed for effective crisis response and recovery.[78]

Notes

1 Example adapted from Stern et al. (2014).
2 Hermann (1963); Allison (1971); Janis (1989); Rosenthal et al. (1989); Brecher (1993).

3 Larsson et al. (2005); Boin et al. (2013).

4 This upscaling is often prescribed in official crisis and disaster plans. In the United States, for instance, once the president declares a certain area officially a disaster area, the Federal Emergency Management Agency (FEMA) – now part of the Department of Homeland Security – becomes active in coordinating the disaster response. See Petak (1985); Waugh (1990); Sylves and Cumming (2004); Sylves (2008).

5 See also Bach (2015).

6 Independent Investigation Commission on the Fukushima Nuclear Accident (2014: 6–7).

7 Preston (2001: 32).

8 Preston (2001: 199).

9 Bush (2011). See Ricks (2006); Badie (2010).

10 Glad (1980); Sick (1985).

11 Hamilton (2011: 480).

12 Preston and 't Hart (1999); Hamilton (2012).

13 A large amount of interdisciplinary literature has documented how they do so, and what factors influence their reasoning. Good summaries include Holsti (1979); Roberts (1988); Vertzberger (1990); Verbeek (2003).

14 Herek et al. (1987). See also Schafer and Crichlow (2010) for an updated study of thirty-nine cases using a similar expert-rating methodology to assess decision outcomes and processes.

15 Post (1993); Peterson et al. (1998); Sweeney (2008).

16 Studies of international crises report that critical decisions tend to be made by small numbers of chief executive officials and their most intimate advisers. See Hermann (1963); Paige (1968); Holsti (1972); Brecher (1979c); Burke et al. (1989); Brecher (1993); George (1993). The same goes for corporate crises. Fernandez and Mazza (2014).

17 As a result, some analysts have turned toward the nexus between leader characteristics and group dynamics to explain crisis decision making. Preston (2001); Verbeek (2003); Schafer and Crichlow (2010).

18 Kaarbo (2008, 2012); Carpenter (2012).

19 Janis (1982); 't Hart (1994); LaFasto and Larson (2001); Sunstein and Hastie (2014).

20 Adomeit (1982: 39).

21 Longley and Pruitt (1980: 87), cited in Stern (1997a). See also Turner (1978).

22 Janis (1982).

23 For detailed accounts of groupthink and crisis decision making, see 't Hart (1994); 't Hart et al. (1997); Mintz and DeRouen (2010); Schafer and Crichlow (2010). Sunstein and Hastie (2014) echo recent cognitive psychology's tendency to "write off" groupthink as a phenomenon because it cannot easily be replicated in laboratory settings. These researchers tend to regard (decades of) case study evidence as "weak."

24 Preston and 't Hart (1999); Houghton (2001); Mintz and DeRouen (2010: 19); Stark (2011); Kaarbo (2012). See also some of the contributions in Lodge and Wegrich (2012).

25 Compare the very similar findings of Ansell and Gash (2008) about collaborative public management more generally and Ellemers et al. (2004) about leadership and group performance.

26 Hoyt and Garrison (1997); Carpenter, Geletkanycz, and Sanders (2004); Nemeth and Goncalo (2004); Fischer et al. (2009); Jetten and Hornsey (2011).

27 Meltsner (1990: 82). See also chapter 4 in 't Hart (2014).

28 Jackall (2009).

29 Rosenthal et al. (1989); Rosenthal et al. (2001). In many international crises studied by Brecher and his associates, the key decisions during the crisis period were made by a variety of what Brecher (1993: 223–25) calls "decisional forums." Likewise, the various country volumes on Baltic and East European post-Cold War crisis decision making produced by the CRISMART team in Stockholm document a strong variation in the composition of decision-making units within and between various types of domestic and international crises (see, e.g., Stern and Nohrstedt [1999]; Stern and Hansén [2000]; Stern et al. [2002]; Lindgren [2003]; Brändström and Malesic [2004]).

30 See 't Hart et al. (1993); Moskowitz et al. (2011); Information Resources Management Association (2014).

31 Weick and Sutcliffe (2007).

32 Turner and Pidgeon (1997); Kott (2006: 115).

33 This example is taken from 't Hart and Pijnenburg (1988).

34 Afterwards, the decision to continue broadcasting the match was severely criticized. The match had been left to proceed in order to allow for a mass mobilization of police forces from all over Belgium, specifically to contain the crowd upon leaving the stadium. Yet to many, the broadcast was taken simply as a manifestation of the apparent feeling among the authorities that "the show must go on."

35 The 9/11 Commission Report (2004: 17).

36 The 9/11 Commission Report (2004: 25).

37 The 9/11 Commission Report (2004: 29).

38 Weick (1988: 312).

39 Schneider (1993); Larsson et al. (2005).

40 Rodriguez et al. (2006); Seifert (2007).

41 Bracken (1983). See also Alberts and Hayes (2005).

42 Cf. Pearce and Fortune (1995).

43 Aghion et al. (2014).

44 Rashid et al. (2013: 119).

45 Kahneman and Klein (2009).

46 Compare many of the case studies in Howitt and Leonard (2009).

47 Leonard and Howitt (2013: 19–20).

48 Moynihan (2012).

49 Painter and Peters (2010).

50 Thompson (1967).

51 Weick (1998).

52 The following section draws largely on Boin and 't Hart (2012).

53 Hilliard (2000).
54 This distinction is further elaborated in Boin and Bynander (2014).
55 Dynes (2006); Boin and Bynander (2014).
56 Clarke (1999).
57 Boin and Rhinard (2008); Keen (2008); Ansell, Boin, and Keller (2010).
58 In that sense, crisis response and recovery can be viewed as merely one manifestation of governance networks and "collaborative public management" that have become the dominant early twenty-first century mechanism for addressing complex policy issues and tackling "wicked" problems. See, e.g., Ansell and Gash (2008); Moynihan (2008; 2009); Waugh (2009); McGuire and Silvia (2010); McGuire et al. (2010).
59 Clarke (1999).
60 Boin, Ekengren, and Rhinard (2014).
61 John DiIulio (1994) describes a shared culture in U.S. federal prisons, which enabled a rapid and unified response to prison riots.
62 Kirschenbaum (2003); Engel et al. (2014).
63 Sylves (2008).
64 Schneider (1993); Kettl (2003).
65 Solnit (2009).
66 See Boin and Bynander (2014) for a more elaborate analysis.
67 Dynes (1970, 2006).
68 www.fema.gov/media-library-data/20130726-1852-25045-2704/fema_fact sheet_nbeoc_final_508.pdf (accessed October 25, 2012).
69 Ekengren and Sundelius (2004).
70 Boin (2001).
71 See Chapter 5; cf. Koliba et al. (2011).
72 See Wachtendorf (2004) on 9/11 in New York City and Telford and Cosgrave (2007) on the 2004 tsunami.
73 Chisholm (1989).
74 This argument is elaborated in Boin and Bynander (2014).
75 Klijn et al. (2010); Lambright et al. (2010).
76 Barton (1969: 297).
77 Koppenjan and Klijn (2004); Johnston et al. (2011).
78 Aldrich et al. (2012).

4 Meaning Making
Constructing a Crisis Narrative

4.1 The Politics of Crisis Communication

Swedish Minister of Foreign Affairs Laila Freivalds paid a high political price for her visit to the theater on the evening on December 26, 2004. The Asian tsunami disaster had killed hundreds of Swedes that very day. Her visit signaled an emotional dissociation from the fate of the 30,000 vacationing Swedes in the affected region. When the prime minister of the day, long-serving Goran Persson, backed her in blaming the government's tardy response on errors committed down the foreign service hierarchy, this did not play well. In early 2005 Persson faced hostile questioning from a parliamentary inquiry, which was broadcast around the nation. A highly critical report was issued, and the tsunami crisis dogged the government all the way until the next election, which it lost.[1]

The charismatic and popular Australian police commissioner Christine Nixon saw her career cut short as a result of her perceived lack of involvement and empathy in times of crisis. During a public inquiry following the deadly "Black Saturday" bushfires on the outskirts of greater Melbourne in February 2009, it transpired that she and her husband had gone out for a pub meal with friends while communities were burning and people were dying. The public never forgave her. Nixon initially defended herself on the basis of fact: she had delegated command responsibilities for the bushfire response to a highly experienced assistant commissioner well before the situation became critical, and she had in fact been at the command center during most of the day before going off duty. It was to no avail. The tabloid press was merciless. Expert support for her conduct at the inquiry was not enough to undo the damage. She resigned in July 2010.[2]

In a crisis, authorities can easily lose control, if only temporarily, over the dramaturgy of political communication. Overtaken by events, they struggle to formulate a message that offers an authoritative definition of the situation, provides hope, shows empathy for victims, and gives assurances that the authorities are doing their best to minimize the consequences of the threat. Leaders do not have much time to come up with such an authoritative take on events. Politicians, citizens, and other opinion makers, all making use of (social) media venues, offer competing interpretations and powerful images crafted for mass consumption.[3] This explains why most crises quickly turn into a "symbolic contest over the social meaning of an issue domain."[4]

We define meaning making as the attempt to reduce public and political uncertainty and inspire confidence in crisis leaders by formulating and imposing a convincing narrative. It is not an easy task. President George W. Bush masterfully framed the events of 9/11 as an attack on the nation that demanded a protracted war effort, but he failed to shape the public understanding of Hurricane Katrina.[5] The Norwegian Prime Minister Stoltenberg effectively framed the national response to the 2011 massacre of young socialist activists by ultranationalist gunman Anders Breivik in terms of democratic resilience and pluralism. Just a year later, a parliamentary inquiry commission criticized the prime minister for the governmental failure to properly prepare for just such a contingency (Stoltenberg lost the ensuing election). The CEO of oil giant BP, Tony Hayward, first failed to offer a convincing account of the Deepwater Horizon disaster in the Gulf of Mexico. He then proceeded to destroy whatever credibility he had left by publicly complaining after a few weeks of high-intensity crisis management that he "wanted his life back" – apparently oblivious to the fact that heritage coastline had been polluted and entire communities had lost their livelihoods.

The *key question* of this chapter is why leaders succeed or fail in shaping a common and widely supported understanding of what the crisis is about and what needs to be done to deal with it. This question is especially intriguing in the context of contemporary information societies, where channels of communication abound, many actors clamor to make the news, and many stakeholders other than governments can transmit powerful facts and images of a crisis around the world in a matter of seconds.

Our *core claim* is that crisis meaning making makes a crucial difference between obtaining and losing the "permissive consensus" that leaders need to make decisions and formulate policies in times of crisis.[6] Effective crisis leadership cannot be brought about by simply "doing the right thing" on the ground. Leaders must manage the meaning-making process. If they fail to do so, others will succeed in getting their message across. As the saying goes, nature abhors a vacuum; in contemporary crises, meaning-making vacuums left by the authorities will be filled instantly, often in ways that severely complicate the efforts and indeed the legitimacy of these authorities.

This meaning-making process, which unfolds during every crisis, consists of two parts. First, leaders must *formulate* a persuasive message (a narrative) that explains what has happened and why, what its repercussions are, how it can be resolved, who can be relied upon to do so, and what lessons will need to be drawn from the episode. Second, leaders must *deliver* their message. Public communication during crisis is a highly competitive business: each and every detail of words, pictures, gestures, timing, and performance matters. This requires a sure-footed manipulation of symbols and enactment of crisis rituals that shape the views and sentiments of the political environment in ways that enhance leadership capacity to act.

Much of the crisis management literature deals primarily with crisis communication rather than meaning making, and does so in a rather instrumental fashion, producing detailed and hands-on prescriptions.[7] Many of these studies are very useful and well borne out by decades of experience; most of them are embedded in management and public relations analysis in the corporate sector.[8] But meaning making is more than crisis communication. Most analysts overlook the specific challenges of meaning making – formulating a convincing message in a *political* setting – which is what this chapter seeks to provide.

4.2   Framing Contests

A crisis marks a breakdown of symbolic frameworks that legitimate the preexisting sociopolitical order.[9] The pillars of "normal" life have fallen down; institutions and policies no longer seem to be working as they should. This creates a "cognitive void" that makes it hard to understand both the roots and future consequences of a crisis. This void plays out at different levels. At the personal level, affected individuals face cognitive conflict: they may still believe in the "normal" order but they confront repeated and undeniable information that things are seriously wrong. At the societal level, this cognitive conflict is emulated in the activities of multiple groups and organizations espousing different definitions of the situation – offering different claims about its causes, impact, and further development, and advocating alternative, and often conflicting, strategies to deal with the situation.

In the ever more densely "mediated" political context of crisis management, the capacity to capture public attention is a fundamental political-administrative asset.[10] In a way, this capacity is inherent to political leadership: people expect leaders to provide a believable and authoritative account that promises a way out of the crisis. They are expected to arbitrate conflicting interpretations of the critical events. But these conflicting story lines build on the implied argument that the very occurrence of the incident or shortcomings of the response and recovery "prove" that something must be wrong. The reputations of leaders and institutions are easily and rapidly undermined by emerging accounts of what went wrong.[11] This is the type of communication challenge crisis leaders always face.[12]

Policy makers seek to impose their definition of the situation in a context that is best conceived of as a triangular relationship between political actors (governmental and nongovernmental), the mass media (news producers: journalists and news organizations), and the citizenry (a pluralistic aggregate of all kinds of individuals, groups, and subcultures).[13] Each of the constituents of this triangle sends, receives, and perceives information about the crisis at hand. Below we briefly discuss each corner of the triangle.

The Political Arena

In a crisis, government actors typically seek to direct or influence both the behavior of citizens that are affected or threatened by the crisis and the beliefs and attitudes of their many other constituencies, for example, political parties, parliament, institutional watchdogs, the press corps, the general public, the international environment. In an operational sense, governments seek to inform (and sometimes instruct) citizens how to protect themselves during a natural or technical disaster. This might include communications about when and how to evacuate a stricken area, how to cope with or avoid contaminated food, or how to avoid contracting an infectious disease such as Ebola. This crisis communication is relatively straightforward, though technically quite complex, but for the most part warning and informing the public tends to be apolitical.

This can change quickly when politicians seek to impose a strategic definition of the situation that identifies culprits and pushes certain solutions that are clearly (or perhaps not so clearly) political in nature. Most governments recognize crises for what they can offer: a podium from which to address a large and attentive audience. Oppositions share this instinct. Both know the stakes are high. Both will seek to push their line of argument and act in a way that enhances their stature and protects or enhances their political capital. This may sound cynical, but analysts and policymakers ignore this political reality at their peril.

Traditional and Social Media

The media have traditionally been a pivotal force in discovering, conveying, and (de-)escalating crises. Journalists often "discover" a threat before the public is aware that something has happened. Sometimes their investigative reporting triggers the crisis: the defining example is Woodward and Bernstein's exposure of the Watergate burglary, which created the political crisis that ended Nixon's presidency.[14]

A crisis provides a golden opportunity for journalists and news organizations to "score." Hot news stories sell well to aroused and captive audiences. In addition, journalists can (and do) claim to perform their civic roles as checks on public power in society. In his classic study on social control in the news room, Breed observed that "newsmen are close to big decisions without having to make them."[15]

If a media organization's coverage is well received and widely followed, the position of that organization is strengthened.[16] If the coverage is poorly received and generally ignored, the position of the organization is weakened. The widely watched and praised coverage of the Gulf Crisis and War following the Iraqi invasion of Kuwait in 1990 was a major breakthrough for CNN. In contrast, the BBC suffered serious reputation problems when one of its stars, Jimmy Savile, was exposed as a serial child abuser. The news broke after his death, but it then became clear that children had been abused in the BBC studios and that BBC executives must have known. When the BBC cancelled one of its own programs that announced an investigatory report into the mother organization, BBC's crisis was complete.

The near accident with the Three Mile Island nuclear reactor in Harrisburg, Pennsylvania (1979), a seminal event in the history of crisis communication and public relations, provides another classic example:

> The press were at the center of Three Mile Island. They were charged with interpreting the event for the nation. Strangely, for accepting this task, they came under the most criticism of any group involved – criticism for sensationalism, for being antinuclear, for being pronuclear and for not keeping reactor specialists on the reporting staff. While the press was searching for information, some involved agencies tried to provide it and others tried to hide it, even to the point of lying to the press and, through them, to the American people.[17]

Many crisis managers routinely complain about the predatory and nihilistic nature of journalism. Some analysts speak of "attack journalism" where "packs" of reporters stray around as "junk-yard dogs" (as opposed to the more benign "watchdogs") looking for consumable dirt on political leaders and other actors inside and outside government. Yet, the memoirs of retired spin doctors tend to emphasize the possibilities for crisis managers to take control of the agenda and lead the media in desirable directions. Some communication scholars argue that the force of contemporary political communication imperatives – the message has to go out fast, it has to be packaged in simple catchphrases, there is no room for any doubts or weaknesses – threatens to undermine the quality of policy deliberation that goes on inside governments as it breeds a siege mentality in their dealing with the news media.[18]

Journalists themselves appear to conceive of their roles in more benign ways: as transmitters of vital public information, as watchdogs or critics of public authorities (more likely to be adopted during politically charged crises such as civil disorder, policy fiascos, and scandals), or as providers of human interest stories (crises tend to create a public climate receptive to sensationalism and emotionalism).[19] They complain that governments and leaders do not want to work with media to get their message across to the public.

The tone of the mass media's crisis reporting varies widely between news organizations, from crisis to crisis, and sometimes even in the course of a single crisis: the spectrum ranges from grim "fault-finding" to uncritical echoing of government pronouncements. Aside from political ideology and editorial policy, the character of crisis reporting is also influenced by organizational factors, such as reporting styles and traditions, and news organizations' crisis response capacities.[20] Some news organizations are better equipped to quickly mobilize than others; some are better at maintaining rigorous reporting standards even in hectic circumstances. This is not just a matter of resources. It also has to do with the quality and experience of news editors and decision-making dynamics within news organizations.[21]

In recent decades, the internet and social media have revolutionized the world of mass communications. Traditional media and social media are intertwined as the distinctions between print and broadcast media have blurred. Today's leaders must deal with the "24/7" news cycle and a cyberspace that produces and distributes instant witness reports of major events and real time feedback on any actions they take, any word they speak, any posture they adopt. Competing for attention in a declining market, traditional media have become more sensational-istic, more aggressive in their surveillance of political-administrative elites. Social media and internet activism have accelerated the development of what has been called "monitory democracy," in which citizens are keen watchers and active co-producers of elite scrutiny.[22]

Social media can serve as both "friend" and "enemy" of crisis leaders. On the one hand, leaders have new means to communicate directly, instantly, and at any time with their organizations, external stakeholders, and the public at large. Leaders make use of social media such as Twitter in order to communicate under both everyday and crisis conditions. For example, immediately following the Paris attacks of November 2015, President François Hollande tweeted a message of confidence in French resilience in the face of terror and capacity mobilize its power, and prevail over terrorists.[23] Furthermore, social media now provide valuable real time – often instantaneous – feedback regarding how messages are being received by various segments of society. Monitoring social media can provide leaders (and their communications teams) with valuable information regarding public concerns as well as rumors or misconceptions.

But social media can also complicate the meaning-making process in various ways. The space limitations of tweets and text messages can cause messages to be blunt or seem (fairly or not) insensitive. When Malaysian Airlines informed some relatives of MH370 passengers via text message that hope could no longer be reasonably sustained and that the passengers were now presumed dead, the text went viral and provoked outrage in social and conventional media.[24] Social media serve as a "communicative equalizer" and provide proponents of alternative – and in some cases scientifically dubious, unethical, or otherwise politically unsavory – views with a means of challenging leaders and leading experts. Similarly, there is considerable potential for social media feeds to be manipulated for purposes of propaganda and disinformation. For example, it has been alleged that some countries have built up "troll factories" to produce large numbers of propaganda social media posts on demand in support of their policy objectives.[25]

The rise of social media is increasingly relevant to societal resilience. Social media and personal communications technology can be used to encourage preparedness, facilitate citizen reporting for improved situational awareness and societal vigilance, coordinate community self-help and mobilization of resources (via crowdsourcing), and for many other purposes relevant to societal security.[26]

The Public

Citizen responses to any particular crisis can vary widely, not just according to what information about the events gets through to them but also by virtue of their demographic and social position or cultural and political orientation.[27] Moreover, in some types of crises – such as civil disasters or social conflicts – citizens play multiple roles. As actors, they may take part in demonstrations or riots. As spectators, they are the objects of media and political efforts to inform and influence them.

As victimized actors, they search for information. As witnesses, they are readily available sources for journalists. As "netizens" on the web, they have the capacity to shape frames and storylines about the event.

The average citizen is no longer a powerless bystander when the response of government is perceived to be late, incomplete, insufficient, or illegitimate. Armed with their cell phones and social media accounts, they share images, data, stories, and opinions. In doing so, they in effect become "co-producers" of both media reporting and government response efforts.[28] When sections of the public are skeptical or angry about government policy, social media provides them with a powerful amplifier (and echo chamber) for questioning the effectiveness or appropriateness of official crisis responses.

Citizens crave information during a crisis, but they will not believe anything they read or see. The average citizen is no expert in the intricacies of the complex systems in which crises occur. But she is no fool, as V. O. Key once observed.[29] In a pluralistic democracy, authorities and journalists cannot mislead the public for a long period of time and get away with it. As Halper explains:

In crisis situations, the public's interest rises sharply, but its knowledge remains at a fairly low level. Initially, then, crises are apt to make the public even more receptive to information emanating from a legitimate government because citizens demand news, and yet are unable to evaluate it adequately. But precisely because the public *does* tend to be more interested during crises, it becomes more alert to basic discrepancies and inconsistencies contained in the official versions, particularly if these flaws are pointed out by a critical press or by well-known and respected political figures.[30]

Public authorities do not help themselves when they rely on rather crude assumptions about citizen behavior during crises in devising their crisis responses and communication strategies. For example, one persistent myth that has proved nearly impossible to dispel is the idea that citizens panic easily in a disaster. This is striking because scores of studies have consistently shown that citizens tend to act quite rationally even in the most extreme circumstances.[31] Much of the behavior that authorities – and journalists, for that matter – describe as panic is better understood as rational improvisation under conditions of very limited or contradictory knowledge about the situation at hand. Authorities who realize this and want to prevent citizens from "panicking" are much more inclined to be proactive in providing citizens with information they actually need.[32] They will avoid patronizing messages that merely suggest that the authorities are "not in touch with reality" and do not respect the public.

4.3   Crafting a Winning Frame

The inherent features of crisis place limits on a government's meaning-making capacity: spectacles of dead bodies, mass destruction of property, people in distress, and widespread violence are difficult to explain away. But there is no space for stonewalling. Leaders (and their crisis teams) will have to come up with a compelling storyline or face the consequences of their inability to do so.

When natural or industrial disasters happen, or foreign powers escalate looming tensions, government leaders have an opportunity to communicate. In the face of a serious, common or external threat, the public tends to defer criticism and lend support to the government of the day. This rally-around-the-flag effect rarely lasts long, but it does give leaders a window of opportunity to offer a "frame" through which the crisis can be understood; one that provides guidance in times of collective stress, and, strategically, one that does not depict them as negligent, oblivious, incompetent, or callous with regard to the misfortune that has occurred.

Successful "framers" may hold the key to defining the appropriate strategies for resolution.[33] They may even emerge as the center of gravity and focal point of the response. Effective framers will likely reap the benefits in terms of political gains and strengthened reputation.[34] But government leaders are not the only ones trying. *Any* actor might successfully have their interpretation of a crisis become accepted by the great majority of the public as the prism through which they make sense of that is happening, and thus gain momentum for whatever crisis management measures they are proposing.

The flipside of an effective frame is its self-binding dynamic. For example, once the response to a particular threat is framed as a "war," it becomes hard not to stage an all-out, hard-line response.[35] Australian Prime Minister-elect Kevin Rudd framed climate change as "the greatest moral challenge of our time." It signaled that he would make combating this threat his government's top priority. But when the carbon trading scheme he eventually proposed encountered political headwinds, he shelved it. The public's response, even among opponents of the scheme, was one of incredulity and indeed contempt. Rudd's hitherto remarkable popularity nosedived, and within a year he was swept from power.[36]

Likewise, when seeking to deter an opponent in a conflict by powerful symbolic language designed to demonstrate resolve, people will remember that commitment when that resolve is tested. For example, U.S. President Obama publicly announced "a red line in the sand" during the Syrian conflict in 2012: if the Assad regime used chemical weapons again, the United States would not stand on the sidelines. When in 2013, a year after that public commitment was made, the Syrian military did in fact use such weapons against its own population, Obama was trapped in his own frame. He did not want to intervene in the Syrian conflict. The "red line" had been crossed, but where was the punishment?[37]

All this prompts the question: what makes for an effective frame? Drawing on political and crisis communication literature, we recognize three clusters of factors that are critical in winning the framing battle: presenting a persuasive narrative, personal and organizational credibility, and effective communication.[38]

Persuasive Narratives

A convincing frame provides actionable advice, a course of action that is best collectively pursued. This can entail specific advice to everybody: President Bush implored American consumers to keep shopping after the 9/11 attacks. It can also be more abstract, suggesting a way of thinking. This may vary from the crude "if you are not with us, you are against us" to the more sophisticated "let's continue to strengthen our democratic institutions."

An effective frame does at least five things: it offers a credible explanation of what happened, it offers guidance, it instills hope, shows empathy, and suggests that leaders are in control. This requires a combination of what David Bromwich calls "moral imagination" and the selective exploitation of data, arguments, and historical analogies.[39] Leadership in crisis always has a moral dimension. Effective leaders embody the hopes and fears of the society under threat; they must offer a message that takes away uncertainty, points to a way forward out of the rubble, and inspires a sense of optimism that in the end things will be better. In short, they appeal to "the better angels of our nature."[40]

In order to be effective, rhetoric is instrumental.[41] Metaphors and emotive concepts can be used as shortcuts to increase or dampen collective anxieties. Labels such as crisis and disaster invoke "archetypical narratives" that shape people's expectations about what can be expected and who is in charge; it creates a context in which heroes but also villains can emerge.[42]

The very act of labeling a situation a "crisis" is in itself a major communicative act with potentially far-reaching political consequences.[43] This phenomenon has been aptly described by Barry Buzan and colleagues who talk about framing events in terms of "securitization:" "an issue is dramatized and presented as an issue of supreme priority; thus, by labelling it as *security*, an agent claims a need for and a right to treat it by extraordinary means."[44] It increases leaders' political room for maneuvering. As Edelman puts it: "Any regime that prides itself on its capacity to manage crises will find crises to manage."[45] The Bush administration, for example, was surprisingly quick and energetic in dramatizing the scope and immediacy of the dangers posed by Saddam Hussein's regime's alleged possession of weapons of mass destruction. Likewise, the Putin regime in Russia has repeatedly used muscular crisis rhetoric to boost its domestic authority.[46]

Emotive language helps to dramatize the seriousness of the situation. For example, in seeking to put pressure on Russian-nationalist rebels in eastern Ukraine to allow international teams' access to the crash site of downed Malaysian Airlines Flight MH 17, Dutch Foreign Minister Frans Timmermans appealed to the hearts of the members of the U.N. Security Council. He presented his case on July 21, 2014, four days after the plane crashed in the middle of a war zone:

We are here to discuss a tragedy: the downing of a commercial airliner and the death of 298 innocent people. Men, women and a staggering number of children lost their lives, on their way to their holiday destinations, their homes, loved ones, their jobs or international obligations. Since Thursday I've been thinking how horrible the final moments of their lives must have been, when they knew the plane was going down. Did they lock hands with their loved ones, did they hold their children close to their hearts, did they look each other in the eyes, one final time, in a wordless goodbye? We will never know. . . . Just imagine for one minute, first to lose your husband and then to have to fear that some thug might steal his wedding ring from his remains. Just imagine that this could be your spouse. To my dying day I will not understand that it took so much time for the rescue workers to be allowed to do their difficult jobs and that human remains should be used in a despicable political game. I hope the world will not have to witness this again, any time in the future. Images of children's toys being tossed around, luggage being opened or passports being shown, are turning our grief and mourning into anger. We demand unimpeded access to the terrain. We demand respectful treatment of the crash site. We demand dignity for the victims and the multitudes who mourn their loss.[47]

Personifying threat and suffering, morally condemning opponents: these factors are instrumental in showing empathy and gaining support for bold action and public sacrifice that under normal conditions would never stand a chance of being accepted.[48]

Leaders can also purposefully use language to depoliticize a crisis. Judicial language creates and supports the expectation that a non-partisan body will be activated to define the situation and assess the performance of key actors. This strategy proved quite effective in Great Britain throughout the 1980s and 1990s when the country experienced a series of inner-city riots as well as a disturbingly high frequency of man-made disasters (a plane crash, a ferry disaster, an oil-platform explosion, a boat collision on the Thames, several major railway crashes, an underground station fire, a stadium crowd disaster). In each case, official inquiries were called for by the government and performed by judges, who – while being tenacious and objective in their pursuit of the immediate causes and implications of these events – by the very nature of their position and terms of reference tended to steer clear of underlying political issues and systemic tensions.[49]

We know since Aristotle that a persuasive narrative combines "logos" (pertinent factual content) with "ethos" (an appeal to shared norms and identities) and "pathos" (an acknowledgment of loss, pain, anger, fear, and other emotional sources of collective stress).[50] President Obama's speech at the vigil for slain schoolchildren in Newtown on December 14, 2012 contained all of these elements. The national leader had to be the mourner-in-chief: he had to be there, look involved, caring, embodying the grief of the community. It is a script that *has* to be performed, but Obama went much further than that: he used the horror of the moment to build a case for social (and implicitly policy and legal) change, drawing powerfully on logos, ethos, and pathos in equal measure. The mourner-in-chief turned into a teacher of reality and an advocate for change, taking on one of the most powerful lobbies in U.S. politics:

This is our first task, caring for our children. It's our first job. If we don't get that right, we don't get anything right. That's how, as a society, we will be judged. And by that measure, can we truly say, as a nation, that we're meeting our obligations? Can we honestly say that we're doing enough to keep our children, all of them, safe from harm? Can we claim, as a nation, that we're all together there, letting them know they are loved and teaching them to love in return? Can we say that we're truly doing enough to give all the children of this country the chance they deserve to live out their lives in happiness and with purpose? I've been reflecting on this the last few days, and if we're honest with ourselves, the answer's no. We're not doing enough. And we will have to change. Since I've been president, this is the fourth time we have come together to comfort a grieving community torn apart by mass shootings, the fourth time we've hugged survivors, the fourth time we've consoled the families of victims. And in between, there have been an endless series of deadly shootings across the country, almost daily reports of victims, many of them children, in small towns and in big cities all across America, victims whose – much of the time their only fault was being at the wrong place at the wrong time. We can't tolerate this anymore. These tragedies must end. And to end them, we must change.[51]

Did Obama's words resonate? Yes and no. For a crisis narrative to be credible and politically effective, there has to be a "fit" between the core message and the key values and state of mind of the targeted audiences. In some segments of U.S. society, Obama's implicit call to rethink the right to bear arms was utterly convincing – they already believed so well before the Newtown massacre; in others, the speech was regarded as offensive and indicative of a government intent on undermining a pillar of the American way of life. This divided reception was a given; what really mattered was how the speech would resonate among the undecided groups in the middle. From that perspective, Obama's speech had only a modest impact; one year later, the country remained almost equally divided on gun control. In September 2015, Obama found it difficult to contain his frustration when speaking on the occasion of the fifteenth shooting spree during his presidency, this time at a community college in Oregon.[52]

Frames can also be too effective, trapping leaders in their own narrative. During the Eurozone sovereign debt crisis that erupted in 2010, virtually all parties agreed that the crisis was deep and potentially existential for the European financial system. But sharply different frames were offered by academics and heads of government and finance ministers within the Eurozone. One group stressed that only fiscal austerity and deep structural reform in debtor countries could resolve the situation. This frame was well received in creditor nations. The other group framed this "solution" as actually aggravating the original problem and imposing intolerable hardship on the population, instead advocating debt relief and renewed investment as the only way out. This alternative frame went down well in Greece, Spain, and other debt-ridden member states. Both frames were therefore effective, but in so doing exacerbated the impasse.[53] There was no effective superordinate, integrative frame that could provide both camps with a cause to rethink their entrenched positions and to start to explore common ground without compromising their credibility among their core constituencies.[54]

Personal and Organizational Credibility

The success of a frame, however effectively crafted, depends to an important degree on the credibility of its proponent.[55] For policy makers who possess it, risky political ventures become possible and major political storms can be ridden out with relative ease. Leaders can only shape public and political meanings during crises when they are seen as credible, trustworthy sources of information.[56] When leaders are trusted, their actions and words are more easily perceived as sincere, competent, and signs of good faith.

Without it, even the most basic tasks become difficult and subject to intense scrutiny by the media and other watchdogs. Where trust has broken down, all actors involved will scrutinize the words and deeds of the "untrustworthy" leader; they will be less likely to believe official announcements, let alone act on them. For a leader or government entering a crisis with low credibility, the dynamics of crisis can quickly trigger a downwards escalatory cycle: low credibility nurtures fault-finding interpretations of crisis frames, which can sink any meaning-making effort. This, in turn, confirms the low credibility, which can make further meaning-making efforts politically perilous.

But crises also provide a unique opportunity to break out of a "low-credibility rut." The expectation bar is low, so leaders can surprise. For example, New York Mayor Rudy Giuliani rose from the political ashes by his performance in the wake of the 9/11 attacks, just as President Hollande did after the Paris attacks in 2015. When they do, citizens may remember why they voted that person into office and rediscover their faith in the leader. This will no doubt boost subsequent meaning-making efforts.

So what determines the level of credibility that leaders bring into a crisis? How can they win or lose credibility during the initial phases of a crisis?

First, the *history and reputation of a leader* affect the ways in which media representatives, network partners, and the public at large interpret his or her credibility. Past performance weighs heavily. Well-publicized instances of successful crisis management increase personal credibility. Even when leaders are not considered particularly popular or successful in the grinding policy processes of the day, their reputation as "trouble shooter," "fixer," or "decider" may provide them with solid capital in the early phases of a crisis. When the relatively unknown economic techno-crat Mario Monti replaced the intensely political and deeply controversial Silvio Berlusconi as Italian prime minister at a time when the country was at the verge of being overwhelmed by its sovereign debt crisis, his status as a non-politician who talked straight and did not sugarcoat the message bought him considerable and much-needed credibility both within and outside the country.

In similar vein, the *reputation of the key organization(s)* can weigh heavily in this equation. An organization that has a history of botched crisis management is unlikely to inspire much trust in its capacity to handle a crisis – this will put a damper on the stellar credibility that a leader may bring to the table. It is hard to make credible promises if those promises depend on the implementation capacity of a distrusted organization, as the Vatican and various national catholic churches learned at great cost in the wake of revelations about decades of sexual abuse by priests and cover-ups by higher clergy. Years of muddling through, perfunctory efforts to investigate, and half-hearted apologies had widened the Church's credibility gap. To restore institutional legit-imacy, the untainted "people's Pope" Francis applied a root and branch approach. In June 2015, he appointed a special tribunal within the Vatican to judge and discipline bishops suspected of covering up pedophilia.[57]

The *initial responses* to a crisis make a huge difference. The first response has to be measured yet decisive. Immediately after being informed of the 2004 tsunami catastrophe in Asia, which had affected many German holidaymakers, German Chancellor Gerhard Schröder cancelled his Christmas holidays, returned to Berlin, and promised €.5 billion of aid – deferring any worries he might have had about how the already strained government budget would pay for this. This picture of compassion and decisiveness gave him much credit domestically as well as abroad. This was in stark contrast to how the Swedish prime minister and his ministers initially responded to the same situation (see opening example of this chapter).

Leaders may be tempted to make strong statements about the crisis and how they will handle it. It is always tricky to "shoot from the hip" when dealing with complex, intractable issues; it is outright foolish to claim publicly that critical problems will be brought under control swiftly when it is not clear whether such a promise can be honored. Quick and ill-considered promises – to "always be there" for victims, to rebuild disaster-stricken communities "brick by brick," to "hunt down and bring to justice" terrorists – prove embarrassing and painful when it turns out they are impossible to deliver.

Some leaders are tempted to downplay the gravity of the situation in the face of clear indicators of critical problems. When the emergence of mad cow disease scared British consumers of beef, the British Agriculture Minister John Gummer tried to reassure the public by eating a beef burger and by feeding one to his reluctant four-year-old. Even after the escalation of the crisis, ministers continued their attempts to reassure the public and their EU partners that British beef was safe. Gummer's successor, Douglas Hogg, for example, stated in November 1995 that "British beef has never been safer," referring to new and tougher safety measures, but completely ignoring the fact that there might already be hundreds of thousands of older infected cattle in the food chain.[58]

Some leaders see greater advantage in concealment than exposure."[59] They self-consciously maintain that crises bestow upon governments the "right to lie."[60] They will engage in a specific form of impression man-agement, which we call *masking*: not telling the full story, downplaying the seriousness of threats and damages, obscuring sensitive aspects of their own crisis response operations. Authoritarian regimes have a long history of masking – up to the point of flatly denying the occurrence of major nuclear accidents and environmental disasters. In times of crisis and war, democratic governments have also gone down this path. Masking efforts may succeed and buy the official or agency time. But if masking efforts are not followed by more substantive remedial actions, they are likely to generate severe backlashes when the "real" problems surface (as they inevitably will).

Some leaders succumb to the temptation of *overemphasizing rosy scenarios*, which find their basis in myopic or highly partisan readings of the situation. When leaders present constituents with optimistic prognoses that have no basis in reality, their future credibility is held hostage to the accuracy of these predictions. President George W. Bush prematurely declared the end of military hostilities in Iraq in a widely publicized, but ill-advised, public relations stunt aboard the aircraft carrier *Abraham Lincoln*. From the flight deck, under a banner proclaiming "Mission Accomplished," the president declared that "major combat operations in Iraq have ended."[61] Even though Bush did caution that difficult work was still to be done, this episode left the U.S. public ill prepared for the ensuing war, which would produce many more casualties than the initial invasion.

Effective Crisis Communication

Meaning making in crises is not just a matter of articulating a powerful message; the message has to be *delivered* to targeted audiences. This is what we mean by crisis communication: to employ deliberate and concerted means to convey information and influence public perceptions and emotions. This is not easy nor is it just a matter of following communication plans; effective crisis communication also entails intuitive and relatively improvised public communication by leaders who are suddenly cast into the hectic pace of crisis reporting.

Based on the extensive crisis communication literature, we can identify at least seven factors that are particularly important in determining the effectiveness of governmental crisis communications efforts:

A clear division of labor – There is a distinct difference between formulating a crisis frame and organizing the delivery of that message. The first is a political act. The second falls in the technical domain of communication experts (who understand the dynamics of crisis). When the crisis communication experts assume the political task of message formulation, the effectiveness of meaning making is undermined. The same happens when politicians try to "run" the entire communication process. A clear division of labor is necessary, even if the tasks are intertwined.

Degree of preparedness – Many public leaders and organizations are ill equipped for crisis communication even in the most basic operational sense. Inexperienced crisis managers do not always understand that crisis communication is fundamentally different from routine communications. Moreover, existing communication infrastructures and mechanisms are quickly overwhelmed and must be reinforced from other parts of the organization or with outside help. Under these conditions, policy makers can easily fall into a reactive mode of "firefighting," which causes them to lose track of the big picture.

Governmental communication has become the domain of public relations (PR) professionals, but these PR officials are not always trained or properly prepared to deal with crises. They do not always understand that a "political brush fire" requires different means of communication than a full-blown crisis. Lack of preparedness translates into a loss of speed and coherence in the first, critical stages of an acute crisis: authorities will be trailing the crisis story instead of shaping it.

Lack of preparedness also tends to produce logistical chaos in dealing with the large army of reporters that besieges authorities in a crisis. Reporters are easily irritated by what they see as an unprofessional communications operation, characterized by inadequate provision of facilities for the media, PR officials who possess limited knowledge and information about the issues at hand, PR officials who do not speak proper English (let alone German, Spanish, or French), and PR officials who are more preoccupied with fencing off and protecting policy makers than with facilitating a dialogue between the media and crisis authorities.

Dealing with experts – It is risky to put technical experts in charge of framing efforts in crises, though their input is often indispensable to the effort. They tend to use technocratic language that many do not understand and that therefore will be wide open to misinterpretation. Information intended to reassure may thus have exactly the opposite effect. For example, following the Chernobyl nuclear accident, Finnish and Swedish government experts told citizens that measured levels were *only* a few hundred times the normal background levels – a degree of contamination that experts knew to be harmless but which sounded ominous to the uninitiated and which exacerbated public confusion.[62]

Or take the example of the 1976 Swine Flu public health crisis in the United States, where a small number of medical experts shaped the political understanding of the crisis, and effectively prescribed what needed to be done (a nationwide inoculation campaign, which in itself posed considerable health hazards): "It mattered a little that the experts could not tell whether the chance of pandemic influenza was 30 percent, or 3 percent, or even less than 1 percent. What the assistant secretary for health, the secretary of [the department of health], the president, and Congress heard, was that there was *some* chance of pandemic flu and this was enough. No responsible politician wished to put himself in the position of opposing the program, thus running the risk that pandemic illness and death might prove him a villain."[63]

Coordination of outgoing information – Getting everyone who publicly represents the government or response network "on-message" is a common mantra of PR and political consultants. As we have seen in Chapter 3, multi-actor, multi-level governance is a typical characteristic of the crisis response. In most crises, there are different places where authorities congregate, decide, and act, if only because of the common differentiation in strategic and operational crisis centers. Reporters will target them all. Moreover, many of these units will feel the need to communicate their part of the story. In many cases there is even rivalry between them, and there might be political and legal incentives for them to point fingers at each other.[64]

While coordination of the message clearly has many virtues, exaggerated forms of message discipline can be counterproductive as they may slow down and inhibit messaging, pending top-down approvals. It can lead to a uniform approach that is counterproductive. In fact, a degree of discord in the messaging can be a valuable warning signal to policymakers about more fundamental uncertainties or policy differences that need to be recognized and resolved.[65] Often, the best approach here too is a more decentralized form of coordination: the various collaborating actors apply general guidelines and communication strategies with discretion.

A social media strategy – Crisis communication used to be a question of rhythm and timing. There was a media cycle punctuated by editorial deadlines for newspapers and specific times at which the nation would tune in to the most important television broadcasts. If you understood that cycle and knew how and where to drop the message, you would be a seasoned crisis professional. Those days are gone. There are no more deadlines, just instant reporting. As people tend to have developed their own unique platforms for news delivery, crisis communication professionalism has increasingly become a matter of understanding how, when, and where defined target groups (the elderly, tourists, young professionals, etc.) get their information. That understanding is the key toward reaching them. In addition, the crisis communication organization needs to prepare for proactive monitoring and rumor-control efforts. This is essential if the organization is to quickly identify and correct information distortions and unsubstantiated rumors, and respond to developing public concerns. The understanding of social media, however, is not well developed in government (more so in big corporations with marketing departments).

Balanced transparency – There will always be situations in which there are justified reasons to withhold key information, at least temporarily. That does not apply to the withholding of embarrassing information, which creates medium- and long-term hazards to individual or organizational integrity and reputation. If an organization that discovers embarrassing facts about its performance voluntarily discloses this information before the media do, it will at least be credited for its openness. But it will also sow doubts as to the capacity of that organization to deal with crisis. If the same information is presented after the story has already broken in the media, the organization will be suspected of attempting to cover up or "spin."

Supportive rituals – The delivery of a message can be greatly enhanced by employing supporting rituals: symbolic behavior that is socially standardized and repetitive. Rituals follow highly structured, more or less standardized sequences and are often enacted at certain places and times, which themselves are endowed with special symbolic meaning. They are an important component of social and governmental responses to many different types of crises as well as politics in normal times (think of election campaigns, annual budget speeches, parliamentary debating procedures).[66] Crisis rituals both shape and conform to public perceptions of grave disturbances of the existing order.

An essential symbolic strategy for leaders in response to an acute and large-scale crisis is to inspect the relevant sites and visit victims and operational staff.[67] The laying of wreaths at the site of an accident or attack or the attendance of funerals are other obvious examples.[68] A more recent phenomenon is the participation of politicians in solidarity marches, such as those which occurred in Paris after the attack on the offices of Charlie Hebdo.[69] As noted earlier, the symbolic importance of publicly displayed compassion for those suffering hardship and those working under dire circumstances cannot be overstated. Failure to engage in this ritual amounts to a serious underestimation of the collective emotion that such crises generate. It is sure to bring officials instant and intense public-relations problems, and, occasionally, political embarrassment.[70] Just think of the Russian leader Putin who was pictured waterskiing while the sailors in the submarine *Kursk* were fighting for their lives.

A notable example of an organization that did understand what was required was Japanese Airlines (JAL) in its response to a big plane crash in 1985 during which 520 people perished:

The airline followed an elaborate protocol to atone. Personal apologies were made by the company's president, memorial services were held [at a cost of over $1.5 million to the company, authors] and financial reparations paid. . . . At the memorial service, JAL's president, Yasumoto Takagi, bowed low and long to relatives of the victims and to a plaque bearing the victims' names. He asked forgiveness, accepted responsibility and offered to resign.[71]

The chief maintenance officer took it one step further, and – in keeping with a streak in Japanese culture – committed suicide. Overall, JAL's response was seen and depicted by the media to be humane, caring, and responsible. After the initial major loss, the company fully recovered its market share.

Another classic crisis ritual is the official investigation. Ritualized and seemingly dispassionate inquiries can help reinvigorate public belief in the rational procedures of government. The terminology used is appropriately evocative: a "full-scale, objective inquiry" to be conducted by "independent experts" or "wise men" where "no expense will be spared," and so on. Such attempts to salvage rationality myths from the turbulence and anxiety of crisis are further amplified by employing a language of "learning." If "the lessons" of the present crisis will be distilled, concerned citizens can at least hope that every effort is made to prevent new traumas (see further Chapter 6). Writing against the backdrop of the massive street protests and riots of the late 1960s in the United States, Edelman argued that such rituals – including judicial rituals resulting in the punishment of perpetrators – help reduce anxiety levels and give the impression that people can exert a certain degree of control over their lives, even though their actual influence is negligible.[72]

Government leaders and agencies will likely face crisis rituals enacted by their political opponents. The burning of enemy portraits and flags is standard practice in international conflicts, while anti-police demonstrations, identifying police as "pigs" or "Nazis," are among the standard animosity rituals practiced by protest groups. More recently, Islamic State terrorists harked back to ancient rituals by beheading their hostages – only today they distribute the pictures to the mass media and the worldwide web, maximizing the psychological effects in the West.

4.4 Effective Meaning-making

Crises generate a context of fundamental ambiguity, confusion, and speculation, conflicting beliefs, and collective arousal. In these circumstances, it is both essential and exceedingly difficult for policy makers to shape the societal and political meaning-making process by which crises come to be labeled, understood, and evaluated – not just in their own right but also in terms of what they tell us about the social and institutional status quo.

Politicians have always understood that crises can be exploited to introduce, defend, or impose a political message that defines society in a certain way, using vocabulary, images, symbols, and rituals that fit both the crisis and the electorate. They do so in competition with other "frame makers." Crises provide opportunities to reshape policies, paradigms, and institutions. Few leaders can resist that sort of opportunity, which may only be provided by a crisis.

A powerful frame may bring benefits but also entails risks. In the months leading up to the 2003 invasion of Iraq, Prime Minister Tony Blair repeatedly emphasized the clear and present danger posed by Iraqi weapons of mass destruction (WMD). Blair quickly became the subject of increasingly bitter attacks from the opposition when no evidence of ongoing WMD programs was turned up in the wake of the military intervention (the same prime minister who had impressed the nation with his frame of the "people's princess" after the death of Princess Diana).

The picture of meaning making that emerges from this chapter is one of adapting to an increasingly complex, nonstop, "wired," and wireless, as well as (socially) mediated communications context. It entails balancing multiple considerations and communicating the right narrative at the right time, in the right way. It involves coordinating an overall message without muzzling individual actors or inhibiting the flow of alternative views that might in fact be warning signals that adjustments to the crisis strategy may be needed. Leaders and their communications teams must be prepared to take the initiative in framing the crisis and strive – though this is not always possible – to take center stage in telling the story of the crisis as well as leading the response and recovery efforts.

This chapter makes it clear that policy makers in liberal democracies (and for that matter even in other political systems) should not overestimate their capacity to control the public's understanding of a crisis. There are limits to what leaders can do to influence how people understand what they see and read, online or in print, even if some of this amounts to the most outlandish conspiracy theories. Despite these clear limitations, however, leaders and their governments can and must continue to engage in meaning-making efforts. Citizens look toward their leaders in crisis. This implicit longing for direction can be channeled toward laying the groundwork for a new and politically attractive future.

Notes

1 Brändström et al. (2008). The authors note strikingly different outcomes of tsunami-induced accountability processes in neighboring Norway and Finland.
2 See her personal, naturally self-serving but still gripping account: Nixon (2011).
3 Combs (1980: 119–21). The distinction between images (general perceptions of events, actors, or conditions as malign or benign) and frames (more specific diagnostic and prognostic issue definitions) is useful here and has been elaborated by Eriksson (2001: 8–16).
4 Schön and Rein (1994: 29).
5 On Bush's 9/11 rhetoric, see Kuypers et al. (2012). On his meaning-making failure during Katrina, see Boin et al. (2010).
6 The term is taken from Key (1961: 35).
7 Nudell and Antokol (1988); Barton (1993); Fearn-Banks (1996); Regester and Larkin (1997); Henry (2000); Fink (2013); Sellnow and Seeger (2013).
8 Outstanding books capturing this literature are Ulmer et al. (2010) and Coombs (2015).
9 See 't Hart (1993), who bases his account on Turner (1978).
10 Bennett and Entman (2001); Meyer (2002); de Vries (2004).
11 Arild and Maor (2015).
12 Walters et al. (1989); Wildavsky (1995).
13 Graber et al. (1998: 4).
14 Woodward and Bernstein (1994).
15 Breed (1955: 331).
16 Miller et al. (2014).
17 Stephens (1980: 5).
18 Meyer (2002); Lloyd (2004).
19 This typology of journalistic roles was first developed in 't Hart and Rijpma (1997: 81).
20 Nimmo and Combs (1985).
21 Olsson (2009a, 2009b); Olsson and Nord (2014).
22 Keane (2009).
23 https://twitter.com/fhollande/status/665308718335070212?lang=en.
24 www.washingtonpost.com/news/worldviews/wp/2014/03/24/this-is-the-text-message-sent-to-mh370-relatives/ (accessed March 25, 2014).
25 Walker (2015).
26 Olsson (2014); Bach (2015); OECD (2015), Wukich (2015).
27 For a case study, see Rosenthal et al. (1994). See further Wildavsky and Dake (1991).
28 Alford (2009); Heinzelman and Waters (2010); Keim and Nojie (2011).
29 Key (1966).
30 Halper (1971: 7).
31 Erikson (1994); Quarantelli (2001). Some governments have actually understood the message and maintain "mythbusting" webpages designed to assist emergency planning efforts. See, e.g., www.cpbr.gov.au/disact/human-response.html (accessed July 20, 2015).

32 Quarantelli (1954); Dynes (1970); Tierney et al. (2001); Aguirre (2004).
33 For an overview of framing research, see Chong and Druckman (2007).
34 Boin et al. (2008; 2009).
35 Butler (2009).
36 Chubb (2014).
37 http://abcnews.go.com/blogs/politics/2013/08/president-obamas-red-line-what-he-actually-said-about-syria-and-chemical-weapons/ (accessed June 12, 2015).
38 See, e.g., Pfetsch (1998); Johnson-Cartee (2005); Coombs (2007); Olsson and Nord (2014).
39 Bromwich (2014); Lebow and Stein (1994); Brändström et al. (2004).
40 Hargrove (1998).
41 Administrative and bargaining languages form the vehicles for behind-the-scenes striving for advantages and deal making (Edelman, 1964, 1977); cf. Entman (1993); Iyengar (1996).
42 Heath (2004).
43 Edelman (1977) uses the term "semantically created crisis."
44 Buzan et al. (1998: 26).
45 Edelman (1977).
46 Judah (2014).
47 www.government.nl/documents/speeches/2014/07/22/meeting-of-the-security-council-new-york-21-july-2014 (accessed September 16, 2015).
48 Edelman (1977: 14); White (1986); Edelman (1988: 66–89).
49 Cf. Platt (1971); Lipsky and Olson (1977); Parker and Dekker (2008).
50 Thompson (1999).
51 www.whitehouse.gov/the-press-office/2012/12/16/remarks-president-sandy-hook-interfaith-prayer-vigil (accessed September 16, 2015).
52 Drake (2013). On the 2015 incident, see http://nos.nl/artikel/2060753-obama-word-boos-over-schietpartijen.html (accessed October 2, 2015).
53 Karyotis and Gerodimos (2015).
54 As conceptualized by Schön and Rein (1994), for instance.
55 Smith (1989: 46).
56 For a survey study of the key components of credibility, see Ohanian (1991).
57 www.ft.com/cms/s/0/b2934a0e-0f89–11e5–94d1–00144feabdc0 .html#axzz3d4e9oYLR (accessed June 15, 2015).
58 Regester and Larkin (1997); Baggot (1998); Grönvall (2001).
59 Halper (1971: 16).
60 As argued by assistant secretary of defense in the Kennedy administration, Arthur Sylvester. Quoted in Halper (1971: 17).
61 http://edition.cnn.com/2003/US/05/01/bush.transcript/ (accessed October 13, 2015).
62 Nohrstedt (1991); Stern (1999: 226).
63 Silverstein (1981: 135), cited in Jervis (1992: 191), italics in original.
64 Stephens (1980).
65 Angela Libertore's (1993) case study of Italy and Chernobyl showed this quite clearly.
66 Bennett (1980); Nimmo and Combs (1990: 54).

67 Leaders who fail to do this may suffer the consequences. For example, Christian-democratic contender for the German chancellorship, Edmund Stoiber, lost his lead in the final stage of the 2002 election race against incumbent Gerhard Schröder when he – unlike Schröder – initially declined to visit flood-stricken areas and seemed to want to play down the issue. Schröder won the election. See Bytzek (2008).

68 Shils (1968); Combs (1980: 41–47); Kertzer (1988: 140–44).

69 Cf. Staelraeve and 't Hart (2008).

70 This is true even when it comes to observing rituals of other nations' crises: the Swedish government and the prime minister in particular faced critical media and parliamentary questions and even ridicule when it turned out that neither the prime minister himself nor any other senior politician or member of the royal family were to participate in the memorial service for the victims of the 2004 Madrid bombings, whereas all of the other EU members were represented by their government leaders. Things got even worse when the prime minister was photographed visiting a farm in rural Sweden at the time the ceremony in Spain took place.

71 Regester and Larkin (1997: 146).

72 Edelman (1971). See also Elder and Cobb (1983: 116).

5 Ending a Crisis
Managing Accountability

5.1 It Ain't Over Till It's Over

In July 1995, Bosnian-Serb forces occupied the town of Srebrenica, a UN safe haven in the Yugoslavian civil war, after a long siege and a brief military campaign.[1] The Dutch military contingent (Dutchbat), the UN protector of the Muslim enclave, surrendered and was allowed a safe retreat. On return, their families, the prime minister, and the Crown Prince welcomed the Dutch troops as national heroes. For the minister of defense, who had spent several days and nights in the government bunker in The Hague from where the Dutch military commanded the besieged troops, the crisis was finally over – or so he thought.

After taking over the enclave, the Bosnian-Serbian troops commanded by Ratko Mladic killed thousands of captives who had been under Dutch protection. The world soon learned that 7,000 men had been murdered, many of them while the Dutch battalion was anxiously awaiting its safe passage home. When the atrocities came to the fore, Dutch sentiment changed quickly. Media reports asserted that the Dutch soldiers had done very little to defend the enclave. Rumors began to circulate to the effect that the Dutch had condoned and even cooperated with the Serbs, thus facilitating the ethnic cleansing.

The Dutch minister of defense, Joris Voorhoeve, would spend the remainder of his political career defending the decision to surrender the enclave. Various investigations were conducted, yet doubts lingered on in the public mind. Finally, under pressure, the prime minister decided to appoint an official inquiry by the National Institute of War Studies. When it reported in the spring of 2002, just before scheduled elections, the report cleared the army of the cowardice charges but roundly criticized the government's decision to send Dutch troops into such a hazardous and badly supported UN mission. The government resigned. Seven years after Srebrenica, the political crisis was finally over.

The civil and criminal court battles continued, however. The "mothers of Srebrenica" proved unrelenting in their efforts to seek justice. Dutch and European courts knocked back their claims, but a Dutch court ruled in 2013 that the Dutchbat squadron did bear legal (though not criminal) liability for the deportations and subsequent killing of Bosnian Muslim men. The Srebrenica tragedy had become a wound that kept bleeding.[2]

Crises can last a surprisingly long time. After the "hot" phase has passed, one would expect a crisis to wind down. A crisis, almost by definition, is a temporary situation – a state of exception.[3] The task of crisis leadership, then, is to restore a sense of normalcy: end hostilities, extinguish the fire, treat the wounded, reaffirm public trust in institutions. But leaders often discover, to their bewilderment and dismay, that the worst for them is yet to come when the initial crisis response operations are "on track" or have ceased. The recovery process often turns out to be surprisingly complex and hard to manage. The shared experience of adversity may foster solidarity and unite people behind the common cause of victim assistance, reconstruction, and institutional reparation, but these crises also provide opportunities for critics of the existing status quo.[4] Crisis leaders may effectively negotiate the challenges of sense making, urgent decision making, and meaning making, only to encounter an unsuspected yet formidable additional challenge: ending the crisis.

This chapter's *key question* is: why do some crises come to a clear, quick, and (relatively) clean ending while others continue to simmer, flare up, and transform? The obvious answer – the bigger the issue, the longer the "tail" – is not adequate. The research findings are clear: the extent of physical and economic damage, the number of deaths, and the crisis behavior of leaders alone do not determine the duration of a crisis.[5] A major influence, we argue, are the dynamics of the accountability processes that crises elicit. The politics of the aftermath can be chaotic and vitriolic. When and how a crisis eventually ends depends to a considerable extent – and this is our *key claim* – on the way these accountability processes are managed. The management of accountability therefore is a pivotal task of crisis leadership.

5.2   How Crises End: Two Scenarios

There are, of course, many ways in which crises develop, escalate, and end. Some are like bolts from the blue: they come and go quickly. Some crises smolder and flare up periodically; some seem to never really end. To facilitate discussion, we discern two ideal-typical crisis trajectories: the fast-burning crisis and the long-shadow crisis.

The Fast-Burning Crisis

A fast-burning crisis is marked by the simultaneous termination of operational response efforts and political attention for the crisis. Think of a natural disaster (a hurricane or a flood). After the winds have died or the water has receded, the stricken community can bury the dead, take care of survivors, and repair the damage. The community can study what went wrong and initiate remedial measures. Once the community "moves on," we might say that the crisis has ended.

The fast-burning crisis is clearly demarcated in time: it comes and goes. It soon is a brief episode in a long history, a page in the book. This does not mean that people will forget this painful and time-defining calamity. It simply means that there is *closure*. Such crises may even become history markers with a positive connotation. This happens when there is a story of leadership success or moral determination; a community views its crisis leaders as sources of collective pride and inspiration. For example, the daring yet successful raids on hijacked planes at Entebbe (1976) and Mogadishu (1977) have set a standard for effective crisis management. The killing of Osama bin Laden had a similar effect in the United States.

The scenario of the fast-burning crisis corresponds best with (technocratic) notions of effective and legitimate crisis management. If a crisis is managed in an effective and legitimate way, we might expect it to be "over" relatively quickly. The burning issue has been tackled; the system can return to "business as usual."

Local experience is a helpful factor. When the scope and impact of a crisis do not transcend local notions of what can be expected and do not overtax the community's and the government's response capacities, a society may quickly come to terms with it. Some communities, in which certain types of crisis happen more often (think of mining and fishing communities), develop resilient subcultures that feature rituals which facilitate closure. These communities have "learned to live" with particular types of crises and disasters.

Another factor is the absence of accountability processes. This absence allows a leader to declare a crisis to be over, to shut down discussion, even to banish its existence from the official record. In authoritarian regimes, leaders can and do manipulate public perceptions of a crisis: they dictate the narrative, which typically points to a combination of bad luck, outside forces, and heroic leadership.

Yet another factor is the serendipitous emergence of something bigger or worse. A crisis can end simply because public attention moves somewhere else. Some crises simply pale in significance when larger crises present themselves. Who remembers what the crises were on September 10, 2001?

The fast-burning crisis clearly is no longer the norm.[6] Most contemporary crises continue to flare long after operational urgencies have been addressed. This can happen even when response operations were quick and decisive. There will still be postmortem inquiries, and when they find that swift crisis operations have had unintended consequences or caused collateral harm, the frame will shift and a "crisis after the crisis" may ensue. Pressures to atone and change can become acute, even if the main characters have vacated their offices a long time ago.

The Long-Shadow Crisis

The norm today appears to be what we call the long-shadow crisis, one that does not end at all when immediate response challenges have been met. Over time, a cascade of major strategic and operational questions about recovery, reconstruction, and reform emerge. Questions about responsibility and accountability come to the fore and remain on the political agenda. Revisionist interpretations of the causes, the quality of the response, and the management of the wider repercussions get airplay in the media and force the crisis back on to political and institutional agendas. Legal proceedings may further complicate the picture. Public apologies may be expected but not given. Turning the page becomes an impossibility.

Why do some crises cast such long shadows? One factor that helps to prolong a crisis is the protracted and contentious nature of the public search for the causes of the crisis. Investigations typically reveal deep-rooted causes, which, in turn, raise thorny issues about leadership, responsibility, and future performance. The 1986 murder of the Swedish Prime Minister Olof Palme is a paradigmatic example. Its very occurrence in one of the most enduringly peaceful polities on earth was as baffling as it was traumatic to the Swedes. The subsequent police investigation caused yet another shock: it was unsuccessful and exposed hitherto invisible and bitter infighting within the Swedish criminal justice system.[7] The crime was never solved and conspiracy theories still emerge periodically.

The duration and costs of recovery processes are another factor. In February 2011, a major earthquake struck the New Zealand city of Christchurch. It killed 185 people and inflicted major damage on its downtown area and eastern suburbs. The government declared a state of emergency that lasted until April 2011. It became clear very quickly that the crisis after the disaster would pose even bigger challenges than the immediate response operation. Economists predicted that it might take half a century to fully recover. A recovery authority with a five-year brief was set up. Hitherto small and sleepy government agencies saw their staff balloon and their workloads explode. The recovery arena quickly became crowded with players: insurers, NGOs, citizen groups, business councils, and city planners all had a part to play. Their interests differed and their actions had to be aligned. Robust claims procedures had to be invented and then administered. Rebuilding plans had to be developed, permits had to be issued. Victims and affected communities demanded quick(er) assistance and action. Meanwhile the cost estimates were adjusted upward (reaching NZ $40 billion in 2013).

Some crises are of such large scope and significance that they retain a special place on governance agendas. These "endemic" crises include global warming, overpopulation, deforestation, and water management. These crises are essentially "unmanageable," at least from a national, short-term perspective. They are "wicked problems": transnational in origins and impact, defying existing governance repertoires and institutional capacities. Combating their origins requires draconic measures that few powerful actors are willing or able to implement. As a result, the problems do not go away and may come to haunt future leaders and policy makers.[8]

The global AIDS epidemic lost its crisis status in the Western world through a combination of painstaking scientific progress and a slow-down in the number of newly HIV-infected people. But the problem has not gone away: it remains a public health crisis in regions like sub-Saharan Africa. The same might well apply to the Ebola epidemic that wrought havoc in Western Africa in 2014. At the peak of the outbreak, international health authorities and even the UN Security Council considered it a major global threat. Transnational mobilization to tackle the crisis was slow in coming but did help contain the outbreak. By mid-2015, the world had moved on, but for deeply affected countries, such as Liberia and Sierra Leone, dealing with Ebola and its consequences will remain a chronic problem, taxing their vulnerable public health systems.

A crisis is sometimes kept alive by so-called policy entrepreneurs who recognize an opportunity to instigate policy or organizational change. They use the crisis to expose the vulnerabilities of the status quo ("see what happens if you turn a blind eye to . . . "). For example, the accident at the Three Mile Island nuclear power station (1979) repoliticized the use of nuclear energy in the United States. The subsequent 1986 Chernobyl and particularly the 2011 Fukushima nuclear accidents had similar agenda-setting effects, prompting significant antinuclear policy changes in countries such as Germany, France, and Italy.[9]

A crisis can also "survive" by morphing into an institutional crisis. This happens when the crisis becomes a symbol of hitherto unknown or neglected risks and vulnerabilities. The filmed beating of Rodney King by a group of officers from the Los Angeles Police Department (LAPD) is a perfect example.[10] The LAPD downplayed the incident and tried to explain (in vain) that King had threatened the officers and refused to obey direct orders. The video of the beating, televised over and over again, signaled that the LAPD had lost its moral bearings. A year later, in 1992, a jury acquitted the policemen. Los Angeles erupted in violence; the rioting lasted for days. More than two decades later, the Rodney King crisis became an oft-invoked historical analogy in the community outrage and critical commentary following a spate of unrelated but evidently "symptomatic" police shootings of young black males, starting with the 2014 slaying of Michael Brown in Ferguson, Missouri. Again, a pattern of police defensiveness in the wake of public accusations of racial profiling (and indeed institutional racism) and court acquittals of accused police officers sparked major rioting, revealing the ugly underbelly of police-community relations in various towns and states.

A crisis may even reemerge from the history books. This typically happens after a regime change, when democracy supplants authoritarianism. Episodes that were erased from the public's mind return on the agenda, as democracy creates opportunities for citizens to demand justice retrospectively, that is, through "truth commissions" or criminal court cases. The drama of the public inquiries that ensues once such proceedings get underway can fuel a societal re-engagement with the unfinished business of the past.[11]

5.3   To End a Crisis: What Role for Leadership?

To end a crisis, closure must be achieved on both the operational and political dimensions of crisis management. *Operationally*, a crisis ends when the response network is deactivated because it is no longer needed. *Strategically*, a crisis reaches closure when crisis-related issues no longer dominate public, political, and policy agendas. This simple distinction helps to explain the intricate challenges that crisis leaders face in their efforts to create a sense of normalcy.

First, crisis leaders have to make an accurate and balanced assessment of the need to keep the crisis response infrastructure in place or to modify it as events unfold. These assessments may pertain to the legal framework of emergency procedures and bylaws, the level of decentralization of decision making authority and the processes for mobilizing critical resources). At some point, this state of emergency is no longer necessary. But when is that point, and how to determine that?

Second, they must assess the political expediency of crisis termination. The key challenge is to recognize when the sense of threat, shock, violation, indignation in the relevant stakeholder communities has dissipated. This is not about achieving complete and utter victory over the problems that triggered the crisis. More likely there may still be lingering concerns among some stakeholders, but the matter is no longer deemed urgent by the majority (and the media have moved on, too). This judgment depends on many considerations, including the perceived political success of the crisis management effort so far as conveyed through media reporting and public opinion data; the positions and momentum of rivals, critics, and advocates; and the presumed ability of all involved to affect and control the public's perception of the crisis.

Juxtaposing the operational and strategic dimensions, we can sketch four ideal-typical states of "closure" (see Figure 5.1). Perfect closure is achieved when operational demands cease while the political and public sense of crisis dissipates as well. This was roughly the case in several Western European countries immediately after World War II, including the Scandinavian countries and the Netherlands: after hostilities had ended, the widespread inclination in societal and political circles was to move on and rebuild. As long as operational definitions of crisis fit with political and societal perceptions, however, there is no reason to end a crisis. In the years after the 9/11 attacks, the American public strongly supported the U.S.-led "global war on terror." The wars in Iraq and Afghanistan eventually became deeply problematic operationally and highly contentious politically. Yet, this crisis has been hard to end.

Figure 5.1 Four Ideal-Typical States of Crisis Closure

The most interesting cases are found in the mismatch between operational and strategic closure. Operational closure often invites termination at the political end of the crisis spectrum, but this rarely happens without a glitch. When members of the Branch Davidians Sect barricaded themselves into a house in Waco, Texas, in 1993, Federal Bureau of Investigation (FBI) and the Bureau of Alcohol, Tobacco, Firearms and Explosives (ATF) agency forces fought their way into the compound, ending the operation quickly with a death toll of seventy-four men, women, and children. For the FBI, the ATF, and Attorney General Janet Reno, however, the crisis had only just begun. The botched operation (which had taken the lives of four ATF agents) provoked a political crisis that gave rise to high-profile investigations and criminal proceedings.[12]

In some cases, leaders terminate the crisis regime before operational activities have ceased. Premature closure occurs when leaders underestimate the complexity and tenacity of the problems at hand, underestimate opponents, or misread the residual stress level existing in the affected community. The danger of premature revocation of the crisis regime is twofold. First, it may create vacuums in policy making and service delivery. Focused, large-scale, and quick activities give way to politics and bureaucracy as usual – disjointed, incremental, and slow. This can undermine the effectiveness of the crisis operation. Second, premature closure is likely to invite disbelief, disappointment, and intense criticism. Especially in a community that is still experiencing acute needs and stress, premature closure exposes policy makers to charges of being "insensitive" and opportunistic ("they forgot their promises as soon as the cameras were gone"). This undermines the trust base, or legitimacy, of a public institution.

Leaders can also *overextend* the crisis regime. They become so focused on the operational dimension of the crisis that they lose sight of the big picture. This happens, for instance, when they get caught up in the myopia-inducing "bunker syndrome": they sit in a command center for weeks on end, where they "manage" the crisis and lose themselves in streams of seemingly urgent communication. The world outside moves on to other concerns, but the authorities have cut themselves off from that part of reality by continuing to allocate all of their attention to a crisis that in many ways is no longer "hot."

Some leaders see strategic or tactical mileage in extending rather than dampening the crisis mood, and in continuing rather than abolishing the crisis governance regime.[13] Authoritarian leaders routinely invoke and prolong states of emergency to consolidate their positions and to vilify and persecute political opponents. Such leaders risk overplaying their hand when they stick to the crisis mode when most perceive that the "real issues" have come to lie elsewhere (for instance in the authoritarian nature, lack of effectiveness, or corruption-inducing nature of the response itself). It leaves them open to charges that they are exploiting the crisis politically as a means to deflect attention. This is a political gamble, which may well turn against them.

5.4   Crisis Accountability: A Contest of Explanations

In their efforts to end a crisis along both operational and political dimensions, democratic leaders must deal with one overriding institutional constraint: the process of accountability. The requirements and dynamics of accountability sharply delineate the playing room for leaders; they also create opportunities for opposition forces to prolong the crisis.

Accountability is one of the pillars of democratic society: it forces elected leaders to explain what went wrong, why, and what they did to limit the consequences of failure.[14] A crisis or disaster nearly always creates accountability pressures for leaders. In modern society, particularly those societies that pride themselves on being stable, well-ordered, peaceful, and safe, crises and disasters are hard to accept.[15] Somebody or some organization must be held responsible. Without some form of public reckoning, it is then very difficult for communities to achieve a new and stable post-crisis equilibrium. As Lee Clarke notes, "crises, disasters and scandals result in public disquiet and in loss of confidence in the body of politics. Confidence can be effectively restored only by thoroughly investigating and establishing the truth and exposing the facts to public scrutiny."[16]

Accountability, however, is not just a way of bringing closure to a crisis; it can also extend its life span and even transform it. In many cases we have studied, crisis-induced accountability pressures gave rise to a "crisis after the crisis." They lift crisis events from the level of operations to the levels of policy and politics. What began as an accident or a series of incidents turns into a story about power, competence, integrity, and legitimacy (or lack of it). Accountability is not just reflective but often intensely political.

Most people still accept that public leaders cannot simply eradicate misfortune. But the burden of the argument has shifted: regulators and managers must establish that they *cannot* be held responsible. When it comes to accounting for actions taken in response to an emerging or an acute crisis, the margins for excusable failure have become even narrower. Governments are assumed to be well prepared for critical contingencies, and to be capable of taking swift and effective measures protecting the public and limiting harm. Any behavior that deviates from this generalized expectation is treated with suspicion and indignation. In short, accounting for crises occurs against the background of an ongoing framing contest about the meaning of the crisis.

Yet, crisis response organizations have much to gain from crises and the accountability processes that they necessitate – provided they do well, and are seen to have done well, in performing their duties. They can flag their successes and boost their image among budget providers, the press, and the public. Effective agencies usually make sure their successes are appropriately marketed to captive audiences, both during and after the accountability process. However, when their operations have experienced problems, the accountability process can be a major threat. Since being good at containing crises is at the heart of political crisis leadership, any evidence to the contrary erodes the legitimacy of political leaders. At the very least, it gives their competitors a chance to discredit them. In such circumstances, beleaguered agencies may resort to cover-up, blame-avoidance, and blame-shifting tactics during the accountability process.

Rendering account involves a delicate blend of factual reconstruction, framing, and lesson-drawing.[17] And there is only a thin line between framing and blaming, which explains why so many crises give rise to political and bureaucratic blame games.[18]

When efforts to investigate crises turn into blame games, the aim of truth-finding and "looking back" loses out against the political dynamics of accusing-defending. This poses a dilemma for incumbents. The integrity of the accountability process has to be guarded against the danger of runaway politicization, but who has the authority and is sufficiently motivated to perform the leadership work of protecting that integrity? Opposition forces will find it easier to engage in blaming, as they do not carry responsibility and can win something by engaging in it.

We view a crisis-induced accountability process as a "contest of explanations." The accountability process constitutes the arena in which victims, responders, planners, regulators, corporations, politicians, investigators, and change advocates try to obtain or preserve position and clout. Their efforts often intersect, partially overlap, and partially conflict – presenting a formidable management challenge to governments and other actors whose performance is placed under the public microscope. Let us take a closer look at the participants in this "contest of explanations" and the forums in which these contests are fought.

Accountability: Actors and Venues

The *legislature* is the principal venue for political accountability. Some groups (notably opposition parties) and individuals (ambitious political entrepreneurs) welcome crises as opportunities for self-dramatization. They seize on a crisis to show their ability to monitor and control government, to demonstrate their toughness as a countervailing power, and, in partisan mode, to inflict damage on or create dissent within the opposing camp.

Legislators can take this proactive stance only when they were not involved in making and approving the very policies and agency statutes they now seek to criticize. Past involvement, in other words, diminishes the opportunity for legislators to exploit the post-crisis accountability process. When today's inquisitors are seen to be conveniently forgetting that they were yesterday's lawmakers, they open themselves to charges of hypocrisy.

Regulatory bodies are often authorized or even obliged to investigate major incidents. Think of environmental protection agencies, transport or food safety bodies, school inspectorates, medical licensing authorities, or health regulators. Regulators tend to be driven by a technical, professional paradigm of accountability. They establish cause and effect and focus on drawing and disseminating lessons for the future. However, in the context of a major crisis, pressures can build on these agencies to be more judgmental, if only to dispel any notions that they themselves have been asleep at the wheel prior to the crisis, allowing their regulatees to take or tolerate excessive risk and to lower the bar on their level of preparedness.

Public regulators are supposed to provide an independent, nonpolitical, professionally sound analysis and formulate recommendations. These bodies are staffed with experts and often command considerable budgets to conduct investigations into ongoing practices and crucial cases in their respective sectors. It is part of their core business to provide high-quality input to the accountability and learning process triggered by crisis, and therefore they experience pressure to perform fast, reliably, and effectively. However, speed and accuracy rarely travel well together. The situation becomes complicated when multiple investigative boards are involved: interagency rivalry does not necessarily improve the quality of the investigation.[19] What's more, it opens up space for blaming processes. One glaring example is found in the aftermath of Hurricane Katrina, which saw several comprehensive inquiries that fueled politicization but did little to establish the underlying causes of the failed response.

The more they are viewed as independent, the higher the likelihood that their reports will be regarded as authoritative by all parties concerned. It is problematic, then, if a public regulator comes under critical scrutiny as part of the crisis process. Many public regulators are also tasked with risk management responsibilities: early warning, vetting proposed legislation, inspecting for safety and security, and so on. When a crisis materializes in spite of these efforts, regulator credibility may suffer. Questions will be asked about their ineffectiveness, their laxness, or even their cooptation by regulatees[20] For example, in the wake of the global financial crisis, the rating agencies – performing a crucial public risk detection function – were widely seen to be part of the problem when they were revealed to be operating on perverse incentives, embedded in unhealthy interdependencies with the very financial institutions they were supposed to rate.[21]

Legal actors may enter the picture. Public prosecutors may launch investigations. Litigation may be sought by victims and other stakeholders. In these legal forums, a forensic paradigm of accountability dominates. The main aim is not just to establish causality but to ascertain responsibility and indeed culpability. The context of high-consequence events such as crises lends these proceedings a particularly grave and potentially adversarial bent. Managerial careers, compensation payments, organizational reputation and autonomy: there is much at stake for those involved.

The legal shadow that major crises cast can be long and costly. Issues of responsibility and liability related to the 1984 explosion of a Union Carbide petrochemical plant at Bhopal, India, that killed over 2,500 people and affected approximately half a million, were being fought over in the U.S. and Indian civil and criminal court systems as late as 2011. The company paid $470 million in compensation in an out of court settlement, but its total expenditure related to the various legal proceedings was much larger. Oil giant Exxon Mobil was in court for two decades following the 1989 massive oil spill in Alaska's Prince William Sound caused by one of its tankers, with the eventual damages being awarded in 2007 exceeding $500 million. That sum pales in comparison with the damages suffered by BP after the 2010 Deepwater Horizon oil spill: BP paid $18.7 billion to settle all federal and state claims.[22]

Crisis-induced court proceedings can also produce legal changes affecting the course and outcomes of future legal action in similar crises. One example is the attempt by the association of victims of the 1987 *Herald of Free Enterprise* ferry disaster to criminally prosecute the executives of the Townsend Thoresen (later P&O ferries) company. The case was dismissed, but it set the precedent that corporate manslaughter was legally admissible in English courts.

Governments can launch an *independent investigation*. Inquiries of an explicitly political nature are often initiated in the wake of crisis, with legislatures (and particularly opposition parties within them) keen to show their involvement and robustness in holding executive power to account. This could take the form of a blue-ribbon panel, an academic authority, a current or former judge, or – in Westminster-style political systems – a Royal Commission. In order to properly fulfill its task, such investigation needs to be bestowed with public authority. This presupposes that people of impeccable, nonpartisan credentials are selected to head it, that they be given a wide brief, unlimited access to information and actors, ample resources, and freedom to organize their work as they see fit. By granting all of that, governments set up a body that can prove to be a major thorn in their own sides.

Blue-ribbon commissions are usually asked to provide "comprehensive" and "independent" assessments of a crisis. These commissions tend to define their own parameters for judgments on political, judicial, and financial accountability. They construct – or at least pretend to – the officially certified version of an important part of a nation's recent history. But they cannot always break the hold that the politics of partisanship exert on the accountability process. In fact, their potential roles as truth tellers, political conflict managers, and institutional agenda setters easily can turn the composition, mandate, and modus operandi of crisis commissions into objects of political contestation. When the investigative work or the findings of commissions become controversial, allegations and counter-allegations will merely perpetuate different versions of the crisis story.

In the not so distant past, *citizens* had little access to accountability processes. It was not easy to get public recognition, compensation, and reconstruction support. Communities had to muster inner strength as they were left to their own devices after the initial flurry of activity had died down and the camera lights had been shut off.[23] Enduring harm suffered by individuals, groups, and communities tended to be dealt with in a rather low-key, bureaucratized manner, if at all. Those who wanted more had a good chance of being bogged down in protracted legal battles or simply being ignored by their political leaders.

Today, citizens have stronger voices. They quickly organize themselves into pressure groups. They proliferate their numbers, voices, and support by leveraging social media. And they are more likely to use their voices and organizational resources when the treatment received from private and public actors involved in crisis response does not meet their standards. During floods, for example, political decisions to conduct preventative evacuations of endangered areas have become the topic of intense controversy in various countries. Not only have governments had a hard time persuading citizens to leave their houses, during the aftermath they have experienced difficulties answering convincingly to charges that they acted overly cautiously at the expense of citizens and businesses. Likewise, public health authorities find it more difficult than in the past to gain compliance for inoculation campaigns for both acute (e.g., the Mexican flu) and chronic (e.g., cervical cancer) health hazards.

Citizens tend not to wait for formal investigation and compensation procedures to run their course. Citizens have learned to organize, mobilize media attention, and forge coalitions with other segments of civil society as well as individual political entrepreneurs seeking to call policy makers and politicians to account for and to "reopen" the crisis; they can evolve from citizen to victim to claimant in a matter of hours and days. Journalists, opposition politicians, interest group activists, and lawyers have plenty of incentives as well as opportunities to empower citizens. The contemporary political climate favors restorative justice, which gives victims a better chance of placing their suffering and traumas high on the public agenda.

Media play a dominant role in accountability processes. The mass media are "all over" the accountability process, ready to cover new information about risks, dangers, mishaps, failures, and flaws that may sustain or transform the running story of the current crisis. Media representatives therefore play a powerful role in shaping the dominant interpretation that emerges from accountability processes. The same rule applies here as it does for initial phases of meaning making: accountability processes do not speak for themselves; they must be interpreted. And media representatives know how to reduce a complex analysis of cause and effect to a simple, evocative story of heroes and villains.

Some media report in fairly objective terms, leaving their audience with the opportunity to make up their own minds. Some assume a proactive stance and try to get to the bottom of the case. Yet others turn into crusading entrepreneurs who exploit the openness of the accountability process in order to argue their preconceived position. They compete on speed, tone, and impact. All of them are now facing the parallel universe of social media, which is unfailingly replete with bluntly expressed opinions and conspiracy theories even if it also features intelligent commentary and remarkable forms of citizen journalism.

5.5 Managing the Accountability Contest

The need to publicly account for crisis can make it hard to end one. The complex and extended accountability processes that often ensue in the wake of a crisis create oxygen for politically and otherwise motivated moves by stakeholders to keep critical events in the spotlight and responsible authorities under pressure.

The political astuteness of crisis leaders is thus tested in the wake of crises and disasters. In negotiating the accountability phase, crisis leaders face three challenges that require a strategy: (a) the interaction with inquiry bodies and media representatives; (b) the response to findings and recommendations produced by inquiry bodies; and (c) the political impact of "public verdicts" produced by inquiries or media investigations.[24]

Facing Inquiries: Stonewalling versus Cooperation

In the immediate aftermath of a large-scale crisis, leaders face questions about possible inquiries. Are they going to set up an inquiry? How are they going to design its brief? How are they going to endow it with resources? Who are they going to appoint in the role of official questioner? And what do they seek to achieve by doing all this – public enlightenment, institutional learning, outflanking the opposition, saving their jobs, or reestablishing legitimacy?[25]

Here leaders face a dilemma. The initiation of an inquiry creates a venue for stakeholders to influence the perception of the crisis management performance (and not necessarily in a way that benefits the crisis managers). At the same time, political leaders usually realize that it is futile to oppose public inquiries into large-scale crises and disasters. There is plenty they can do to constrain inquiry mandates. Frontloading tactics include restricting the terms of reference of the investigation, hand-picking "friendly" or malleable chairpersons, and limiting the time and resources made available. Such tactics may rebound. To be seen as compromising the search for "the truth" undermines public support for incumbent leaders and governments.

When a crisis gives rise to an inquiry, authorities have choices to make when it comes to instigating, designing, and cooperating with the inquiries. Leaders can choose to be proactive or reactive, cooperative or combative, matter of fact or emotional in how they handle themselves in the face of strong and often unrelenting accountability pressures. All of this is deeply political, and there is a lot at stake for many of the parties involved.[26]

Affecting the way the inquiry process itself is designed and run is one way to exercise such influence. Incumbents benefit from inquiries that are expert-driven, operate on a targeted brief, with a no-blame ethics and a non-adversarial stance. Their political opponents naturally benefit more from inquiries that are all but that.

Leaders will be expected to provide access to information and government witnesses. They may be reluctant to do so, for obvious reasons.

Leaders can "stonewall" fact-finding efforts by keeping tabs on files, people, and other sources of information. They can also pretend to cooperate and flood their inquisitors with truckloads of mostly tangential records. They can try and put a positive spin on all of the information they provide to investigators and reporters. But stonewalling tactics are unlikely to be fully effective when the full force of journalistic, political, and sometimes judicial inquiry ihto executive actions is unleashed.

To some extent incumbents and investigators have overlapping interests: an inquiry needs "inside" material and political leaders want to be seen as cooperative. A typical solution, then, is to negotiate terms of access and cooperation, for example whether and how leaders can be interviewed, which documents and officials will be made available, and whether the conclusions of the inquiry will be first discussed with the incumbent leaders (which provides them with time to prepare their "spin" following publication).

Leaders can adopt a more cooperative stance. They can endorse the creation of a genuinely independent and/or bipartisan legislative inquiry that is chaired by highly reputable, independently minded public figures. One that has wide terms of reference and is well resourced. This may work well for all involved. After all, a politically dangerous crisis is truly defused when incumbent leaders have been cleared or exonerated by an official inquiry widely perceived as thorough and independent.

Responding to Revelations: Denying Versus Acknowledging Error

The accountability process typically brings two types of difficult questions for leaders. When a crisis occurs on their turf, so to speak, they face charges of having failed to prevent it: why did they not foresee the crisis? And why were they unable to prevent simmering problems from escalating?

Think of the criticism directed toward the U.S. intelligence community after the September 11 attacks. Think of how the tragedy of Hurricane Katrina revealed a lack of preparedness for hurricane-induced flash flooding in and around New Orleans.[27] Or think of the Chinese public health agencies, which stood accused of underplaying the dangers of SARS and misinforming their political superiors and international colleagues about the scale of the problem in China. But even when an agency had nothing to do with the outbreak of crisis and was merely called in to help combat the problem, it can be criticized as an ill-prepared, sluggish, and uncooperative partner in crisis response. For instance, specialized crisis response agencies such as the police or the fire brigade often complain about the disorganized or rigid "bureaucratic" nature of the non-emergency services (e.g., housing services, social work, public transport, and public utilities) that they must work with during major disasters.

There are many possible answers to these questions, and consensus may not be easy to achieve. Leaders may accept responsibility or deny it and blame *force majeure* or other actors for damages, glitches, and errors. Much depends on the formal division of labor and responsibility between policy makers and agencies. When policy implementation and service delivery have been delegated to private actors, quasi-independent agencies, or lower levels of government, it is easy for policy makers to deflect blame on them. Seen in this light, a side effect of decentralization, delegation, outsourcing, and other techniques of new public management that became *en vogue* in the 1990s is that they provide policy makers and regulators with protective coating in cases of failure and crisis. Policy makers will not hesitate to point out that they were no longer determining the nature, level, and quality of policy implementation. They were far removed from the source of trouble; hence their causal impact on the crisis outbreak was negligible. They redirect questions to the implementing actors. This explains why ducking, diffusing, and deflecting responsibility are much more likely initial responses to crisis-induced accountability pressures than taking responsibility and absorbing the blame that comes with it.[28]

Coping with Verdicts: Perseverance Versus Resignation

When accountability forums are highly critical of the government's conduct, the apotheosis of the accountability process hinges on the leadership's conceptions of what "taking responsibility" entails. They can try to hold out. They can deploy several tactics to defuse criticism and maintain their legitimacy. They can argue that continuity is vital in a time of crisis and rebuilding.

Leaders who stand condemned by accountability forums can attempt to escape the searchlights of the accountability debate by referring to a set of recurrent defensive scripts such as accusing the accusers, disqualifying critics, blaming the messenger, extenuating their own behavior, shifting the burden of proof onto critics, or blaming others.[29] Table 5.1 summarizes the various argumentative tactics that can be used. The viability of any particular tactic or argument varies: when they are used (timing), where they are used (forum), by whom they are used (credibility), and how well they are presented (staging, delivery). Nor are these tactics mutually exclusive. They are often used simultaneously in various forums addressing different accountability questions. They can also be

Table 5.1 *Playing the Blame Game: Argumentative Tactics*

Accountability Dimension	Tactic	Argument
Severity	Denial	Nothing bad happened.
	Mitigation	Harm was negligible.
		Harm was compensated.
		You can't make an omelet without breaking some eggs.
	Positive spin	It was a success.
Agency	Combating causation	It was not my doing.
		I was only a small contributor.
		Uncontrollable forces reigned.
	Combating capacity	I was not informed.
		Others made vital decisions.
		I was under orders.
	Blaming messenger	Publicity caused the harm.
	Disqualifying investigators	Investigation was unfair.
		Investigators are incompetent.
		Report is unprofessional.
Responsibility	Justification	I chose the lesser evil.
		I prevented worse by others.
	Preventing labeling	This was atypical behavior.
	Scapegoating	I have punished the culprit(s).
	Repentance	I apologize, please forgive me.
		I have learned my lesson.
	Symbolic reform	I have changed policies.

Source: adapted from Bovens et al. (1999)

used sequentially, for example when the emphasis in the blame game gradually shifts from issues of agency to issues of responsibility, or when earlier use of particular tactics has proved ineffective.

Some leaders seem better at dodging the blame bullet than others, even in the most adverse circumstances.[30] Personality and persona come into play. The British Prime Minister "Teflon Tony" Blair managed to dissociate himself from whatever mire or difficulties he himself or his ministers became involved in – until the Iraq war proved to be one crisis too many. Some have the resilience (or the luck) of becoming "comeback leaders," demonstrating astute leadership during a crisis. French president Francois Hollande is a case in point: dogged by entrenched unpopularity and personal scandal, he managed to turn around (at least temporarily) the French public's perception of his leadership by his response to the 2015 terrorist attacks in Paris.[31]

Given the fact that most humans lack such Teflon or luck, what can leaders do who are under the gun of crisis-induced allegations to duck responsibility? They can try to depict the failures committed as technical, operational matters for which blame remains limited to lower-level operators. They can argue that any deeper failures or weaknesses that have occurred are incidental (as opposed to structural). They can argue that they have already taken measures to address the problems that were revealed by the investigation. They can deflect blame toward "lightning rods" within or beyond the wider structure of government.[32] Responsibility for unpopular or risky endeavors can be limited through delegation by design, providing officeholders with the option to survive scandal, and demonstrating resolve to "learn the lessons."

In contrast, leaders can also choose to embrace responsibility for what happened prior to and during a crisis. They can admit partial responsibility but at the same time point out that there were many other fingerprints on the problems, not hard to do in an age of distributed authority and network governance. They can agree to pay compensations. They can engage in public displays of empathy and dramatize their commitment to "caring government" or a "socially responsible" corporation by their presence, their rhetoric, or a commitment to new projects and initiatives for victims and affected communities.

Contrition – the art of apology – is one step down the ladder of symbolic displays of empathy.[33] Research suggests that elite apologies can be usefully understood and evaluated in terms of: (1) truthfulness – an apology needs to be accompanied by full disclosure of relevant information; (2) sincerity – an apology needs to come across as an authentic attempt to reconcile rather than a desire to escape further scrutiny, (3) timing – apologies loose force when they come late (i.e., well after an actor has first tried to ignore or deny responsibility), (4) voluntarism – contrition in the absence of duress makes has more impact than apology that is perceived to be forced, (5) comprehensiveness – the degree to which it encompasses all victims and affected parties, and (6) dramaturgy – the extent to which it is performed in an appropriate, dignified public context.

5.6   Accountability, Blame Games, and Democracy

This chapter has documented a tension between the characteristics of the accountability process and the "smoothness" of crisis termination. For instance, it is often said that transparency is a key value of democratic governance. It follows that accountability requires full transparency in the wake of a crisis. Yet, full transparency may simply be impossible, dangerous, or illegal.

The latent tensions that exist in any polity between public, the opposition's, and government interests do not melt away during crises. On the contrary, since the visibility and political stakes of crises are so high, these tensions will be even more pronounced than usual. Crises induce or amplify divisions not just among and between (segments of) society and the government, but also between officials, groups, and organizations within government. The same leaders who seek to centralize authority and decision-making powers during the crisis are quick to point out that they cannot be held responsible for policies whose implementation they themselves have delegated to agencies or local governments. These, in turn, will seek to argue that they were given the tasks and the formal authority to deal with certain matters but never obtained the necessary (financial) means or the *de facto* freedom to maneuver. The big risk is that both parties end up sharing blame and public embarrassment in a game where everybody loses.

Blaming others is an attractive strategy after a crisis. Whether a strategy of blame deflection actually works in this fashion depends on many factors.[34] But there are certainly telling examples of instances in which it did. When the British prison service faced a string of embarrassing incidents in 1994–1995, Home Secretary Michael Howard argued that he could not be held responsible for incidents. Pointing to the operational responsibilities of the prison agency, the home secretary removed Director General Derek Lewis from his post in the prison service. Lewis did not go quietly, but Howard survived – notwithstanding a grueling and history-making television interview in which the BBC's Jeremy Paxman asked Howard twelve times whether he had threatened Lewis with overruling him.[35]

Brändström and Kuipers picture a crisis-induced blame game as a decision tree that consists of the strategic choices actors face in the accountability process (see Figure 5.2).[36] All actors make choices on three dimensions: severity (how bad was the situation?), agency (how could it happen?), and responsibility (who is to be sanctioned?). First, they must assess the events: what values and interests are at stake and in which respect have these been violated or threatened? When they conclude that core values have been violated, or when the dominant opinion among other powerful actors suggests this has been the case, they need to position themselves by giving accounts of their own behavior and that of others.

The second key question is whether the situation should be seen as an incident – which it is when it can be argued that it was produced

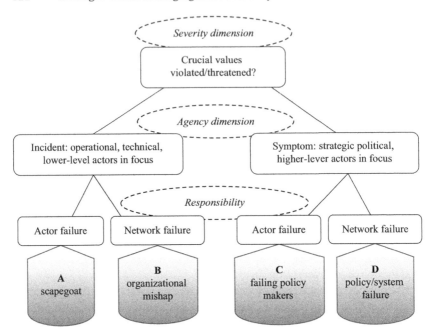

Figure 5.2 Actor Choices in Crisis-Induced Blame Games
Source: adapted from Brändström and Kuipers (2003: 302).

by ad-hoc failures at the operational level – or as a symptom of under-lying policy failures. In the latter case, the crisis is usually depicted as "an accident waiting to happen" for which neither operators nor executive agencies should be blamed but rather those officials and institutions that designed the contested policy.

The third question is how central any single actor (individual but more likely organizational) was in producing the undesirable situation. Were the crucial acts or omissions produced by a single organization or an entire network of organizations?

The dominant judgment that results from the combination of choices that the various participants in the blame game make can take four forms (outcomes A–D in Figure 5.2). When the participants arrive at outcome A (scapegoating), blame is deflected toward specific sectoral or crisis response agencies (see further below). When they collectively decide on network failure (outcome B), sanctions against an entire range of operational organizations become a possibility. This may set the stage for adjustment of policies, rules, and procedures that govern the implementation network in the policy sector at hand.

Politically, the most explosive outcome, at least from a blaming perspective, is C. The crisis is interpreted as a product of errors or other shortcomings that a set of clearly identifiable senior policy makers have committed. From a dispassionate researcher's position, outcome D is perhaps the most salient one. This collective judgment implies that not individual human errors or misjudgments but rather flawed systems of policy making or service delivery lie at the heart of the crisis. "When crises are defined in this manner, some sort of institutional reform or major policy change becomes hard to avoid, irrespective of the political fate of the incumbent elites."[37]

The alternative to a blaming strategy is accepting responsibility. Grand gestures of this kind ("the buck stops here") and the use of restorative rhetoric are honorable, and sometimes work.[38] After the 2004 tsunami, the Norwegian government accepted responsibility for the slow and ineffective procedures that slowed down its efforts to assist the many Norwegians caught in the catastrophe. In this case, squarely absorbing the blame actually enhanced the government's political legitimacy.[39]

To be sure, it is not only politics in accounting for crises. A parallel universe to the political domain is the professional domain of specialists in many different disciplines who look back on a crisis and consider the possible lessons these events may harbor for the future. As will be explained in Chapter 6, institutional learning requires a safe environment, where the drive for improvement and not the desire to score points or avoid losses dominates. This is hard to accomplish when the professional accountability process is engulfed by the political and legal domains, where different rules apply.

There is no single, self-evident institutional design solution readily available to overcome these tensions. Even independent investigation boards cannot always fully escape the dangers of agency capture. Nor can their reports substitute for parliamentary dialogue and legal judgment. Ultimately, the quality of crisis accountability depends upon the extent to which key actors display a sense of proportionality and self-restraint. Political scientists have argued that democratic accountability is not just a way of putting structures of checks and balances in place; it is also about developing and maintaining a culture in which transparency is the norm, and political debate about past performance is not completely overshadowed by politicking.[40] This is particularly true in the context of political crisis management. Only those who have the wisdom and the courage to prioritize the effectiveness and legitimacy of the system as a whole rather than their short-term personal and organizational interests can hope to escape self-defeating blame games.

Crises put not just the response capabilities of authorities to the test but also the democratic authenticity of the governance systems in which crises occur. They test the strength of the institutional mechanisms for calling elites to account.[41] To what extent does the accountability process become a truth-finding dialogue, and to what extent does it escalate into inquisition and blame games? Policy makers cannot take for granted that a perfect correlation exists between what actually happened prior to and during a crisis and the political distribution of praise, blame, and sanctions that follows in its wake. A deeply institutionalized system of accountability sets democratic polities apart from non-democratic ones, but this in itself does not guarantee that democratic accountability works after crises in ways that are predictable, fair, or controllable. Moral entrepreneurs, political ambulance chasers, spin doctors, cover-up artists, bureaucratic zealots, and media guerrillas: the crisis accountability arena harbors a colorful cast of characters. Their interaction provides for a dynamic process, which in and of itself is not guaranteed to result in outcomes that pass the test of fairness, efficiency, lawfulness, or citizen well-being.

In formulating their strategy, leaders have to negotiate a deeply entrenched tension: they must consolidate, restore, and show faith in the security and validity of preexisting social, institutional, and political arrangements; yet, they also face pressures to criticize and reform these same arrangements. They must try to adopt an open, reflective, responsibility-accepting stance that may leave them politically vulnerable and avoid a defensive, responsibility-denying stance that may deflect blame at the price of eroding the system's long-term legitimacy.

Notes

1 Honig and Both (1997); Honig (2001).
2 www.nrc.nl/next/van/2014/juli/17/srebrenica-een-wond-die-steeds-weer-open gaat-1401693 (accessed June 10, 2015).
3 Schmitt (1985).
4 Cuny (1983) noted that natural disasters often undermine the legitimacy of governments in third world countries. Cuny himself disappeared in Chechnya while doing research on that protracted crisis.
5 Bovens and 't Hart (1996); Quarantelli (1998); Quarantelli and Perry (2005).
6 Some scholars suggest it was at one time. See Rosenthal (1998).
7 See further Hansén and Stern (2001) who analyze the case as a national trauma.
8 Dror (2014) is particularly insistent that these are the key challenges of the future and that existing government structures and leadership practices are woefully inadequate for dealing with them.

9 't Hart (2013). See also Birkland (2006).
10 This example is taken from Miller (2001).
11 Elster (2004); Torpey (2006).
12 Vizzard (1997).
13 Linz and Stepan (1978).
14 Accountability is here defined as an institutional relation or arrangement in which an agent can be held to account by a forum (another agent or an institution). See Bovens et al. (2014: 8).
15 This section draws on Kuipers and 't Hart (2014).
16 Clarke (2000: 8).
17 Mulgan (2014).
18 Hood (2011).
19 Charles (2001) offers a detailed account of the investigation into the crash of TWA Flight 800.
20 Sparrow (2000, 2008).
21 Sinclair (2012).
22 www.wsj.com/articles/bp-agrees-to-pay-18-7-billion-to-settle-deepwater-hori zon-oil-spill-claims-1435842739 (accessed July 2, 2015).
23 Erikson (1976, 1994).
24 The three challenges discerned here are adapted from Boin et al. (2010).
25 Sulitzeanu-Kenan (2010).
26 Stark (2010; 2011).
27 Preston (2008); Boin et al. (2010).
28 Bovens et al. (1999); Hood et al. (2007).
29 Hood (2011); Brändström (2015).
30 The growing literature on ministerial survival offers some clues to this, though only a minor part of it examines the impact of behavioral and stylistic factors. See, e.g., Dowding et al. (2012).
31 On "comeback leaders," see 't Hart (2014).
32 Ellis (1994).
33 Hearit (2006); Nobles (2008).
34 For a more detailed analysis, see Hood (2011).
35 This example is taken from Resodihardjo (2006). See Lewis (1997) for an inside account of this crisis.
36 Brändström and Kuipers (2003).
37 Brändström and Kuipers (2003: 303).
38 Griffin-Padgett and Allison (2010).
39 Brändström, Kuipers, and Daléus (2008).
40 Olsen (2014); Warren (2014).
41 Douglas and Wildavsky (1982); Douglas (1992).

6   Learning and Changing
From Crisis to Reform

6.1   Never Again!

Conventional wisdom suggests that human progress requires that we learn from our failures. As crises unearth failing policies, procedures, and organizations, they provide clear-cut opportunities to learn and adapt. We would therefore expect policy makers to study what went wrong before and during a crisis and to change ideas, policies, structures, and processes in accordance with their findings.

In a context of competing accounts of what happened it is, however, not so easy to determine what went wrong and what should be adapted to prevent similar crises from happening again. Many different and sometimes contradictory lessons can be distilled from one and the same crisis experience. Moreover, stakeholders often disagree on what the right lessons are. As we have seen in Chapter 5, the post-crisis period is not necessarily one of social unity, mindful inquiry, and dispassionate reflection. The adversarial politics of the aftermath will affect the identification and selection of the lessons to be learned from crisis. Even when there is agreement on certain measures to be taken, there is no guarantee that lessons learned will actually be implemented. And consensus about lessons does not necessarily mean that the lessons will be sufficient to prevent similar mistakes from happening in the future.[1]

Consider the rash of new policies, legal changes, and major institutional reforms and reorganizations that were pushed through the legislature at unprecedented speed after the 9/11 events – in the United States, the European Union, and many other countries. In the U.S., the so-called Patriot Act was adopted in near unanimity, enacting policy changes in the judicial system, in the handling of immigrants and resident aliens, and in the allocation of government funds for national security and public safety. In a major administrative reorganization effort, many security-related and emergency management agencies were merged at the stroke of a pen into the vast Department of Homeland Security. The department, with its 170,000 employees and wide responsibilities for dealing with different contingencies, could not prevent – and some would say contributed to – a botched response to Hurricane Katrina (summer of 2005).[2]

The European Union learned and changed in much more incremental fashion. A uniform definition of terrorism was accepted; extradition rules for potentially terrorism-related crimes were extended. Police units can now track suspected criminals across national borders and, if necessary, act with full authority on foreign soil. Europol, the European agency for police cooperation, has been strengthened; Eurojust, a similar agency designed to foster cooperation in public prosecution, was created. The EU accorded higher priority to the protection of its external borders; a special agency (FRONTEX) was created. The EU Lisbon Treaty contains the so-called Solidarity Clause, which urges member states to help each other in case of a terror attack or natural disaster. But while the scope and depth of cooperation in the field of justice and home affairs deepened markedly after 9/11, Madrid (2004), and London (2005), the EU failed to produce a coordinated response to the recent financial and refugee crises.[3]

It is clear that governments can and do learn from crises. But they learn different lessons and implement them in different ways. And it is not always clear if the lessons serve their purported aim. The *key question* of this chapter, therefore, asks why some countries and organizations learn appropriate lessons and implement the lessons learned, whereas others do not. There are two sides to this question: "puzzling" and "powering."[4] The puzzling side refers to the capacity to learn: what went wrong, why, and what needs to be changed so that it will not happen again? The powering side pertains to the capacity to reform: can policy makers instigate substantive changes in the wake of a crisis?

Strong leadership during a crisis does not necessarily translate into effective management of post-crisis learning and reform processes. Learning is a highly complex process, all the more so in the post-crisis context of public organizations and high politics. While the perceived need for change may seem high, politics-as-usual makes it hard to enact far-reaching changes.[5] Our *core claim* is that the capacity of governments to learn and change is constrained by fundamental tensions between the imperatives of political crisis management and the conditions for effective reform.

Our argument unfolds in four steps. We begin by analyzing how crises constrain but also create opportunities for learning. We then explain how the politics of the crisis aftermath can also create opportunities for stakeholders to push drastic policy changes that may have little to do with any lessons learned. We explain why many leaders – contrary to conventional wisdom – shy away from exploiting reform opportunities (and why that may be a wise strategy for them). The final part of our argument takes us to what perhaps is a somewhat pessimistic conclusion, as we posit our claim that crisis leadership, learning, and reform typically demand skills and strategies that are at odds with each other.

6.2   Learning from Crisis: Lessons from the Literature

The literature can be easily summarized: "learning is a golden concept: everybody is for it."[6] While many scholars recognize that learning is hard, they seem to agree that crises provide golden opportunities to learn and reform. This is especially true when a crisis is a jointly experienced, exogenous threat to a widely valued status quo. In such situations – where no thorny political and institutional issues arise and all parties concerned are motivated to ensure that never again can such adversity reoccur – learning seems to be both desirable and possible.

Scholars have defined learning in many different ways, but most would agree that it involves purposeful efforts to (re)examine, (re)assess, and (re)calibrate existing and proposed beliefs, policies, and institutional arrangements. Learning involves the gathering of new information and ideas, applying them to policy issues, and determining under which conditions all of this can take place.[7] In order to learn, governments need to have not only some institutional capacity for lesson-drawing but also a (sustained) motivation to use this capacity and work with its products.[8]

The classic distinction between single-loop and double-loop learning made by Argyris and Schön is especially useful here.[9] Single-loop learning refers to the correction of practices without having to change core beliefs and fundamental rules of the game. This type of learning is most common after crises: the reports of crisis commissions and investigation bodies contain many recommendations for minor rule adjustments, innovations in equipment and training, improved communication routines, and so on.[10]

Single-loop learning is obviously helpful, but it may not always be sufficient. Many crises have a "paradigm-shattering" quality to them. Their very occurrence or the haphazard response to them exposes fundamental limitations, weaknesses, and contradictions in existing policies and institutional arrangements. To deal with these, double-loop learning is required.

Double-loop learning refers to actions that "resolve incompatible organizational norms by setting new priorities and weightings of norms, or by restructuring the norms themselves together with associated strategies and assumptions."[11] In learning processes of this kind, lessons do not pertain to "the strategies and assumptions for effective performance [as in single-loop learning] but to the very norms which define effective performance."[12] Double-loop learning initiatives are likely to touch sensitive nerves because they call into question fundamental tenets of the status quo, including the core beliefs that policy makers hold about the nature of the world around them.

The most effective type of learning is what Argyris and Schön call "deutero learning." This third type refers to what we might call "meta learning" or "learning how to learn" from crises. The research on high-reliability organizations (HROs) discussed in Chapter 2 suggests that organizational leaders can build and maintain safety cultures in organizations that facilitate continuous and effective learning.[13] The HRO is not only good at sensing potential threats and dealing with them quickly; this capacity is in fact boosted by a strong learning culture. For instance, HROs treat even small incidents and near misses as opportunities to re-assess organizational belief systems and practices. This allows them to adapt their way of working before incidents develop into full-blown crises.

A well-developed learning capacity combines at least three types of learning.[14] The first type is *experience based*. Direct exposure to a crisis is a powerful, to some literally unforgettable, experience. This experience may help an individual or organization to develop insights with regard to the causes of crisis and the effectiveness of the response. Experiential learning presupposes memory: organized recording, recollection, and retrieval of past events and actions. In addition, it requires some sort of mechanism to translate memories into lessons.[15] This type of learning occurs most naturally within professions that more or less routinely deal with certain types of crises through standardized procedures for recording and re-examining past experience (think of airplane pilots who anonymously share their experiences with near misses, which allows the industry to learn quickly and effectively).

A complementary form of learning is *explanation based*. Learning then becomes a rational-scientific search for the causes of failure and the effects of the response. This type of learning requires a critical mass of people qualified to tease out cause-and-effect relations and determine their validity. It also assumes a considerable level of autonomy to protect these "crisis auditors" from political interference. Moreover, it requires time and resources to allow them to do their job in an unhurried and meticulous manner. Some inquiry committees actually manage to do all of this. Some organizations have set up their own machinery to generate explanation-based learning.

In some sectors, explanation-based learning mechanisms are particularly well developed. For instance, in many countries some type of safety board is set up for the transport sector. The U.S. National Transportation Safety Board is probably the best known: it leads post-crisis investigations into the causes of disaster, with the explicit aim of learning lessons that will help prevent similar disasters from reoccurring. Another example is NASA, which has an institutionalized capacity to study and explain causes of even minor failures.[16] The aviation sector has particularly well-developed mechanisms for learning, which has resulted in spectacular safety improvements over time.

A third type of learning is *competence* or *skill based*. When a crisis exposes a deficit between a threat and the governmental capacity to deal with it – crises almost by definition do exactly that – new skills and competences may be in order. Emerging epidemics, such as AIDS, Ebola, and SARS, typically require that doctors and health workers learn new techniques (the general approach to epidemics is well established). Technology-driven crises – think of computer viruses or cyber attacks – also demand fresh skills. Professionals tend to develop new skills through experimenting in direct response to a crisis. This type of learning is quick, but it may not always be effective (as it does not allow for systematic yet timely evaluation of the new skills). Exercises are necessary complements to identify gaps and shortcomings and to engage in systematic evaluations in a forgiving atmosphere.

Why Learning from Crisis Is Hard

Despite the many ways in which crises induce governments and their organizations to learn, the result is often disappointing. If there are lessons, these are often symbolic, ineffective, or the source of unintended consequences. Few organizations seem to truly learn after a crisis. This finding chimes with the general consensus in the literature that it is hard to learn (from crises or otherwise). This is due to a wide variety of constraints that operate on both individual and organizational learning capacity.[17]

Social-psychological researchers are especially pessimistic when it comes to the capacity of small groups to learn from crises. The so-called threat-rigidity hypothesis explains that the conditions of crisis make it hard if not impossible to learn.[18] It argues that people tend to respond in a rigid and inflexible manner to threats and uncertainty. They can no longer process information in an adequate manner; they fall back on learned routines and instilled reflexes. Fear is another impeding factor: leaders who fear for their position and organizations that dread negative publicity are unlikely to encourage others to investigate thoroughly what exactly went wrong before and during the crisis.[19]

The research on organizational learning is equally pessimistic.[20] In Chapter 2, we introduced Barry Turner's work, which details the collective failure within many organizations to heed signals of impending danger.[21] His work, like the work of many other organization theorists, explains the underlying problem: organizations cannot properly communicate and understand information.[22] They fail to collect sufficient relevant data. They find it hard to distil cause-and-effect relations from their limited and flawed pool of data (and even if they do, they have no way of testing their n=1 findings).[23] They rarely possess a systematically organized "institutional memory."[24] Moreover, they generally do not have "uncommitted resources" that can be used to deal with these shortcomings and improve their information-handling capacity.[25] Taken together, these findings suggest that there is no such thing as "crisis-induced learning" – even if organizations do try to learn, the results are likely to be suboptimal at best.

Widely visible and costly errors prior to or during crises invite sweeping policy revisions and reversals. This strategy has the virtue of simplicity and cognitive parsimony, but it is fundamentally risky. No causal links have been established between cause and effect; the strategy draws on a presumed analogy with the most immediate past. This is likely to be self-defeating in the long run, when the future turns out to be not the past repeated.[26] Moreover, some crises might simply be too big an experience for organizations and polities to absorb in a reflective and evenhanded way. We may then expect "over-learning": premature, one-sided, and rigid application of hastily drawn inferences supported by the dominant coalition, at the price of a more open, inquisitive, and contingent approach to lesson-drawing.[27]

A particularly subversive type of learning has been observed in organizations that have *successfully* responded to a crisis. When leaders feel that the response system has done well during the last crisis, this will lead them to repeat their strategies and actions in similar events. The crisis is embraced as a formative experience and is carefully nurtured into an instructive legend; it becomes the bedrock of organizational stamina and perseverance. The perverse effect, however, is noted only in the long run. As crises never return in the same shape or form, lessons from the past are likely to become tomorrow's blind corners. Hence the saying "nothing fails like success."[28]

The politics of accountability, discussed in Chapter 5, further undermine the capacity to learn. The escalation of blame games has a particularly debilitating effect. When blaming takes prevalence, many involved policy makers will gather comprehensive and minute information about everything that went on prior to, during, and after the crisis episode in order to deflect blame. Information is tailored to be used as ammunition. Data are selected and molded to construct winning arguments in a battle for personal and institutional survival. Individuals and organizations manipulate their memories: when it is opportune to remember, they will; if needed, they "forget" – until other actors force them out of their strategic amnesia.

So, there may be a paradox here: when the need to learn is at its peak, the institutional capacity of public leaders and their organizations is often disappointingly low.[29] This is especially true when "politics" undermines the motivation to learn: the powering required to survive crises politically can overtake the drive to engage in the puzzling that lesson-drawing presupposes.[30]

Some crises induce a strong motivation in people at all layers of the organizations involved not to be caught unaware or incapable in the future. They give rise to what we may call enabling factors: external pressure to improve performance; a persuasive diagnosis of existing problems coupled with feasible proposals for change; a coalition of motivated change advocates who are influential in both the political arena and the civil society; a capable and responsive public service. These factors seem to be required to produce radical, yet widely supported and effectively implemented departures from past policies.[31] When leaders share this motivation to learn, they can act as pivotal forces in making sure that lessons are translated into organizational or system-wide policy changes.[32] The best example may well be the Cuban Missile Crisis that came dangerously close to all-out war: the fear of a nuclear holocaust is said to have pushed U.S. and Soviet leaders to deterrence rather than escalation – a paradigmatic change – in the long aftermath of this international crisis.[33]

Effective learning also requires *the capacity to reform*. Here we find one of the most persistent barriers to crisis learning. We will discuss these barriers, and ways to overcome them, in the following sections.

6.3   From Crisis to Reforms?

Some leaders recognize a crisis as an opportunity to instigate major policy and institutional changes (as will other stakeholders inside and outside of government). In the early phase of President Obama's tenure, which coincided with the depths of the financial crisis, his Chief of Staff Rahm Emanuel famously remarked "You never want a serious crisis to go to waste."[34] When crises are construed as a failure of plans, policies, or practices, the idea of institutional renewal becomes attractive.

In fact, more than a few crises are followed by speedy reform proposals that hardly build upon the type of analytical underpinnings discussed above. Political logic rather than learning requirements dictate the pace of the action: creating a public appearance of responsible and forceful action *now* is given priority over launching more highly informed proposals later.[35]

The relation between crises and reform is often noted in both academic theorizing and popular wisdom.[36] The received wisdom builds on the insight that reform of public policy and organizations appears to be nearly impossible under normal circumstances.[37] In order for a reform proposal to become successful, it must survive bureau-political infighting in its conception phase, political conflict in its birth stage, and entrenched opposition in its early years.[38]

Institutional frameworks are hard to change because they typically are the long-term product of trust, successful performance, and coherence between policy ideas and organizational forms. A solid institutional framework is important because it determines to a considerable degree how policies are made and how they are administered. It brings stability to government behavior, provided it stays in tune with the dominant societal and political conceptions of what is appropriate. An institutional framework helps to create "believable futures": we know what to expect from a stable policy sector.[39]

Crises change all that, or so many scholars think. In political science, for instance, students of democratization have posited that crisis is a necessary condition for change.[40] Students of government argue that governance unfolds as a pattern of "punctuated equilibria" – long eras of stability alternated with short-lived periods of uncertainty and conflict.[41] They point to critical junctures during which existing polity settings, policy goals, and institutional arrangements for policy making come under pressure. This pressure may jeopardize their self-evident legitimacy and deinstitutionalize governance. These notions suggest the reform potential of crises, which can be fully exploited by leaders acting on these critical junctures.[42]

The idea that crises often precipitate deep institutional change finds much support in practice.[43] When crises become viewed as symptoms of underlying societal vulnerabilities and governance problems, existing institutions (and office-holders responsible for them) are no longer viewed as part of the solution but become part of the problem (to paraphrase a famous Ronald Reagan dictum). Accordingly, many crises give birth to ambitious efforts to reform the policies and institutions of government.[44] Many crises are followed by the rotation of elites, the revision of policies, and the redesigning of institutions. They create opportunities for critics of the status quo and proposals for policy reforms and institutional changes that in normal times are simply unthinkable or politically infeasible.[45]

Upon closer scrutiny, however, the relation between crisis and reform is less straightforward than commonly assumed. In many crises, elites desperately struggle to preserve rather than reform the status quo. Many policy changes announced with fanfare during or in the wake of crises are reforms in name only and are better described as thinly veiled efforts to preserve pre-crisis structures and practices. Even when reform proposals are truly intended to bring about double-loop lessons and structural changes, they rarely materialize in the long run. The belief that crisis and reform make a happy couple is, therefore, in need of qualification. Let us now elaborate on both parts of this thesis.

Why Crises Enable Reform

Every now and then crisis lessons or reform proposals do survive and "stick." Explanations of such apparent successes are usually couched in terms of either enlightened leadership or deep crisis.[46] The real explanation is a bit more complex.

A crisis creates an opportunity for reform when it highlights a performance deficit. This happens when a government agency or policy either is shown to have contributed to the development of that crisis or has proven evidently incapable of responding adequately to it.[47] Under normal circumstances, a performance deficit is explainable and usually acceptable (the police cannot catch all thieves; a hospital cannot heal all patients etc.). In a crisis, however, when good governance is needed most, a performance deficit can become a source of contention and controversy. The effectiveness, efficiency, and appropriateness of existing policy-making procedures, organizational routines, and traditional modes of public service delivery then becomes subjected to intense criticism.[48] Justified or not, such criticism strongly implies that the "old way of doing things" is no longer feasible. Tried-and-trusted routines are suddenly weighed against promising (yet in many respects uncertain) alternatives. In other words, political and public support for the pre-crisis policy or organization is disappearing swiftly.

The BBC experienced an institutional crisis when it turned out that one of its star presenters, Jimmy Savile, had abused many children (often in the BBC studios). The allegations were substantiated only after his death in 2011, but it soon became clear that rumors to this effect had circulated within the organization for years. When one BBC program (Panorama) on the Savile case claimed that another program's exposé on

Savile (Newsnight) was shelved to avoid a scandal, the BBC experienced an immediate and deep loss of public and political trust. Reforms followed quickly.

There are three reasons why an institutional crisis may create an opportunity for structural and fundamental reform. First, and perhaps most important, a crisis relaxes the structural constraints that tend to keep institutions in place.[49] It focuses attention on their previously unnoticed vulnerabilities. Instead of devoting periodic, diluted attention to many different problems, policy makers, media, and mass publics alike are consumed by one single set of issues for some time. The sheer force of physical events or political representations of their meaning raises public anxiety to such levels that there is an increased willingness to follow leaders who claim to be able to resolve the problem and an equal readiness to support unconventional and risky policy options. Far-reaching mandates may be delegated to centralized authorities and the number of potential veto points in the policy process is temporarily reduced to "let the government govern." Some crises trigger the "rally around the flag effect": substantive conflicts over issues, entrenched modes of adversarial behavior, and ongoing institutional battles between different players in the policy arena are temporarily suspended.

Second, these crises challenge the core beliefs that guide the formulation and implementation of policies and practices within a particular area of government.[50] As the routine way of working and thinking becomes discredited in the eyes of outsiders, room for alternatives suddenly emerges. The chief characteristic of a stable public institution is that its modus operandi remains unexamined and is taken for granted. A crisis invites everybody to take a close look; it prompts the question whether this institution and the way in which it operates are effective and beneficial to all. In short, the loosening of institutionalized structure makes it possible for new structures to be considered.

Third, a crisis "unfreezes" entrenched ways of thinking not only at the top but throughout the policy sector in which a crisis has occurred.[51] As we know from the research on policy implementation, it is ultimately the way that middle-level and street-level bureaucrats "walk the walk and talk the talk" that determines the success and failure of public policies.[52] A crisis tends to shatter their confidence in those trusted routines because of the very fact that they have proven unreliable in the face of pressure.

Combined, these factors allow for a radical break in the chains of historical legacies.[53] A window of opportunity opens for implementing lessons learned and making the system more robust. Much, however, depends on what happens during the crisis and its immediate aftermath.

Critical Factors for Effective Reform

Whether lessons learned are actually implemented depends to a considerable extent on the management strategy that is adopted to deal with the crisis. The continuum of possible positions is marked by two extreme ends: the conservative approach and the reformist approach.[54]

When leaders adopt a *reformist approach*, they aim to change policies or redesign the institutional features of a public organization in order to ensure a new fit with the changed environment. This strategy attempts to bridge the exposed performance gap and restore faith in the sector by breaking with past practices and adopting lessons learned. It usually requires bold, risk-taking forms of leadership, as crisis lessons tend to move away from (rather than back to) the status quo. Policy makers adopting this approach amplify rather than dampen the crisis mood; they must "sell" the new alternatives for the pre-crisis status quo in both political and bureaucratic arenas.[55]

A *conservative approach* aims to defend and maintain the preexisting institutional essence in the face of pressures to change it. The core idea is that incremental improvement rather than radical redesign will close the performance gap and restore legitimacy. This leadership strategy amounts to a form of "dynamic conservatism": adapting policy instruments and organizational structures and processes to accommodate external pressures for change while preserving core values.[56]

It is often not wise for leaders to automatically embark on the path of reform when confronted with a crisis. To understand why this is so, one must recall the essence of crisis: it constitutes a threat to valued ways of working and thinking. The political-administrative elite that deals with this threat will prefer to curb it before trying to change organizations or policies. The centralization reflex common to most government crisis-response systems endows them with special authority, with the unstated aim to preserve what exists: as a rule, hierarchies do not funnel authority to those who seek to change their very modus operandi.

We may thus expect the political calculus of crisis managers to advise against reform-oriented strategies. Consider the four most likely futures that leaders can expect, depending on their choice of strategy (reform or repair) and the way the crisis outcome will be perceived (see Figure 6.1). A conservative approach is relatively low risk. If a state of order returns, leaders can claim credit. If things change for the better, leaders can still claim credit. Reform is the risky road to choose. Leaders may win big when they promise and accomplish long-overdue reforms, but they also run the risk of disillusion and deep credibility losses.

Figure 6.1 *Alternative Post-Crisis Futures*

		Perceived level of institutional change	
		High	*Low*
Crisis management strategy	*Reformist*	Reform	Disillusion
	Conservative	Unintended change	Restoration

Our argument can thus be summarized as follows: *in response to crisis, incumbent policy elites are more likely to aim for conservation than reform.* This thesis is firmly rooted in the psychological literature on decision making and commitment. It also fits the dominant view of public policy making in established democracies, which suggests that public policy normally evolves in a slow, incremental fashion.[57]

If this claim is accurate, it follows that there must be one or more special factors at play when a double-loop learning, reform-oriented approach comes to prevail in a crisis. After all, reform *does* occur – if only sporadically – in the wake of crises. Policy makers must, in other words, either be induced or enabled by specific circumstances to adopt a reformist approach. Four factors seem especially relevant.

Perceived inevitability – Crisis leaders may consider reform inevitable, indeed the only way to deal with the crisis. This is most likely to happen when a crisis is seen as the outcome of shifts in the external environment. External shifts such as war, climate change, economic depressions, and energy shortages can acutely threaten the very existence of a policy sector. Repair is not an option, as the threats cannot be managed; nothing short of all-out reform will save the day. This perception of inevitability may be self-evident or it may grow in the wake of ineffective restoration efforts.

Annoyance – Leaders are, obviously, more likely to adopt far-reaching changes the more annoyed they are with the existing institutional make-up (and the less politically committed they are to uphold it). As argued before in this book, we should never forget that crises put people under immense pressure and provoke emotional reactions. When leaders perceive the crisis as a result of previously noted or long-standing problems, they may be tempted to exploit the crisis to rid the sector of the underlying problem. Even when rational considerations would suggest a more incremental, deliberative course, leaders can get so annoyed with the "foot dragging" of policy organizations that they decide to move swiftly and decisively.

Political survival – Policy plans tend to be informed by an assessment of what is politically and technically feasible. After a crisis, however, the political calculus may outweigh considerations of technical feasibility. If a sufficient number of powerful actors in the political arena favor reform initiatives over conservation efforts, a reformist strategy is more likely to be adopted. Having presided over the development of the crisis and at risk of being blamed for its occurrence, incumbent elites will be especially sensitive to political moods and majority preferences. It becomes nearly impossible for them to argue against reform on the basis of technical arguments only.

Structural opportunities – It becomes much easier to contemplate more unorthodox policy alternatives for dealing with a crisis when a leader experiences few checks and balances. In some types of emergencies, most notably natural disasters, civil disturbances, or near-war situations, authorities can invoke formal powers and create bylaws that amount to a significant centralization of authority. This allows them to temporarily bypass routine bureaucratic and parliamentary procedures, curb media activity, or even relax legal constraints on state actions. The more veto power is removed from the scene, the higher the chances that a reform coalition may triumph.

Conditions for Success

Whichever strategy crisis leaders select (reform or restoration), the question is whether they can effectuate it. Their strategy must gain political ascendance and acceptance, it must be implemented, and finally it must restore trust in the problem-solving capacity of a public policy or organization. We surmise that three preconditions are required to make this happen.

A first condition is that *the chosen strategy corresponds with political and societal conceptions of the future.* Conservation efforts can be effective only when the core values and beliefs underpinning the pre-crisis institutional regime have survived the crisis. Likewise, reform efforts stand a chance only when a widespread feeling has emerged that status-quo actors and institutions should lose their prominent position in the system.

A second condition is that *crisis leaders manage to seize and retain the initiative in the crisis process.* Timing is a crucial factor. They must demonstrate that they have recognized the impending crisis and have begun to address it well before their own actions become portrayed by others as part of the problem. The sense of urgency that lesson-drawing enjoys in the wake of a crisis evaporates quickly. Early recognition (and acceptance, which is not self-evident) of a widening performance gap and decreasing legitimacy increases the probability that crisis management strategies will be effective. A crisis investigation that takes years to produce its findings should not expect an army of eager political entrepreneurs waiting to run with the ball. Nor is it realistic to expect that pending such long investigations, major financial resources are being kept in reserve to cover the often considerable costs of major policy changes.

A final condition is that *leaders are adept at playing the game of post-crisis reform politics*. There is no such thing as the "ten golden rules" that will help play this game. Leaders must avoid the obvious mistakes, such as sacrificing their public credibility in pursuit of short-term relief from media pressure. They should avoid the temptation of heroism: adopting a leadership style of "going at it alone" is likely to prove quixotic at a time when their political stature is weak and they need allies more than ever.[58] However, the challenges of post-crisis politics may require skills that are fundamentally at odds with all of those other challenges outlined in this book.

6.4   The Tension Between Crisis Management and Reform Leadership[59]

One would be justified in asking how policy makers can be expected to learn the right lessons and smoothly implement them, making use of the opportunity window that crises tend to open. Consider what we expect from them. While they are still busy coordinating all sorts of operational challenges that directly relate to the crisis at hand, they must exercise reform leadership. They need to articulate that the status quo is untenable, propose a coherent set of radical and politically sanctioned reforms, and guard their integrity during reform implementation. They must embrace novel policy ideas, sell them to diverse audiences, and wield power to see them enacted.[60] All of this in an environment of inherent uncertainty and considerable resistance in societal, political, and bureaucratic arenas.

Hence, a compounding tension for crisis leadership comes to the fore: the imperatives of effective crisis management conflict with the imperatives of crisis reform. It suggests, at the very least, that crisis management and reform leadership cannot be the province of the same executives. Two sets of tension seem especially relevant in this discussion.

Repair or Reform?

Reform leadership is an exercise in "creative destruction."[61] Old structures must be destroyed before new ones can be implemented. In order to be effective reformers, leaders will want to seize upon the damage done. They dramatize the seriousness of the situation, yet at the same time externalize its causes. Leaders can use the language of crisis only if they themselves are not at risk of being blamed for the crisis at hand (newly incumbent leaders are, ceteris paribus, in a much better position to do so than veteran leaders).

In the thick of crisis, leaders rarely prioritize learning and reform. They are under tremendous pressure to restore a sense of normalcy. Core values and proven methods then become anchors in stormy seas; crisis is not a time for critical self-reflection and exploring new options that pay off in the long run only. The use of reform rhetoric at this time of turbulence may compound rather than alleviate the collective stress that has been generated by crisis. It will surely evoke resistance among stakeholders. Even new leaders who have emerged on a platform of change prior to the occurrence of crisis may be forced to suspend their reform ambitions.

Persuasion or Muscle?

Reform leadership is about persuasion. Commands and intimidation do not work in pluralistic polities. Reform leaders, in particular, have much persuading to do because their plans differ markedly from what exists. They have to convince multiple audiences that what they want is good, realistic, and inevitable. Moreover, they must convince stakeholders that the benefits of the proposed reforms outweigh the sunk costs of existing structures and policies. This requires not only effective command and selection of facts, and the rhetorical skills to present them; it also touches on the socio-emotional bond between leaders and citizens. Leaders need to reassure followers that they have a plan that will work.

During a crisis, many policy makers are tempted to employ a top-down, command-and-control style. Short-circuiting the decision-making process speeds up the government's response capacity in the face of urgent threats. Instead of brokering painstaking compromises, leaders actually make decisions and issue orders. Gone are the endless negotiations with many stakeholders.

Stakeholders will likely understand and accept (at least temporarily) these centralization tendencies. In the early phases of crisis, political support is granted near-automatically. It usually begins to wane, however, as soon as the first shock has been absorbed and the first revelations of causes surface. Leaders who seek to gain momentum for reform by exploiting their temporary powers of authority are taking a big risk. They may gain political support at large by demonstrating the willingness to make big decisions, but leaders do so at the price of antagonizing many of the stakeholders they have to deal with on a day-to-day basis long after the crisis is gone.[62] A "crash-through" strategy of pushing controversial reform can easily unleash a backlash.

6.5 Ambivalent Opportunities: From Crisis-Induced Reforms to Reform-Induced Crises

To some leaders, crises may be more of an opportunity than a threat. Crises enable such leaders to temporarily stop "muddling through" and push through radical reform packages that would be unimaginable during "normal" times. It is by no means guaranteed that they succeed: even in deep crises the resilience of the institutional status quo and its political, bureaucratic, and societal veto players should not be underestimated.

But even when long-established, deeply entrenched policy trajectories are reformed, this does not always mean that learning has taken place. It does not necessarily mean policies have been specifically redesigned with the primary aim of reducing crisis vulnerabilities or increasing crisis-response capacities. A critical observer may well conclude that the flurry of immediate measures and organizational adjustments is more a product of political and bureaucratic needs to deflect blame, communicate resolve, and demonstrate competence – or opportunistic attempts to push through pet projects – than of careful and reflective learning closely tied to the crisis experience in question.

The urge to project political determination and to alter quickly the conditions that gave rise to the crisis is perfectly understandable. Yet while reformers may be able to grasp the direct consequences of their own proposals, the potential second-order effects of big and sudden changes are rarely considered. A more informed learning process is thus required, one that is aimed at upgrading crisis management performance in a more fundamental and forward-looking fashion.

It may be true that the great leaders in history are those who turned crisis into prosperity, but it should be remembered that many have failed in the attempt. Explanations of the development of administrative and political systems often feature crises. For instance, one significant force propelling advances in European integration was the periodic occurrence of political crises. These episodes altered the political agendas and calculus of European leaders. More importantly, the need to respond to them often produced constructive innovations of collaborative institutions and programs. However, studies of imperial decline document the serial *mis*management of crises.

Crises tend to cast long shadows upon the political systems in which they occur. It is only when we study these longer-term processes that we are able to assess their full impact. Unfortunately, such studies are quite rare.[63] Most studies of the "crisis aftermath" of emergencies have been about community reconstruction, individual and collective trauma, and legal battles. We need to complement these studies by taking a broader macro-social perspective that looks at collective learning for an entire nation, polity, or society in the aftermath of crisis. It remains an open question whether crises trigger more fundamental forms of systemic change or whether they forestall such change, and to what extent these processes can be channeled by good crisis governance.

Notes

1 See Schiffino et al. (2015) for a useful overview and dialogue on these issues.
2 The intelligence communities retained their autonomy, however. See Kettl (2004) for an analysis of this period in U.S. politics. See also Brown (2015) for the customary critique on the response to Katrina.
3 Boin et al. (2013). See also Nohrstedt and Hansén (2010).
4 We are keeping here with the two dimensions of political learning that Heclo (1974) discusses.
5 Brunsson and Olsen (1993); Olsen and Peters (1996); Peters and Pierre (2001), Patashnik (2008).
6 Wildavsky (1984: 245).
7 Haas (1990); Hall (1993); Sabatier (1999); Busenberg (2001).
8 Rose (1993).
9 Argyris and Schön (1978).
10 Van Duin (1992); Birkland (2006).
11 Argyris and Schön (1978: 24).
12 Argyris and Schön (1978: 22).
13 Roberts (1993). Note the caution in LaPorte (1996). See Weick et al. (1999) for a discussion of potential lessons from HRO research. But also see Sagan (1993); Perrow (1994); Marais et al. (2004) for penetrating criticisms of High Reliability research findings.
14 Stern (1997b).
15 Rose (1993).
16 See Vaughan (1996) for a detailed description of this system and a penetrating analysis of its shortcomings.
17 For overviews, see Etheredge (1985); Fiol and Lyles (1985); Stern (1997b); Smith and Elliott (2007); Moynihan (2008); Deverell (2010). For case-based findings, see Jacobs (1989); Rosenthal and 't Hart (1989); Boin et al. (2008).
18 Staw et al. (1981).
19 Carrel (2000).
20 This literature is pessimistic with regard to *crisis* learning (see Carley and Harrald, 1997 for an interesting discussion; see also Sagan, 1993). It has

slightly more upbeat news when it comes to the capacity to learn from routine events and policy delivery.

21 Turner (1976); Turner and Pidgeon (1997).
22 Pidgeon (1997).
23 To learn the right lessons, one would have to test hypotheses in organizations that have experienced crises and in organizations that have remained free from them (Turner, 1978; Perrow, 1994).
24 Vertzberger (1990).
25 Deutsch (1966: 166).
26 Quarantelli (1996).
27 May (1972); Neustadt and May (1986); Rosenthal et al. (1989); Stern and Sundelius (1997).
28 Sitkin (1992). See Hargrove (1994) for an intriguing analysis of this phenomenon.
29 The paradox is introduced by Dekker and Hansén (2004). But the empirical evidence on the crisis-learning is, in effect, mixed. See Deverell (2009; 2010); Broekema (2015).
30 Pidgeon (1997).
31 Van Duin (1992); Birkland (1997); Thomas (1999); Busenberg (2001); Cobb and Primo (2003); Dekker and Hansén (2004); Broekema (2015).
32 See, e.g., Scanlon (1989).
33 Blight and Welch (1989).
34 www.wsj.com/articles/SB122721278056345271 (accessed October 18, 2015).
35 Boin et al. (2008, 2009).
36 It is often observed that the Chinese character for crisis denotes both threat and opportunity.
37 Leemans (1976); Caiden (1991); Wilsford (1994); Shepsle (2001).
38 Patashnik (2008).
39 Selznick (1957); Suchman (1995); LaPorte (1996).
40 Almond et al. (1973).
41 Baumgartner and Jones (1993).
42 Hay (2002); Kuipers (2006).
43 Mackintosh (2014).
44 We define reform here as a purposeful, planned effort to structurally alter a policy or organization.
45 Keeler (1993); Kingdon (1995); Cortell and Peterson (1999).
46 Keeler (1993); Kingdon (1995); Goldfinch and 't Hart (2003).
47 See Boin and 't Hart (2000) for a set of hypotheses with regard to the process that gives rise to such a judgment. See Ansell, Boin and Kuipers (in press) for an elaboration.
48 Boin and 't Hart (2000). The legitimacy of a sector is the long-term resultant of societal, political, and legal support and acceptance. It cannot be measured in absolute terms. It is possible, however, to assess and detect significant alterations in levels of legitimacy. Steep declines in a fairly short time period are telltale signs of (impending) institutional crisis. Researchers can gauge these by examining the extent and content of media coverage, the amount and content of parliamentary attention for the sector, and the

number and nature of administrative appeals, court, and Ombudsman rulings concerning the sector.

49 Pierson (2000); Hay (2002); Kuipers (2006).

50 These core beliefs are also referred to in the literature as policy paradigms (Hall, 1993; Sabatier and Jenkins-Smith, 1993).

51 Hay (2002).

52 Lipsky (1980); Wilson (1989).

53 This represents something of a departure from conventional wisdom. Early macro-political theories of crisis development were quite deterministic and optimistic. Crises were viewed as necessary breakdowns on the way to a better future (Almond et al., 1973). Even after structural functionalism's demise, the deterministic tendency among crisis theorists remained well alive in their emphasis on overloaded politics and limited administrative capacities as inherent crisis generators in contemporary governance. See, e.g., Dror (1986); Kaase and Newton (1995). We beg to differ. Moreover, by treating the crisis management strategies of actors as a key factor, we depart from the political science mainstream which tells us that the institutional characteristics and historical legacies are all that matter, and that we should not assume "that the talkers and the legislators could ever straightforwardly shape outcomes" (Skocpol, 1985: 93). See also Dryzek (1992).

54 Lanzara (1998) offers a very similar distinction between "exploitation" and "exploration" strategies.

55 't Hart and Goldfinch (2003).

56 Schön (1971); Terry (1995); Ansell et al. (2015).

57 On the former, see Janis and Mann (1977); Janis (1989); Staw (2003). On the latter, see Lindblom (1979); Rose and Davies (1994).

58 Goldfinch and 't Hart (2003).

59 We draw here on the insights of Boin and 't Hart (2003).

60 For the required skills of reform craft, see Bryson and Crosby (1992); Moon (1995).

61 Schumpeter (1943).

62 Boin and Otten (1996).

63 But see Birkland (1997); Broekema (2015). See also a symposium on crisis management (Kurtz and Browne, 2004).

7   How to Deal with Crisis
Lessons for Prudent Leadership

7.1   Navigating Crises

In this book, we have presented a number of claims about leadership in times of crisis. These are based on the findings of several decades of crisis research, direct observation of crisis managers in action (in real-world settings and simulated contexts), and ongoing dialogue with experienced and reflective practitioners. In this final chapter, we translate key observations from the evolving body of crisis management research into recommendations for improving crisis management practices.

Navigating crises prudently is a complex leadership challenge. Trade-offs must be made among various key values and constraints. Policy makers must make decisions and live with the consequences of their actions or inactions. Citizens either suffer the effects of governmental unpreparedness or reap the benefits secured by well-prepared leaders and resilient institutions. Effective crisis navigation requires leaders to prepare themselves and their organizations to deal with this challenge well ahead of the moment when they find themselves in the "hot seat" of crisis. Our recommendations do not tell policy makers *what* to do but offer ideas and suggestions about *how* prudent crisis leadership might be facilitated, organized, and exercised.

7.2   Grasping the Nature of Crises

Let us begin with the nature of the beast. What is it that makes crises so difficult to handle? And what should policy makers understand about crises when they seek to enhance their crisis leadership capacities?

One of the most important things to keep in mind is that crisis is a label, a semantic construction people use to characterize situations that they somehow regard as extraordinary, volatile, and potentially far-reaching in their negative implications. Why people collectively label and experience a situation as a crisis remains something of a mystery. Physical facts, numbers, and other seemingly objective indicators are

145

important factors, but they are not decisive. A flood that kills 200 people is a more or less routine emergency in Bangladesh, but it would be experienced as a major crisis in, let's say, New Jersey or Poland. Similarly, seasonal influenza kills somewhere between three thousand and fifty thousand persons per year in the U.S., a fact easily obscured in the media and public consciousness by the threat posed by a relatively small number of vividly portrayed imported Ebola cases.[1]

Crises are in the eye of the beholder. It is people's frames of reference, experience, memory, values, and interests that determine their perceptions of crisis. A sense of collective stress results not just from some objective threat but also from the intricate interaction between events, individual perceptions and fears, media representations, political reactions, and, as we have argued throughout the book, government efforts at meaning making.

This process of collective understanding is one of escalation and deescalation. It is subject to the influence of actors who have a stake in playing up a crisis mood or playing it down. And this is exactly what happens when unexpected incidents or major disruptions are predicted or actually occur: not only will different political, bureaucratic, and societal (private and nonprofit sector) stakeholders form their own picture of the situation and classify it in terms of threats and opportunities, but many of them will actively seek to influence the public perception of the situation. Once a particular definition of the situation has taken hold in leaders' minds or in public discourse, it may be resistant to change (even in the face of mounting evidence pointing to other interpretations). It becomes a political reality that policy makers have to take into account, act upon, and sometimes work hard to adjust.[2]

Policy makers should therefore actively consider what a particular, potentially crisis-triggering event means to them and their overall political strategies, and should take a proactive part in shaping the public understanding of it. If they don't, others will, leaving policy makers to respond to an agenda that is not necessarily favorable to their view of the common good or to the interests they cherish.

The second thing to keep in mind is that incidents and disturbances are much more likely today than ever before to be viewed not as unfortunate events that just "happen" but as the avoidable consequences of deficient political choices, government policies, and organizational practices. The "Act of God" argument or its profane corollary ("shit happens") no longer suffices to account for the occurrence and severity of a crisis. Ironically, despite today's rapid pace of change, citizens and opinion leaders expect comprehensive security and a comfortable degree of stability, even when they may recognize in the abstract that their world has become increasingly dynamic, complex, and risky.

Leadership in crisis response will inevitably require a two-pronged strategy: dealing with the events "on the ground" (whether literally as in natural disasters or metaphorically as in an economic crisis) and dealing with the political upheaval and instability triggered by these events. Neglecting one or the other is detrimental to any attempt to exercise public leadership in a crisis.

Thirdly, one should accept that even the richest and most competent government can never guarantee that major disruptions will not occur. Policy makers cannot escape the dilemmas of crisis response by banking solely on crisis prevention. Crisis prevention is a necessary, indeed vital task, but it works best for familiar contingencies, such as those that have occurred previously and exhibit telltale signs at an early stage. Prevention is very difficult when it comes to the "unknowable" and "unimaginable" events at the heart of many crises. There is, in other words, no alternative to investing serious time and energy in thinking in a more generic sense about the "rude surprises" that will inevitably occur: the unpleasant, undesirable, unexpected, unorthodox, uncertain, and often inconceivable contingencies that cannot be met by the available repertoires and resources of society and government.[3]

Policy makers do not like to think about potentially nasty and as yet purely hypothetical events since it is psychologically unsettling and because there are so many other pressing issues. However, if they do not lead the way in breaking through the natural tendency for organizations to ignore risks by demonstrating personal and sustained commitment to organizational preparedness, they should not expect much to happen in this regard. It is politically prudent to think about and prepare for future crises. In the wake of a crisis, a laissez-faire approach in the pre-crisis stage tends to be viewed as negligence and can cause much trouble for the leaders who bear final responsibility.

This may all seem rather ominous. Yet leaders should keep an open mind to the fundamental ambiguity of crises: they entail threats, but they may also harbor opportunities. Leadership makes a crucial difference in our perspective. Let us recapitulate what we regard as the five key tasks of crisis leadership:

- *sense making*: detecting an emerging threat and making sure that policy makers get a firm grasp on what is going on and what might happen next;
- *decision making and coordinating*: shaping the overall direction and coherence of the collective efforts to respond to the crisis;

- *meaning making*: actively shaping the public understanding of the crisis as much as is feasible in a democratic, mediatized political system, in order to align the collective definition of the crisis in such a way that it becomes possible to work purposefully toward a set of desirable crisis outcomes;
- *accounting*: contributing to the democratic process of explaining one's ideas and actions to forums of "legitimate value judges"[4] in order to achieve closure of the crisis and allow a community and its political system to move on;
- *learning*: drawing lessons and grasping opportunities to reconsider and perhaps reform those features of existing institutions, policies, and practices that have been found wanting beyond repair in the crisis process.

In the following sections, we summarize our recommendations for each of these critical leadership tasks in a number of maxims. In addition, we will examine the leadership challenge of preparing organizations for the rigors of crisis management. Taken together, they constitute an agenda for developing leadership capacity in and organizational preparedness for times of crisis.

7.3   Improving Crisis Sense Making

To See Crises Coming

Threats that policy makers and their organizations spot in time are the ones that can be managed best. An early-warning system that works gives them a chance to nip at least some evolving threats and risks in the bud. Moreover, accurate early warning of an impending crisis gives policy makers a chance to mitigate its consequences when it is too late or otherwise impossible to avert its occurrence. This buys them time to deal with the impact in a more orderly and effective fashion than is likely to happen in the case of a surprise. Speaking politically, effective warning gives leaders important advantages over those who do not see the crisis coming. It allows them to think in advance not only about threats to stave off but also about the strategic or tactical opportunities that every crisis harbors.

This is something that leaders should get their staffers to do as a matter of routine: scan potential crises issues consistently for both threats and opportunities.[5] If leaders and their staffers fail to see them and act upon them, other players in the political arena might be more astute, and this may complicate rather than facilitate a leader's prospects of handling a crisis successfully.

Policy makers should be alert to factors that inhibit the flow of vital information and limit their capacity for early, flexible, and imaginative threat assessments. More often than not, they are caught by surprise in the event of hostile attacks, large-scale accidents, or civil disorders. In spite of vast investments in information-gathering agencies, intelligence analysts, and a close reading of the daily news, senior officials appear genuinely baffled time and again.

Crises surprise leaders in various ways. In some cases, no one in their surroundings was looking in the right direction. Leaders should therefore take steps to reduce the likelihood of such blind spots, and be alert to what they are *not* told and what they might *not* get to see of the surrounding world. They should hone their intuition and develop their capacity for detecting the silences and omissions in the midst of the incoming flow of information and the talk of their advisers.[6] Leaders must make sure that their intelligence and advisory system operates on a principle of "managed diversity": diversity of technical expertise, of values, of cultural backgrounds, in short of predispositions and perspectives in scanning and interpreting the environment for possible major contingencies. If they do not actively organize diversity and redundancy in their advisory system, there is a real risk that existing policy paradigms and organizational traditions will reproduce a limited and sometimes outright biased view of the situation.

Secondly, surprise may occur because various officials and agencies have parts of the puzzle but fail to put the pieces together in time. Sharing information and joint sense making are by no means given, particularly not when organizations compete for turf, money, prestige, or simply the top official's attention. Policy makers must actively create strong incentives for hitherto separated, closed, competitive segments of the bureaucracy to share and compare information.

This does not mean they should demand uniform outlooks and consensus-based advice. They must simply nurture interaction. It is a leadership task to balance expert outlooks and recommendations, and weigh them against other equally important perspectives.[7] This leadership skill must be informed by sensitivity to the wider political landscape. An ideologically based or personally constructed normative compass for any public action is a source of inner strength, but does not suffice. Leadership also requires the ability to understand and connect with the evolving public view of what constitutes a reasonable course of action in a given crisis. Active monitoring of social media, personally or through the efforts of aides tasked to do so, provides an invaluable real-time window into public sentiment that today's leaders ignore to their peril.

Finally, a crisis may surprise a leader because no one had the guts to tell the leader the bad news of its suspected arrival. The inner circle around a chief executive may shield him from unpleasant news. The less sure advisers feel about their position in the corridors of power, and particularly *vis-à-vis* the leader, the stronger the incentives for them to tell the chief executive what they think they want to hear – and thus to avoid mentioning anything that might be controversial or upsetting to them.

Consistently asking for candid reporting from advisers, including worst-case scenarios, is essential but not sufficient. Policy makers must also show by their attitudes and actions that they value those who bring them bad news or have the courage to argue unpopular viewpoints. In any system where hierarchy is the bottom line, anticipatory compliance and risk minimization are always right around the corner, even in seemingly informal, collegial, "professional" groupings. Leaders must be continuously aware of the distorting influence their presence might have on the frankness of discussion among their advisers. Sometimes the best leadership is not to provide vision and direction, indeed even not to be present, when advisers seek to ascertain threats and make sense of contingencies. Leaders are better off getting the fruits of their deliberation, including any important or persisting disagreements, before they engage with them directly.[8]

Develop a Clear and Timely Picture of the Unfolding Events and Their Implications

Crises generate a search for information by all parties involved. If one does not manage the flow of incoming information there is a serious risk that one will be swept away by a deluge of data, communications, and "news." The effects of this deluge are amplified by colleagues, staffers, and advisers who all diagnose the needs of the situation according to their personal inclinations, professional identities, and institutional roles.

To make sense of a crisis, leaders must make sure that robust systems of data collection and information verification are in place. They should encourage staff to look methodically for the relevant facts in the explosion of data, yet remain aware of how information is filtered and summarized before it reaches their desk. They should probe behind the seductive phrasings in texts and the compelling charts in briefings, verify key facts, check assumptions underlying major intervention proposals, and test these assumptions against their own values and political objectives.

While the first step in sense making is to develop situational awareness – an adequate and relatively up to date picture of what is happening – a second and equally important step is to probe the situation and the context in an attempt to identify key uncertainties, action imperatives, and to understand better the potential impact of crisis developments on key actors, stakeholders and constituencies.[9] This should be done in a relatively systematic fashion as crisis stress tends to narrow the perspective and can easily produce "tunnel vision." We use the components of our crisis definition to formulate a set of diagnostic questions that can prove useful in probing a crisis situation.[10]

What are the core values at stake (and for whom) in this situation? This question helps crisis managers to identify key constituencies, threats, and opportunities embedded in the contingency at hand. It also encourages them to craft solutions that attend to them in a consciously balanced and measured way. A common source of difficulty in crises is when initial or early ways of framing problems do not identify the full range of salient values at stake in the situation. Sometimes policymakers rush to develop options for action without taking the time to think hard and deliberate vigorously on the nature of the problem facing them. Unbalanced response strategies can easily be the result. Crises commonly demand hard choices; dilemmas and value conflict arise frequently. Generally speaking, the capacity of decision makers to formulate strategies well adapted to the situation and which protect the values they cherish most dearly will be increased if they engage in this kind of active value-probing.

What are the key uncertainties associated with the situation and how can they be reduced? This question enables decision makers to identify critical variables and parameters and better prioritize intelligence and analytical resources. A simple but effective means of coping with uncertainty is to make the consideration of multiple scenarios a standard practice of crisis sense making. Development of best-, worst-, and middle-case scenarios can be helpful.

First of all, such an approach forces sense makers to extrapolate from current information and formulate prognoses. This type of thinking can help crisis sense makers break out of a reactive mode and be more proactive in their response to the crisis. Second, comparison of the scenarios can help policymakers to identify critical variables, which can be monitored closely for indications of how and in which direction the crisis is developing. Thirdly, recognition of and preparation for the worst case is almost always good politics. The general public and journalists alike tend to be more critical of complacency or negligence in the face of a previously uncertain threat which subsequently occurs than of vigilant overreaction (which is generally forgiven if perceived to have been in good faith). Among the illustrations of the latter are the "Y2K bug" – which proved ultimately to be rather expensive but not particularly controversial – and many post-9/11 terror alarms in the United States. The precautionary principle (*better safe than sorry*) is relatively easy to defend in today's risk society.

How much time is available (or can be "bought") to deal with this situation? Effective and legitimate crisis response strategies may look very different depending upon whether the time frame is measured in minutes, hours, days, weeks, or months. As the time frame widens, there is increasing room for analytical, deliberative, consultative, and coalition building processes. Effective systems for early warning accompanied by vigilant, proactive response to warning create larger temporal windows for pre-vention, mitigation, and preparation of policy and operational responses.

In the thick of a crisis, a leader should dare to take the time to evaluate the available information and contemplate the dilemmas that seem to emerge from that information. This does not mean leaders should pro-crastinate in the hope that the threat will evaporate or incremental improvement will occur. But they should dare to take time to think about the meaning of a crisis.

Rumors Are a Potential Source of Information

Information flows should be properly organized and this should be done in advance. This is not to say that all information flows can be controlled. Rumors, for instance, are part and parcel of any crisis. Leaders should try to address them through developing (in advance) a rumor-control regime: proactive engagements with the mass media and direct channels of communication to the relevant publics should help them in their struggle with unfounded but widely accepted images of the situation.

Leaders should remember that rumors are not purely dysfunctional: they may provide vital warnings or indicate key uncertainties. Rumors should be read as pointers for effective communication and action. Moreover, particularly in adversarial types of crises, the flip side of rumor control may be rumor diffusion: it sometimes helps to keep one's oppon-ents guessing about one's state of mind, intentions, and capabilities.

Dealing with the Stress of Crisis

Part of leadership mythology is that true leaders are impervious to stress. Crisis reality is that they are not. Images of devastation and loss can affect policy makers deeply. Some crises hurt their friends or loved ones dir-ectly. Some may present them with dilemmas that touch their deepest fears about holding high office and the awesome responsibilities it entails. Some crises are simply too demanding and last too long.

These kinds of crisis characteristics do more to people than just arouse them into maximum alertness. They wear policy makers down. Here we are reminded that leaders are humans too: they are not immune to stressors. It takes wisdom and courage to admit as much, particularly in the midst of an ongoing crisis. This awareness facilitates coping.

A leader who lacks the capacity for self-monitoring and has failed to assign it to deeply trusted others in his inner circle runs the risk of falling prey to high stress and fatigue, with potentially ruinous consequences. Distressed and weary leaders may slide into adopting simplistic images of the situation, stereotypes of other parties, and may be prone to either passivity or haste and recklessness. When that happens, their ability to make a sober diagnosis and provide a beacon of calmness and prudence diminishes.

Rigorous adherence to elementary rules of stress control is essential for leaders in times of crisis. This includes a suitable regime of waking, working, eating, drinking, and sleeping hours; a prearranged delegation of competence and trust to deputies so that they can act with authority; and getting some of the most experienced and trusted advisers to monitor a leader's condition and performance during the crisis, with the explicit assignment to issue warnings when executive stress is beginning to take its toll. These rules should inform all efforts to prepare for crises.

7.4   Improving Crisis Decision Making and Coordination

Centralizing Authority Is Overrated

The success or failure of the crisis response does not always hinge on a single all-or-nothing, do-or-die decision delivered by the crisis leader.[11] To be sure, crises are often best engaged through a combination of strategic choices and concerted action. But it is not always a single boss or a small team at the top of the governmental hierarchy who should make all decisions and who should coordinate each and every action. Crises produce control paradoxes: everybody assumes and expects leaders to be in charge, but the very circumstances of the crisis make it both very difficult and sometimes rather undesirable that they are.

However powerful they might seem, leaders are never wholly free agents. They are institutionally embedded actors: the institutional features of administration shape the discretionary space for leaders in dealing with crises. Part of a proactive crisis management strategy is to reflect upon the institutional setting of crisis leadership and, if necessary, try to alter it for the better. Crisis leadership is more than proactive crisis responses; it also involves fundamental questions of institutional design.

One such question concerns the division of labor between the various layers of authority and nodes of action in a governance system that is preparing for, or responding to, crisis. What should central, top-level executives reserve for themselves and what should they delegate to other officials and organizations – and, in turn, to their respective chains of command?

These are perennial – and rather complex questions – in government. Easy answers do not exist even under normal circumstances, but during a crisis there is often little time and small margins for resolving such thorny issues. Achieving a "whole of government" response is in fact an extremely difficult challenge in its own right. To complicate matters further, it is increasingly recognized from the local to the global level that major crises tend to require not only whole of government responses, but whole of community engagement. The public sector must be able to both effectively deploy its own capabilities *and* partner effectively with the private and nonprofit sectors and community-based initiatives.[12]

A second design issue concerns the management of heterogeneity and conflict in crisis response systems. Crisis response operations mobilize many distinct, partly overlapping, and sometimes openly competing organizational units. Each draws upon its mandate, professional repertoire, and ethos in the fulfillment of the task at hand. Cooperation across such professional boundaries has proven to be at least as difficult as cooperation across geographical or institutional borders. When a crisis hits, leaders are ill-served when significant parts of the response operation are marred by interorganizational miscommunications and rivalries right down to the operational level. Trying to arbitrate such issues in the midst of a crisis consumes an inordinate amount of a government's time and energy.

Both design issues are often best addressed by intelligent decentralization. When a crisis materializes, senior leaders must be able to rely on the capacity of professional units to improvise and synchronize their actions with others. They should therefore invest in creating the institutional and social conditions that facilitate effective network coordination during crises. During a crisis, they should monitor if and how coordination emerges, and they should be available to "trouble shoot" when frictions do occur – as they surely will no matter how solid the pre-crisis network formation. Inadequacies must be swiftly recognized and addressed, even if that entails serious departures from pre-crisis planning (see further below).

But the Critical Decisions Should Be Made by Strategic Leaders

The ash-heap of history is filled with examples of leaders who failed to rise to the responsibility of high office when no one else could make the call. The craft of governing requires a judgment call: leaders must resist the temptation of impetuous moves in the heat of crisis, but they cannot endlessly postpone decisions just because of lingering uncertainty or daunting potential consequences. Somewhere between the irresponsible flight into symbolic action and the paralysis prompted by fear, leaders must identify the critical decisions that they alone can make.

Among the toughest decisions in crises are those that force leaders to choose between whether or not to take draconian measures. Effective intervention in a crisis may be deemed to require relaxation of some of the usual constraints that come with democratic governance and the rule of law. When a leader decides to take that route, and is seen as successful in addressing the threat and stabilizing the situation, he may at first be heralded by the media as a courageous and forceful leader. But as is bound to happen in a democracy, soon after stakeholders and account-ability fora (including these very same mass media) will scrutinize his actions. A few key questions are certain to emerge. Did leaders exercise good judgment, or did they allow themselves to be captured by some hardline faction among their advisers? Did they try to protect the general interest or did they seek to exploit the opportunities offered by the crisis to strike out against political enemies?

If short-term considerations prevail over longer-term ones, leaders set the stage for a critical discussion on their performance. The core ques-tion, then, becomes at what cost to public values, civil liberties, freedom of the press, and reputation abroad do leaders seek to gain the upper hand in crises by means of rash moves? Even in the heat of crisis, broader strategic and normative considerations must prevail in leaders' reasoning and choices. One such consideration must be how various actions taken during peak moments in the crisis process will play out in the long run. When the ordinary grind of political life takes hold again, draconic crisis measures will appear in another light. The trade-offs leaders make between effectiveness and appropriateness will be reframed and reassessed by pivotal forces in their political environment.

Crisis Planning Helps More than Crisis Plans Ever Will

Even if all possible crises could be imagined, and even if money were not an issue, governments would still experience many problems in the implementation of their crisis contingency plans. This is not surprising: students of public administration have stocked libraries with their research findings identifying the various inherent shortcomings of modern government. Hence leaders should *assume* that even if their associates correctly identify and agree on the nature of future threats, they are likely to fall short of the mark when it comes to designing the right plan, securing sufficient funding, training the officials who should do the job, controlling the entire process, or correcting deviations when they occur. Thus even if the crisis plan is really good, the situation may not fit or key preconditions for effective implementation of the plan may not be in place. In fact, as we will see below, securing and sustaining improved preparedness stands out as a significant leadership challenge in its own right.

As Russell Dynes observed for disaster management: "The composition of the emerging structure seldom fits neatly with the pre-disaster patterns of community organization or with the images of coordination which are specified in planning."[13] This observation rings true for most of the crisis cases we have studied. Whether we look at textbook examples of perfect response or devastating failures, crisis plans rarely occupy center stage in the heat of the moment. A crisis plan may exert some influence in the establishment of a crisis center, but the existence and use of a formal plan do not by any means determine the effectiveness of the crisis response.[14]

There is a good reason why detailed plans tend not to work well when implemented too religiously. A fundamental tension exists between the idea of planning and the nature of crisis decision making. Planning presupposes knowledge of what will happen. In routine and rather stable environments, we may be able to predict with a certain degree of precision how many people will require medical attention, attend school, draw unemployment, or commit crimes. Planning can thus begin. A crisis, by definition, disturbs stable environments and creates uncertainty. It presents authorities with unfamiliar challenges that can never fully be dealt with in preconceived plans. Any crisis response operation will therefore necessarily contain elements of improvisation, which requires creativity, flexibility, and resilience rather than rigid adherence to paper plans.[15]

Crisis decision making and coordination are much more effective when they are not dictated by detailed plans and allow for a healthy degree of improvisation. In most crises, lives are saved because of alert and decisive individuals and because organizations worked together in innovative ways. Lives are, of course, also lost because of individual errors and organizational miscommunications, but it is hard to see how an excessively detailed and constraining plan would have improved coordination. Indeed, it is much easier to see how a plan would suffocate individual initiative and spontaneous, organic cooperation.

The absence of detailed plans allows for new organizational forms to emerge, which can replace overloaded, disgraced, or demolished public organizations originally tasked with crisis management. This is vital to effective crisis management operations, and it should be facilitated by keeping contingency plans simple. These plans should formulate clear principles about aims to be achieved and the core preconditions that apply; they should be flexible and low on details about how the various professionals are supposed to do their jobs.

It is important for leaders to keep in mind that planning is subject to many pressures, obstacles, and constraints that can easily impinge on the quality and the utility of plans. There are countless examples of crisis/emergency plans based on flawed assumptions divorced from the reality of crisis operations and resource availability – resulting in so-called fantasy documents. Still, when approached, packaged, and implemented properly, planning may have great value.

Vigilant planning proceeds from several key insights discernible in the literature. First, it is important to distinguish between planning for structured, well understood contingencies (e.g., plane crashes) as opposed to other relatively less structured and somewhat less familiar challenges (e.g., traffic disruptions associated with volcanic ash clouds). While coping with plane crashes may be facilitated by very detailed, scripted plans that ensure that key actions are resourced and implemented in proper sequence, unexpected challenges require enactment of problem identification and application of creative problem solving.

Given the propensity for unanticipated problems to arise in crisis, a modular, capability-based approach tends to be best. A key planning function is to identify capabilities and resources that can be deployed in novel and creative ways – much like children's Lego pieces can be combined in a wide variety of constellations for different purposes. Planning does not have to be rigid and should not be an obstacle to improvisation. Rather, like training (explained further in this chapter) it provides a basis for achieving more qualified improvisation.[16] Though it is has become something of a truism, the planning *process* (which builds familiarity with organizational contexts, capabilities, social networks, and enhances psychological preparedness) is often far more valuable than the plans themselves.

By working together on plans and reflecting upon the challenges associated with particular contingencies, participants become sensitive to problems that may emerge during a crisis. They develop an understanding for the needs and capacities of other potential crisis management actors. This helps to build social capital that facilitates smooth interactions in the heat of crisis. When planning is viewed in terms of social capital building, the use of simulations immediately comes to mind. Well-designed and implemented simulations can help foster more realistic expectations and build mutual trust, precisely the characteristics that inform effective coordination. The Mayor of New York City, Rudolph Giuliani, referred directly to a series of simulation exercises held in the years before September 2001 in his explanation of the relatively coordinated response to the World Trade Center collapse.

Similarly, planning scenarios can be used to encourage leaders and other officials to think the unthinkable, combat complacency and over-confidence, and motivate investment in preparedness. In the United States, emergency management agency FEMA has helped to revitalize planning efforts by encouraging leaders and emergency managers to "think bigger" about potential threats, encouraging leaders and emergency managers to plan and prepare for "maximum of maximums" (MoMS), in other words, worst-case scenarios.[17] The logic is based on the plausible assumption that systems prepared for MoMs will be able to cope effectively with a broader range of challenges than those prepared for more moderate and commonly occurring types of contingencies.

Finally, the real driver of coordinated crisis networks is found in the shared values that guide the actions of the various actors involved.[18] This explains why coordination and cooperation often emerge in the early phases of many crises (the value of saving lives becoming powerfully dominant), only to dissolve as the various actors begin to champion different values (as the threat to life recedes). This insight also helps to think through issues of preparation and planning. Leaders may thus be better off in using crisis-planning processes to explore what binds actors together and then try to reinforce and codify that through institutionalized coordination arrangements.

7.5   Improving Crisis Meaning Making

Leaders Who Do Not Communicate Persuasively Will Fail

A crisis never speaks for itself. In the uncertainty that such a period of discontinuity provokes, people will try to attach meaning to their plight. They will want to know why this happened and why it was not prevented. They will want to find out what their leaders did to prevent or at least minimize the scope of the crisis. Through a process of collective meaning making, in which many different actors promote their version of the events, some sort of shared (or contested) assessment will arise.

Nor can leaders rely upon their crisis management performance to speak for itself. If they want to be favorably assessed – in democracies a condition *sine qua non* for a post-crisis leadership career – they will have to "market" their version of events. This may be a humbling and perhaps humiliating experience if it is approached as a chore to be performed to satisfy the ungrateful. But leaders who understand that crisis management is nothing more than governance under extreme conditions will see this as an opportunity to explain the past and define possible futures. The ability to shape images of recent adversity is extremely helpful in charting new courses. Leaders must therefore build on their crisis performance and surf the wave it provides for them.

Policy makers who seek to influence the process of meaning making in crises must tell their story to the public, the media, and the politicians in a convincing way. Crisis communication is one of the most effective yet least understood means of imposing a degree of order on a highly dynamic environment. Through effective communication, leaders can shape perceptions that channel behavior. That is why sloppy or clumsy communications may have perverse effects: the behavior of individuals will be informed by some alternative picture of the situation – a frame that may motivate people to act in counterproductive ways. This should not be read as a cue for Machiavellian leadership. It just reminds leaders not to take for granted that their interpretation of the situation will match the dominant one among stakeholders or the general public. Leaders must therefore become skilled in the art of crisis communication before they must deal with crisis. The onslaught of social media activities during crises represents a novel and ever growing leadership challenge to be mastered. In the absence of these skills, crisis leaders become dangerously dependent on media advisers, spin doctors, spokespersons, or other surrogates.

Meaning making, however, entails more than effective media management, a sound public relations policy, or a spin-doctoring wizard. To be sure, media management requires a Herculean effort if one wants to do it well. And yes, having a spin doctor in the team certainly helps to package the message the right way. But thinking in terms of media management and "spin" evokes a tactical approach from leaders where a strategic one is required. Meaning making requires a philosophy of crisis management, which reminds leaders of core values that must be preserved, structural weaknesses that must be repaired, and opportunities to be explored.

Shaken by the onslaught of crisis, citizens look to their leaders for hope, courage, motivation, and empathy. Leaders are able to provide these things through communications that are well formulated, well-timed, well-staged (in terms of the visual backdrops and circumstances), and memorable. When they are unable or too slow to deliver communication of this kind, the citizenry will be disappointed, angry even, and a political vacuum ripe for exploitation by others is created.

Leader credibility is a particularly helpful resource in times of crisis. Under threatening uncertainty, people look toward leaders and will gladly put their fate in the hands of those they trust. Few leaders, however, are trusted to this extent. Leaders are easily tempted to make up for this "trust deficit" by making tall promises and delivering reassuring explanations. This is a mistake. Credibility is won the hard way but is lost easily. A leader who enters a crisis with low credibility status is facing an uphill struggle. He will have to earn credits under trying conditions. This can only be done by performing well under very difficult circumstances. Mayor Giuliani, again, constitutes a good example: highly controversial and all but written off prior to 9/11; a national hero after it – by virtue of his determined, dignified, and honest leadership style during the crisis. In contrast, empty promises and false assurances will be exposed by at least some segments of the mass media army that congregates around the story of a major crisis, and will then be fully exploited by political opponents to erode the support base on which a leader depends.

7.6   Improving Crisis Accounting

Crises Must Be Brought to Closure

It is tempting to consider the cessation of operational crisis management activities as the end of the crisis. It usually does not work that way because the political aftermath assumes its own dynamics. Different actors explore the aftermath for opportunities to attack opponents, attract praise, initiate reform – or gain in any other way from the temporary state of "unfreezed" structures. All these activities nurture a process of escalation, which leads surprised and exhausted leaders into what is known as the "crisis after the crisis."

Crisis leaders must therefore manage both the operational and the political dimensions of crisis. They cannot afford to view operational crisis management purely or even predominantly in functional terms – they should "delegate" this perspective to senior officials who are further removed from the political domain and stand closer to the operational heat. A crisis leader must play the political game throughout the crisis, starting the moment a crisis begins. That means operating in the political domain, which inevitably takes away from operational command duties.

Leaders should engage in high politics even if normal politics have been suspended because of the crisis.

Accounting for Crises is Inevitable – and Risky

Crises cast long shadows. And so they should, to some extent. Major breakdowns in public order, safety, health, and prosperity do not occur every day in most Western societies. Their very occurrence should provoke serious reflection, and should – as a matter of democratic principle – compel leaders to account for their actions and those of the people and agencies in their sphere of responsibility prior to, during, and following a crisis. Crises require an open and active accountability process, one that makes it possible to release tensions, to reequilibrate the social and political system, and to engage in meaningful learning.

The massive media onslaught that is the hallmark of contemporary crises guarantees that questions of responsibility, accountability, blame, and compensation will be on the agenda. All actors involved are likely to continuously assess and perhaps even defend their positions, in particular those who bear final responsibility. Apart from the mass and social media, many formal, institutional accountability practices will be set in motion in judicial, political, and professional arenas. These various and sometimes closely intertwined accountability processes need not necessarily escalate into tough, aggressive blame games, but they do often enough for any leader to take that option into account.

Leaders should therefore prepare themselves and their staff for the cascading political and possibly legal developments that may feature in the wake of a crisis. Throughout the crisis, they should carefully document the crisis response as well as the process which produced it. In addition, they should closely monitor the events and the stances taken by major political actors for possible long-run, second-order consequences, those that come back to haunt leaders if they ignore them. They should monitor how the media report the crisis and the government's handling of it. They need to follow and contribute to social media debates and narratives. Fluid images of success or fiasco are framed through media reports of what leaders seemingly did and did not do during the crisis.

The evolution of the crisis narrative during the accountability process can deprive leaders of control and drive them out of office. Leaders should therefore beware not to immediately disband their crisis team as the acute crisis stages seem to pass. The crisis aftermath is not a time to take a low profile or return to "business as usual." Leaders should remain visibly on top and be proactive in rendering account: open and forthright if possible, alert and disciplined, repentant if necessary. Leaders should not render their political fate dependent upon interpretations of the crisis put forward by their critics and other stakeholders who may not necessarily have an interest in a fair and balanced evaluation of the crisis process.

Avoid Blame Games

It is sometimes said that in an earlier era, governmental leaders could count on public sympathy in times of trouble. If bad things happened, these were attributed to exogenous factors (enemies, nature, or "acts of God"), and government was seen as part of the cavalry that came to the rescue. Regardless of whether this is an accurate or merely nostalgic view of past crises, today it is certainly not the case. Leaders must struggle to obtain public support. So instead of assuming that most crises generate the rally-around-the-flag effect as seen in the United States following the 9/11 attacks and the 22/7 attacks in Norway, leaders must seriously entertain the alternative scenario: that they become scapegoats. In times where governments are often already deeply unpopular, leaders run a serious risk of bearing the brunt of a societal blaming process.

When they come under fire in the wake of a crisis, it may be comforting for a leader to point the finger at somebody or something else. They can try to claim, for example, that it was the rumor mill of the media that inflamed a difficult situation into a crisis. With a more responsible media, the crisis would not have erupted at all, or their ability to manage the situation would have been much better, or so they may argue. Unfortunately, the chances of success for this type of blame-shifting strategy are slim. Experience suggests that it is counterproductive for public leaders to blame the media for what can easily be construed as their own shortcomings.

Finding scapegoats lower down the bureaucratic hierarchy or across the partisan divide may also seem an expedient blame-avoidance strategy for an embattled leader. Here the chances of getting away with it are somewhat bigger. History is filled with examples of how mid-level officials face charges linked to crises while the top leadership escapes from being held liable. Yet this strategy may come at a hefty price. It earns a leader the lasting distrust if not enmity of the people and organizations that must work for them in years to come; some of these "lightning rods" might not take their victimization lying down. When they put up a fight, a blame game is started that is likely to feed on itself and escalate into a situation where everybody loses.

By denying their role in the crisis, leaders forfeit a rare opportunity for significant self-evaluation and reflection. In the end, buck passing only undermines one's authority, whereas proactive, genuine, and well-communicated responsibility-taking may well underpin it.

7.7 Improving Crisis Learning and Reform Craft

Learn – Don't Just Copy or 'Implement Recommendations'

Over the course of their careers, seasoned policy makers gather experiential lessons. When they face a new crisis, they may assume it resembles previous ones, and rely upon a tried-and-tested repertoire of techniques and stratagems. To the extent that the current challenge resembles the recollected past, this is a sensible thing to do. It reduces a policy maker's sense of uncertainty and may increase the speed and efficiency of crisis responses.

The present is not a carbon copy of any past, however. Policy makers are easily led astray rather than helped by a strong reliance upon historical analogies with past crises. Direct personal experiences with crises are valuable, but scarce and inherently ambivalent diagnostic resources. It is naturally tempting for people to overgeneralize from the experience of one or two vividly remembered personal experiences to the neglect of the wider experience base. For this reason alone, personal experiences of crisis can and should be complemented by knowledge of the experiences of others. This experience may be drawn from the history of one's own country or organization, or be vicarious – drawn from the experience of other organizations in one's own country or from that of organizations in other countries. Before they draw lessons, policy makers should make sure they are informed by multiple, systematic, and unbiased accounts and analyses of not just the most recent but a range of relevant crisis experiences.[19]

If learning is to amount to more than the idiosyncratic use of analogies or the unreflective copying of past practices, it should entail an intelligent investigation of a range of crises. Commissions, investigation boards, and consulting firms play a role. The research on so-called high reliability organizations suggests that there are ways to build a safety culture that facilitates effective learning. Moreover, the blossoming field of crisis consultancy has developed several techniques – such as executive debriefings, postmortem analyses, and the use of scenarios – that may facilitate crisis learning.[20]

If they are to have any impact on future public performance, the findings of such systematic examinations, the lessons learned, must be transmitted among individuals and embedded within the collective learning dynamics of governments. The lessons must become part of a shared and institutionalized memory bank, maintained by organizational units close enough to the heart of the policy-making machinery to be relevant, but shielded as much as possible from post-crisis politicking. From this reservoir of experience-based crisis management knowledge, guidelines for future governmental action can be formulated and disseminated. Hence a pivotal leadership task is to make sure the institutional preconditions exist for this to happen. They should win top-level support for the way lessons are formulated, even when the resulting lessons are controversial. Crisis-aware public leaders stimulate the quest for meta-learning (i.e., learning to learn) in the public sector.[21]

Effective learning involves a multi-step process. Individual and collective experience of an event must be captured, analyzed, and placed in the broader context of other comparable events. Constructing meaningful lessons and reform proposals generally requires significant investment of time and resources as well as a willingness to delve into politically and organizationally sensitive matters. It also is best served by a balanced approach that combs the crisis in question not only for apparent failures, but also identifies successes that may be taken for granted or overlooked in a hyper-critical, post-crisis climate dominated by fault-finding and blame games. Once lessons are identified and sensible reform proposals formulated, it is common to publish them under the banner of lessons learned. But are the lessons really learned at this stage? Rather these are lessons identified and remedies proposed. In our view, it is only after a successful implementation of these reforms that these lessons have been truly learned in a more profound sense.

'Sweeping' Reforms Are Not the Only Way to Learn From Crises

Deep crises often generate strong media and political pressures for sweeping overhauls of preexisting policies and organizations. If things went wrong so badly, the institutional fabric must have been really flawed. This line of thinking is predicated on the premise that big events must have big causes. It is supported by the long lists of missed signals, unheeded warnings, and response problems that post hoc examinations tend to produce. But the more sophisticated of these examinations also reveal another truth: crises are all too often the result of escalated chain reactions in policy systems or high-risk technologies. Moreover, crises are labels that do not correspond one-on-one with the performance of organizations or operators.

Sweeping organizational reforms may look good politically. They reassert the capacity to lead and they hold the promise of serendipitous gains from adversity. But sweeping, hastily conceived, and readily pushed through reforms tend to come at a price of unease, dissent, and unintended consequences, which may only be noted after the crisis momentum has faded. Leaders are thus well advised to subject crisis-induced reform plans to the same level of scrutiny and debate accorded to such proposals in normal times, even if the political temptation to utilize momentary windows of opportunity is strong and the urgency of systemic overhauls seemingly high.

In fact, there is something to be said for the idea that in many instances the worst-case situation (the entire system has failed, therefore everything must change) does not exist, and that more effective crisis-induced learning is better guided by a leadership strategy of "dynamic conserva-tism."[22] This strategy prioritizes the defense of core values and insti-tutional commitments. It urges leaders to flexibly adapt policy-making structures and modus operandi of public organizations to the high-pressure context of crisis rather than to succumb to the temptation of grand reform rhetoric.

It is, of course, not easy to determine what must change so that the rest can remain the same. Leaders therefore need some kind of policy compass or roadmap, which helps them negotiate this inherent tension between stewardship and change mastership. They must have a clear idea of what is worth preserving in their society, policy field, or organ-ization. This can guide them once they are forced into the unfamiliar, chaotic terrain of a major crisis. Such a philosophy of crisis manage-ment should help prevent the occurrence of common crisis response modes, such as ad hocery, improvisation, and stress-induced rigidity. It should prevent leaders from making immediate, "knee-jerk" deci-sions; it focuses attention on long-term consequences of any reform plans.

The implementation of reform programs is a long-term process that generates complex problems. Contrary to popular expectations, as we have shown, crisis-induced reforms do not escape this iron law; it is quite the contrary. Crisis-induced reform is often a product of centralized and opportunistic policy management (matching preexisting reform packages to now-salient critical problems). In this context of "seizing the moment," due process and deliberative democracy make way for pro-cedural shortcuts, and forceful crisis rhetoric masks the implementation dilemmas attached to the reforms advocated.

Whereas successful reform leaders take an inclusive approach and co-opt key officials and groups who will become involved during the implementation process, rapid-fire reform strategies in crisis decision making tend to hinge upon exclusive, inner-circle modes of making policy. As a consequence, the appreciative gap that separates policy makers from implementers is not bridged but widened.[23] As soon as the sense of crisis urgency passes, leaders will have to deal with this gap. Hence the paradox: crisis-induced reforms may well give rise to reform-induced crises.

7.8   Being Prepared

Pulling together some of the key threads of the discussion above points to a continuous, ongoing challenge for the leaders of today and tomorrow: preparing themselves, their staffs, and their organizations for crisis management.[24] Crisis preparations consist of several subtasks to be addressed before crisis hits, each of which will be discussed in turn below.

Organizing and Selecting

A key responsibility of leaders is to ensure that an appropriate set of organizational roles, structures, and processes are in place ahead of time to enable effective and flexible work under crisis conditions and to select suitable staff for key functions in that crisis organization. There is no single optimal form of organizing for crisis management; rather a crisis organization should be designed taking into account the characteristics and context of a given setting. Organizations that fail to develop a specialized crisis organization in fact make a design choice as well – often by default. That choice is likely to be suboptimal as most organizations are not designed and have not "organically" developed in ways that facilitate coping with the extraordinary pressures, information flows, and pace associated with crises. Even organizations – such as media and first responder organizations – used to rapid real-time operations may be overwhelmed when the scale, scope, complexity, and operational tempo increases dramatically.

Key challenges include specifying the role of top leadership (do they keep running the everyday organization, the crisis organization, or both?), developing surge capacity to deal with increased crisis-related work while keeping up with essential ongoing tasks, developing means of coping with information deficit and overload in periods of acute crisis, and cultivating sustainable staffing and stress monitoring functions. Selecting senior and mid-level leaders for crisis management roles is also challenging. Many officials are promoted on the basis of skills, personality traits, and management styles that are primarily demonstrated and enacted under "steady state" operational conditions. Such leaders may, or may not, be equipped by personality, background, previous education, and training (explained in the following section) for managing effectively in crisis. If, as is often suggested, we are living in increasingly crisis prone times, it may be that crisis management aptitude should play more of a role in leader selection in general.

Educating, Training, and Exercising

Leaders must be (and try to ensure that their team members, key subordinates, and key partners are) educated, trained, and exercised in preparation for crisis management. It is increasingly recognized in many countries that the management of crises, disasters, and emergencies requires a specialized political-administrative skill set. One approach is to emphasize the need to educate and develop a cadre of crisis professionals.[25] Such a profession could depart from military, medical, legal, or other professional "models." Professionalization entails the identification of a body of knowledge, core skills and standards, including a code of ethics. Suitably specified, this can be helpful; care must be taken, however, to prevent the emergence of a static orthodoxy and excessive homogeneity.

When facing major crises, partnership between political leaders and "professionals" is essential. This means that political leaders who are not "professionals" must be educated as to the nature of crisis management, informed of what is required of them in crisis, familiarized with crisis planning and organization, and equipped to engage in meaningful communicative interaction with others inside and outside of their organizations. In this sense, crisis management education must be both conceptual and practical. Individual and collective crisis management skills are best acquired and honed through hands-on practice. There are a wide variety of powerful instructional designs and techniques (both traditional and technology enhanced) suitable for crisis management training and exercises. Instructional designs and techniques should be consciously and explicitly adapted to the goals and purposes of a given training or exercise. One size (and one instructional design) does not and cannot fit all.[26]

Cultivating Vigilance

One of the great challenges, especially in organizations and communities that have been spared from frequent exposure to disasters and crises, is to break through inertia and defense mechanisms which detract from psychological and organizational preparedness.[27] A common mentality is "it won't happen here" syndrome, in which threats and hazards which have impacted other organizations and communities are dismissed as irrelevant. In order to motivate (and secure funding for) preparedness efforts, leaders must cultivate an "it could happen here" mentality for themselves and those who follow them. This entails actively monitoring the crisis experiences of others and asking the tough questions of "Are we ready to cope with a contingency like this?" and "What can we do now to be more prepared when it is our turn?" In the absence of, or in between crises such as those mentioned above, leaders must protect preparedness budgets and provide resources – a particularly difficult task in the contemporary climate of budget austerity.

Senior leaders should champion preparedness activities as an ongoing effort. They should espouse a holistic view of the requirements for crisis management performance, in contrast to narrow, sector-based, and mechanistic perspectives grounded in distinct professions. Such a shared paradigm for professional coordination can only be built in advance of the next major crisis. Leaders can do this by showing personal commitment to crisis preparedness. Without leadership commitment, the work toward improving organizational crisis capacity will soon slide into a low-prestige ritual without adequate staff motivation. Leaders must free up some of their own time and allocate ample resources for joint socialization and concerted action among the units or organizations most likely to form the nucleus of crisis response operations. Joint training and rigorously designed and executed exercises of the kind suggested above must become institutionalized rather than isolated and incidental occurrences in the government system.

Leaders must stimulate their organizations to launch an enduring awareness-raising and training program, which engages the leadership and their immediate staffs. Active leadership involvement in preparedness activities is critical. Through such involvement, leaders develop intimate knowledge of the strategic and operational capabilities of their crisis organizations. Furthermore, leaders set a powerful example for subordinates and peers by participating in exercises, making good calls – and mistakes – in relatively safe environments, and learning from that experience.

7.9   Prudent Crisis Leadership

Citizens expect many things of their governments and their leaders. Being an effective crisis manager is not always at the top of the mental checklists that voters use to evaluate candidates for high office, but many political executives will find out during the course of their tenure that it is a crucial quality they must possess if they want to stay in office and remain effective. In crises, the leadership potential of public officeholders is put to the test, and the testing is done in full public view thanks to the relentless media scrutiny that crises generate.

Many government leaders have failed to live up to the multifaceted requirements of successful crisis management: being effective, being moral, respecting democratic constraints – and being seen to be this way. Often, short-term imperatives for visible, forceful, and symbolic action have won out over considerations of democratic legitimacy. In other instances, a legalistic drive to adhere strictly to the book has generated a public impression of a timid, ineffectual, or insensitive government in the face of grave threats. Effective leadership requires policy makers to devise, enact, and legitimize a workable balance between these contradictory imperatives.

Moreover, leaders should also display an awareness of the fact that crisis management is situated on the dividing line between stability and change in policies and polities. Many historic revolutions, for instance, began as public order crises that escalated due to ineffectual leadership. Many revolutions were shaped by leaders who well understood the dynamics of crisis.

For public leaders, taking the time for strategic reflection on their crisis management capacity is a good investment in a political future. It prepares them for their role in this unfolding script of turmoil between stability and change. It forces them to consider their legacy: what is worth defending and for what change can a crisis be exploited?

A pivotal strategic question of crisis leadership is where a reasonable defense of incumbency and stability ends and a debilitating, and potentially self-defeating, posture of rigidity begins. When may imminent threats justifiably be met by what will seem disproportionate measures to at least some people? How far can crisis management responses go before democracy itself is fatally wounded?

These questions were topical in the tumultuous years of the 1960s; they have been rediscovered after the 9/11 events and the devastating terrorist attacks on European capitals such as Madrid, London, Paris, and Oslo. Other hazards and contingencies pose somewhat different but no less difficult challenges to our values, sensibilities, and ways of life. We have no doubt that such dilemmas will continue to plague us in the near and distant future.

These are difficult questions. They surely are a far cry from the reassuring "ten principles of effective crisis management" found in best-selling crisis management handbooks, many of which sell an illusion of control (top-down, linear, straightforward) which does not fit particularly well with the context of contemporary crises. Difficult questions and dilemmas of leadership in crises need to be faced and addressed, not denied.

Notes

1 See the webpages of the Center for Disease Control: www.cdc.gov/vhf/ebola/outbreaks/2014-west-africa/united-states-imported-case.html and www.cdc.gov/flu/about/qa/disease.htm (accessed May 12, 2015).
2 Hermann and Hagan (1998); Mitroff and Silver (2010).
3 The term "rude surprises" was coined by LaPorte (2003).
4 The term is taken from Dror (1986).
5 Regester and Larkin (1997); Jaques (2014).
6 Gladwell (2005).
7 George and Stern (2002).
8 Janis (1989). To understand the dynamics and effects of crisis response, we must cast our net wider and consider the institutional context in which leaders operate and crisis decision making takes place. For such an approach, see Stern and Sundelius (2002).
9 Stern (2009).
10 Stern (2009; 2014).
11 't Hart (2014).
12 Baubion (2013); Bach (2015).
13 Dynes (1970: 208). For a discussion of the symbolic value of planning, see Clarke (1999).
14 All this should not be interpreted as a postmodern rejection of bureaucratic structures. Bureaucracies – think of the Salvation Army or a local transportation company – can prove a powerful source of improvisation during a crisis. The secret of these types of organizations is that their structure revolves around commonly shared values. In routine situations, bureaucratic structure helps to optimize efficiency; during a crisis, these structures can be temporarily abandoned as the shared values guide improvisation.
15 Kendra and Wachtendorf (2003).
16 Cf. Kendra and Wachtendorf (2003).
17 www.ready.gov/press-release/release-101020 (accessed October 25, 2012).
18 Douglas (1992).
19 Lagadec (1997); Boin et al. (2004). Following a crisis, it is common to initiate exercises in formulating lessons learned from such an episode. However, the step from observing the recent performances of oneself and others in the heat of a crisis to formulating lessons learned of enduring value is quite formidable. For one, one needs to distinguish between the many lessons observed and the fewer lessons learned.
20 For a theoretical introduction, see Argyris and Schön (1978); Weick and Sutcliffe (2002). See also Stern et al. (2014).
21 Schön (1971); Deverell and Hansén (2009); Deverell and Olsson (2011).

22 Ansell et al. (2015). See also Zelikow and Rice (1995).
23 Boin and Otten (1996).
24 This section draws heavily on Stern (2013).
25 Cf. Stevens (2013).
26 Stern (2014).
27 Parker and Stern (2005); Parker et al. (2009).

References

Adomeit, H. (1982). *Soviet Risk-taking and Crisis Behavior: A Theoretical and Empirical Analysis.* Boston: Allen & Unwin.

Aghion, P., Bloom, N., Sadun, R., and Van Reenen, J. (2014). Never Waste a Good Crisis? Growth and Decentralization in the Recession. www.people.hbs.edu/rsadun/GoodCrisis_December2014.pdf (accessed August 8, 2016).

Agrell, W. (2013). *The Black Swan and Its Opponents: Early Warning Aspects of the Norway Attacks on 22 July 2011.* Stockholm: Swedish National Defence College.

Aguirre, B. E. (2004). Homeland Security Warnings: Lessons Learned and Unlearned. *International Journal of Mass Emergencies and Disasters,* 22(2): 103–15.

Alberts, D. S. and Hayes, R. E. (2005). *Power to the Edge: Command and Control in the Information Age.* Washington, DC: CCRP Publication Series.

Aldrich, D. P. (2012). *Building Resilience: Social Capital in Post-Disaster Recovery.* Chicago: University of Chicago Press.

Alford, J. (2009). *Engaging Public Sector Clients: From Delivery to Co-Production.* Basingstoke: Palgrave Macmillan.

Alink, F., Boin, A., and 't Hart, P. (2001). Institutional Crises and Reforms in Policy Sectors: The Case of Asylum Policy in Europe. *Journal of European Public Policy* 8(2): 286–306.

Allison, G. T. (1971). *Essence of Decision: Explaining the Cuban Missile Crisis.* Boston: Little Brown.

Almond, G. A., Flanagan, S., and Mundt, R. (eds.) (1973). *Crisis, Choice, and Change: Historical Studies of Political Development.* Boston: Little Brown.

Ansell, C., Boin, R. A., and Farjoun, M. (2015). Dynamic Conservatism: How Institutions Change to Remain the Same. In M. S. Kraatz, ed., *Institutions and Ideals: Philip Selznick's Legacy for Organizational Studies. Research in the Sociology of Organizations,* vol. 44. Bingley, UK: Emerald Group Publishing, 89–119.

Ansell, C., Boin, R. A., and Keller, A. (2010). Managing Transboundary Crises: Identifying the Building Blocks of an Effective Response System. *Journal of Contingencies and Crisis Management,* 18(4): 195–207.

Ansell, C., Boin, R. A., and Kuipers, S. (in press). Institutional Crisis and the Policy Agenda. In N. Zahariadis, ed., *Handbook of Public Policy Agenda-Setting.* Cheltenham: Edward Elgar.

Ansell, C. and Gash, A. (2008). Collaborative Governance in Theory and Practice. *Journal of Public Administration Research and Theory*, 18(4): 543–71.

Argyris, C. and Schön, D. A. (1978). *Organizational Learning: A Theory of Action Perspective*. Amsterdam: Addison-Wesley.

Arild, W. and Maor, M. (eds.) (2015). *Organizational Reputation in the Public Sector*. New York: Routledge.

Bach, R. (ed.) (2015). *Strategies for Supporting Community Resilience: Multinational Experiences*. Stockholm: Swedish National Defence University.

Badie, D. (2010). Groupthink, Iraq and the War on Terror. *Foreign Policy Analysis*, 6(4): 277–96.

Baggot, R. (1998). The BSE Crisis: Public Health and the "Risk Society." In P. Gray and P. 't Hart, eds., *Public Policy Disasters in Western Europe*. London: *Routledge*, 61–78.

Barnard, C. (1938). *The Functions of the Executive*. Cambridge, MA: Harvard University Press.

Barton, A. H. (1969). *Communities in Disaster: A Sociological Analysis of Collective Stress Situations*. New York: Doubleday.

Barton, L. (1993). *Crisis in Organizations: Managing and Communicating in the Heat of Chaos*. Cincinnati: South-Western Publishing.

Baubion, C. (2013). *OECD Risk Management: Strategic Crisis Management*. OECD Working Papers on Public Governance, 23. Paris: OECD Publishing.

Baumgartner, F. R. and Jones, B. D. (1993). *Agendas and Instability in American Politics*. Chicago: University of Chicago Press.

Beck, U. (1992). *Risk Society: Toward a New Modernity*. London: Sage Publications.

Bennett, A. (1999). *Condemned to Repetition? The Rise, Fall and Reprise of Soviet-Russian Military Interventionism, 1973–1996*. Cambridge, MA: MIT Press.

Bennett, W. L. (1980). Myth, Ritual and Political Control. *Journal of Communication*, 30(4): 166–79.

Bennett, W. L. and Entman, R. M. (eds.) (2001). *Mediated Politics: Communication in the Future of Democracy*. Cambridge: Cambridge University Press.

Bernstein, S., Lebow, R. N., Stein, J. G., and Weber, S. (2000). God Gave Physics the Easy Problems: Adapting Social Science to an Unpredictable World. *European Journal of International Relations*, 6(1): 43–76.

Birkland, T. A. (1997). *After Disaster: Agenda-Setting, Public Policy, and Focusing Events*. Washington: Georgetown University Press.

(2006). *Lessons of Disaster: Policy Change after Catastrophic Events*. Washington: Georgetown University Press.

Blight, J. G. and Welch, D. A. (1989). *On the Brink: Americans and Soviets Reexamine the Cuban Missile Crisis*. New York: Hill and Wang.

Blinder, A. S. (2013). *After the Music Stopped: The Financial Crisis, the Response, and the Work Ahead*. New York: Penguin Books.

Blumler, J. and Gurevitch, M. (1995). *The Crisis of Public Communication*. London: Routledge.

Boin, R. A. (2001). *Crafting Public Institutions: Leadership in Two Prison Systems*. Boulder, CO: Lynne Rienner.

(2005). From Crisis to Disaster: Toward an Integrative Perspective. In E. Quarantelli, ed., *What is a Disaster? A Dozen Perspectives on the Question*. London: Routledge.

Boin, R. A. and Bynander, F. (2014). Explaining Success and Failure in Crisis Coordination. *Geografiska Annaler: Series A, Physical Geography*, 97(1): 123–35.

Boin, R. A., Ekengren, M., and Rhinard, M. (2013). *The European Union as Crisis Manager: Patterns and Prospects*. Cambridge: Cambridge University Press.

Boin, R. A., Kofman-Bos, C., and Overdijk, W. I. E. (2004). Crisis Simulations: Exploring Tomorrow's Vulnerabilities and Threats. *Simulation and Gaming: An International Journal of Theory, Practice and Research*, 35(3): 378–93.

Boin, R. A., McConnell, A., and 't Hart, P. (2009). Crisis Exploitation: Political and Policy Impacts of Framing Contests. *Journal of European Public Policy*, 16(1): 81–106.

Boin, R. A. and Otten, M. H. P. (1996). Beyond the Crisis Window for Reform: Some Ramifications for Implementation. *Journal of Contingencies and Crisis Management* 4(3): 149–61.

Boin, R. A. and Renaud, C. (2013). Orchestrating Joint Sensemaking Across Government Levels: Challenges and Requirements for Crisis Leadership. *Journal of Leadership Studies*, 7(3): 41–6.

Boin, R. A. and Rhinard, M. (2008). Managing Transboundary Crises: What Role for the European Union? *International Studies Review*, 10(1): 1–26.

Boin, R. A., Rhinard, M., and Ekengren, M. (2014). Managing Transboundary Crises: The Emergence of European Union Capacity. *Journal of Contingencies and Crisis Management*, 22(3): 131–42.

Boin, R. A. and 't Hart, P. (2000). Institutional Crises in Policy Sectors: An Exploration of Characteristics, Conditions and Consequences. In H. Wagenaar, ed., *Government Institutions: Effects, Changes and Normative Foundations*. Dordrecht: Kluwer Press, 9–31.

(2003). Public Leadership in Times of Crisis: Mission Impossible? *Public Administration Review*, 63(5): 544–53.

(2012). Aligning Executive Action in Times of Adversity: The Politics of Crisis Co-ordination. In M. Lodge and K. Wegrich, eds., *Executive Politics in Times of Crisis*. Houndmills: Palgrave, 179–96.

Boin, R. A., 't Hart, P., and McConnell, A. (eds.) (2008). *Governing after Crises: The Politics of Investigation, Accountability and Learning*. Cambridge: Cambridge University Press.

Boin, R. A., 't Hart, P., McConnell, A., and Preston, T. (2010). Leadership Style, Crisis Response and Blame Management: The Case of Hurricane Katrina. *Public Administration*, 88(3): 706–23.

Boutelier, H. (2004). *The Safety Utopia*. Heidelberg: Springer.

Bovens, M., Schillemans, T., and Goodin, R. (eds) (2014). *Oxford Handbook of Public Accountability*. Oxford: Oxford University Press.

Bovens, M., 't Hart, P., Dekker, S., and Verheuvel, G. (1999). The Politics of Blame Avoidance: Defensive Tactics in a Dutch Crime-Fighting Fiasco. In H. K. Anheier, ed., *When Things Go Wrong: Organizational Failures and Breakdowns*. London: Sage, 123–47.

Bovens, M. and 't Hart, P. (1996). *Understanding Policy Fiascoes*. New Brunswick: Transaction Publishers.

Bracken, P. (1983). *The Command and Control of Nuclear Forces*. New Haven: Yale University Press.

Brändström, A. (2015). Crisis Accountability: Ministerial Resignations in Sweden. *Scandinavian Political Studies*, 38(3): 301–20.

Brändström, A. and Kuipers, S. L. (2003). From 'Normal Incidents' to Political Crises: Understanding the Selective Politicization of Policy Failures. *Government and Opposition*, 38(3): 279–305.

Brändström, A., Kuipers, S., and Daléus, P. (2008). The Politics of Blame Management in Scandinavia after the Tsunami Disaster. In R. A. Boin, P. 't Hart, and A. McConnell, eds., *Governing after Crisis: The Politics of Investigation, Accountability and Learning*. Cambridge: Cambridge University Press, 114–47.

Brändström, A. and Malesic, M. (eds.) (2004). *Crisis Management in Slovenia: Comparative Perspectives*. Stockholm: Swedish National Defence College.

Brändström, A., 't Hart, P., and Bynander F. (2004). Governing by Looking Back: Historical Analogies and Crisis Management. *Public Administration*, 82(1): 191–210.

Branigan, T. (2011). Chinese Anger over Alleged Cover-Up of High-Speed Rail Crash. *The Guardian*, July 25, 2011. www.theguardian.com/world/2011/jul/25/chinese-rail-crash-cover-up-claims.

Brecher, M. (1979a). "Vertical" Case Studies: A Summary of Findings. In M. Brecher, ed., *Studies in Crisis Behavior*, 267–72.

(1979b). State Behavior in International Crisis: A Model. *Journal of Conflict Resolution*, 23(3): 446–80.

(ed.) (1979c). *Studies in Crisis Behavior*. New Brunswick: Transaction Books.

(1980). *Decisions in Crisis: Israel 1967 and 1973*. Berkeley: University of California Press.

(1993). *Crises in World Politics: Theory and Reality*. Oxford: Pergamon Press.

Breed, W. (1955). Social Control in the Newsroom: A Functional Analysis. *Social Forces*, 33(4): 326–35.

Brinkley, D. (2006). *The Great Deluge: Hurricane Katrina*. New York: Morrow.

Broekema, W. (2015). Crisis-Induced Learning and Issue Politicization in the EU: The Braer, Sea Empress, Erika, and Prestige Oil Spill Disasters. *Public Administration*, 94(2): 381–398.

Bromwich, D. (2014). *Moral Imagination: Essays*, Princeton: Princeton University Press.

Brown, C. (2015). *The 2005 Hurricane Katrina Response Failure*. PhD diss., Radboud University, Nijmegen. www.diva-portal.org/smash/get/diva2:885098/FULLTEXT01.pdf.

Brunsson, N. and Olsen, J. P. (1993). *The Reforming Organization*. London: Routledge.

Bryson, J. M. and Crosby, B. C. (1992). *Leadership for the Common Good: Tackling Public Problems in a Shared-Power World*. San Francisco: Jossey-Bass.

Buchanan, M. (2000). *Ubiquity: Why Catastrophes Happen*. New York: Three Rivers Press.

Burke, J. P., Greenstein, F. I., Berman, L., and Immerman, R. H. (1989). *How Presidents Test Reality: Decisions on Vietnam, 1954 and 1965*. New York: Russell Sage Foundation.

Busenberg, G. J. (2001). Learning in Organizations and Public Policy. *Journal of Public Policy*, 21(2): 173–89.

Bush, G. W. (2011). *Decision Points*. New York: Broadway Books.

Butler, J. (2009). *Frames of War*. London: Verso.

Buzan, B., Waever, O., and de Wilde, J. (1998). *Security: A New Framework for Analysis*. London: Lynne Rienner.

Bytzek, E. (2008). Flood Response and Political Survival: Gerhard Schröder and the 2002 Elbe Flood in Germany. In R. A. Boin, A. McConnell, and P. 't Hart, eds., *Governing After Crisis: The Politics of Investigation, Accountability and Learning*. Cambridge: Cambridge University Press, 85–114.

Caiden, G. E. (1991) *Administrative Reform Comes of Age*. New York: Walter de Gruyter.

Carley, K. M. and Harrald, J. R. (1997). Organizational Learning under Fire: Theory and Practice. *American Behavioral Scientist*, 40(3): 310–32.

Carpenter, M. A. (ed.) (2012). *The Handbook of Research on Top Management Teams*. Cheltenham: Edward Elgar.

Carpenter, M . A., Geletkanycz, M., and Sanders, W. (2004). Upper Echelons Theory Revisited: Antecedents, Elements and Consequences of Top Management Team Composition. *Journal of Management*, 30(6): 749–78.

Carrel, L. F. (2000). Training Civil Servants for Crisis Management. *Journal of Contingencies and Crisis Management*, 8(4): 192–96.

Charles, M. T. (2001). The Fall of TWA Flight 800. In U. Rosenthal, R. A. Boin, and L. K. Comfort, eds., *Managing Crises: Threats, Dilemmas, Opportunities*. Springfield: Charles C. Thomas, 216–34.

Chisholm, D. (1989). *Coordination Without Hierarchy: Informal Structures in Multi-Organizational Systems*. Berkeley: University of California Press.

Chong, D. and Druckman, J. N. (2007). Framing Theory. *Annual Review of Political Science*, 10: 103–26.

Chubb, P. (2014). *Power Failure: The Inside Story of Climate Politics under Rudd and Gillard*. Melbourne: Black Inc. Agenda.

Clarke, A. (2000). *Thames Safety Inquiry: Final Report*. London: Her Majesty's Stationary Office.

Clarke, L. (1999). *Mission Improbable: Using Fantasy Documents to Tame Disasters*. Chicago: University of Chicago Press.

(2005). *Worst Cases: Terror and Catastrophe in the Popular Imagination*. Chicago: University of Chicago Press.

Coates, J. (2012). *The Hour Between Dog and Wolf: Risk Taking, Gut Feelings and the Biology of Boom and Bust*. New York: Penguin Press.

Cobb, R. W. and Primo, D. M. (2003). *The Plane Truth: Airline Crashes, the Media and Transportation Policy*. Washington, DC: Brookings Institution.

Cobb, R. W. and Ross, M. H. (eds.) (1997). *Cultural Strategies of Agenda Denial: Avoidance, Attack and Redefinition*. Lawrence: University Press of Kansas.

Combs, J. E. (1980). *Dimensions of Political Drama*. Santa Monica: Goodyear.

Comfort, L. K. (1989). The San Salvador earthquake. In U. Rosenthal, M. T. Charles, and P. 't Hart, eds., *Coping with Crises: The Management of Disasters, Riots and Terrorism*. Illinois: Charles C. Thomas.

Comfort, L., Boin, R. A., and Demchak, C. (eds) (2010) *Designing Resilience*. Pittsburgh: University of Pittsburgh Press.

Committee of Privy Counsellors (2004). *Review on Intelligence of Weapons of Mass Destruction*. London: The Stationery Office.

Coombs, W. T. (2007). *Ongoing Crisis Communication: Planning, Managing, and Responding*. 2nd ed. London: Sage.

(2015). *Ongoing Crisis Communication: Planning, Managing and Responding*. 4th ed. London: Sage.

Coombs, W. T. and Holladay, S. J. (eds.) (2009). *The Handbook of Crisis Communication*. Malden, MA: Wiley-Blackwell.

Cortell, A. P. and Peterson, S. (1999). Altered States: Explaining Domestic Institutional Change. *British Journal of Political Science*, 29(1): 177–203.

Crandall, C. S., Bahns, A. J., Warner, R., and Schaller, M. (2011). Stereotypes as Justifications of Prejudice. *Personality and Social Psychology Bulletin*, 37(11): 1488–98.

Cuny, F. L. (1983). *Disasters and Development*. New York: Oxford University Press.

Cyert R. M., March J. G,. and Clarkson, G. P. E. (1963). *A Behavioral Theory of the Firm*. Englewood Cliffs, NJ: Prentice-Hall.

De Vries, M. (2004). Framing Crises: Response Patterns to Explosions in Fireworks Factories. *Administration and Society*, 36(5): 594–614.

Dekker, S. and Hansén, D. (2004). Learning under Pressure: The Effects of Politicization on Organizational Learning in Public Bureaucracies. *Journal of Public Administration Research and Theory*, 14(2): 211–30.

Deutsch, K. W. (1966). *The Nerves of Government: Models for Political Communication and Control*. New York: The Free Press.

Deverell, E. (2009). Crises as Learning Triggers: Exploring a Conceptual Framework of Crisis-Induced Learning. *Journal of Contingencies and Crisis Management*, 17(3): 179–88.

(2010). *Crisis-Induced Learning in the Public Sector Organizations*. Stockholm: Elanders Sverige.

Deverell, E. and Hansén, D. (2009). Learning from Crises and Major Incidents: From Post-Crisis Fantasy Documents to Actual Learning in the Heat of Crisis. *Journal of Contingencies and Crisis Management*, 17(3): 143–45.

Deverell, E. and Olsson, E. K. (2011). Hur organisationsteori påverkar strategi och anpassningsförmåga i kriser. In J. Falkheimer and M. Heide, eds., *Strategisk Kommunikation: Forskning och praktik*. Lund: Studentlitteratur, 169–90.

Devine, P. G., Hamilton, D. L., and Ostrom, T. M. (eds.) (1994). *Social Cognition: Impact on Social Psychology*. San Diego: Academic Press.

Dijksterhuis, A. and Aarts, H. (2010). Goals, Attention, and (Un)Consciousness. *Annual Review of Psychology*, 61, 467–90.

Dilulio, J. (1994). Principled Agents: The Cultural Bases of Behavior in a Federal Government Bureaucracy. *Journal of Public Administration Research and Theory*, 4(3): 227–318.

Douglas, M. (1992). *Risk and Blame: Essays in Cultural Theory*. London: Routledge.

Douglas, M. and Wildavsky, A. (1982). *Risk and Culture: An Essay on the Selection of Environmental Dangers*. Berkeley: University of California Press.

Dowding, K., Berlinski, S., and Dewan, T. (2012). *Accounting for Ministers: Scandal and Survival in British Government, 1945–2007*. Cambridge: Cambridge University Press.

Drabek, T. E. and Quarantelli, E. L. (1967). Scapegoats, Villains, and Disasters. *Transaction*, 4(4): 12–17.

Drake, B. (2013). A Year after Newtown, Little Change in Public Opinion on Guns. Pew Research Center. www.pewresearch.org/fact-tank/2013/12/12/a-year-after-newtown-little-change-in-public-opinion-on-guns/ (accessed June 15, 2015).

Drennan, L., McConnell, A., and Stark, A. (2014). *Risk and Crisis Management in the Public Sector*. London: Routledge.

Dror, Y. (1986). *Policymaking under Adversity*. New Brunswick, NJ: Transaction Books.

(2014). *Avant-Garde Politician: Leaders for a New Epoch*. New York: Westphalia Press.

Dryzek, J. S. (1992). The Good Society versus the State: Freedom and Necessity in Political Innovation. *Journal of Politics*, 54(2): 518–40.

Dubrin, A. (ed.) (2013). *Handbook of Research on Crisis Leadership in Organizations*. Cheltenham: Edward Elgar.

Dynes, R. R. (1970). *Organized Behaviour in Disaster*. Lexington: D. C. Heath and Company.

(2006). Community Processes: Coordination. In H. Rodriquez, E. L. Quarantelli, and R. R. Dynes, eds., *Handbook of Disaster Research*. New York: Springer, 217–33.

Dyson, S. B. and Preston, T. (2003). *Lenses for Leaders: The Role of Complexity and Prior Expertise in Shaping the Use of Analogy in Foreign Policy Decision Making*. Pullman: Department of Political Science, Washington State University.

Dyson, S. B. and 't Hart, P. (2013). Crisis Management. In L. Huddy, O. D. Sears, and J. S. Levy, eds., *Oxford Handbook of Political Psychology*. New York: Oxford University Press.

Edelman, M. J. (1964). *The Symbolic Uses of Politics*. Urbana: University of Illinois Press.

(1971). *Politics as Symbolic Action: Mass Arousal and Quiescence.* Chicago: Markham.

(1977). *Political Language: Words that Succeed and Policies that Fail.* New York: Academic Press.

(1988). *Constructing the Political Spectacle.* Chicago: The University of Chicago Press.

Eichengreen, B. (2002). *Financial Crises: And What to Do about Them.* New York: Oxford University Press.

Ekengren, M. and Sundelius, B. (2004). National Foreign Policy Co-Ordination. In H. Sjursen, W. Carlsnaes, and B. White, eds., *Contemporary European Foreign Policy.* London: Sage Publications, 110–22.

Elder, C. D. and Cobb, R. W. (1983). *The Political Uses of Symbols.* New York: Longman.

Ellemers, N., De Wilder, D., and Haslam, S. A. (2004). Motivating Individuals and Groups at Work: A Social Identity Perspective on Leadership and Group Performance. *Academy of Management Review,* 29(3): 459–78.

Ellis, R. J. (1994). *Presidential Lightning Rods: The Politics of Blame Avoidance.* Lawrence: University of Kansas Press.

Elster, J. (2004). *Closing the Books: Transitional Justice in Historical Perspective.* Cambridge: Cambridge University Press.

Engel, K., Frerks, G., Velotti, L, Warner, J., and Weijs, B. (2014). Flood Disaster Subcultures in the Netherlands: The Parishes of Borgharen and Itteren. *Natural Hazards,* 73(2): 859–82.

Entman, R. M. (1993). Framing: Toward a Clarification of a Fractured Paradigm. *Journal of Communication,* 43(4): 51–58.

Erikson, K. T. (1976). *Everything in Its Path: Destruction of Community in the Buffalo Creek Flood.* New York: Simon and Schuster.

(1994). *A New Species of Trouble: Explorations in Disaster, Trauma and Community.* New York: W. W. Norton.

Eriksson, J. (2001). Introduction. In J. Eriksson, ed., *Threat Politics: New Perspectives on Security, Risk and Crisis Management.* Aldershot: Ashgate, 8–16.

Etheredge, L. S. (1985). *Can Governments Learn? American Foreign Policy and Central American Revolutions.* New York: Pergamon Press.

Fearn-Banks, K. (1996). *Crisis Communications: A Casebook Approach.* Mahwah: Lawrence Erlbaum Associates.

Feldman, M. S. and March, J. G. (1981). Information in Organizations as Signal and Symbol. *Administrative Science Quarterly,* 26(2): 174–86.

(1988). Information in Organizations as Signal and Symbol. In J. G. March, ed., *Decisions and Organizations.* Oxford: Blackwell, 409–28.

Fernandez, A. and Mazza, C. (2014). *Boards under Crisis: Board Action under Pressure.* New York: Palgrave.

Fink, S. (2013). *Crisis Communications: The Definitive Guide to Managing the Message.* New York: McGraw-Hill.

Fiol, C. M. and Lyles, M. A. (1985). Organizational Learning. *Academy of Management Review,* 10(4): 803–13.

Fischer, P., Greitemeyer, T., Morton, T. Kastenmüller, A., Postmes, T., Frey, D., Kubitzki, J., and Odenwälder, J. (2009). The Racing-Game Effect: Why Do Video Racing Games Increase Risk-Taking Inclinations? *Personality and Social Psychology Bulletin*, 35(10): 1395–409.

Fleischer, J. (2013). Time and Crisis. *Public Management Review*, 15(3): 313–29.

Flin, R. (1996). *Sitting in the Hot Seat: Leaders and Teams for Critical Incidents*. West Sussex: Wiley.

Fortress (2014). Deliverable D3.1: Crisis Case Studies of Cascading and/or Crossborder Disasters. Report. http://fortress-project.eu/wp-content/uploads/2014/04/FORTRESS-D3.1_Crisis-case-studies-of-cascading-and-or-crossborder-disasters.pdf (accessed August 8, 2016).

Furedi, F. (2005). *The Politics of Fear: Beyond Left and Right*. London: Continuum.

Galaz, V., Moberg, F., Olsson, E. K., Paglia, E., and Parker, C. (2011). Institutional and Political Leadership Dimensions of Cascading Ecological Crises. *Public Administration*, 89(2): 361–80.

George, A. L. (1986). The Impact of Crisis-Induced Stress on Decision Making. In F. Solomon and R. Q. Marston, eds., *The Medical Implications of Nuclear War*. Washington, DC: National Academy Press, 529–52.

  (1993). *Bridging the Gap: Theory and Practice in Foreign Policy*. Washington, DC: United States Institute of Peace Press.

George, A. L. and Stern, E. K. (2002). Harnessing Conflict in Foreign Policy Making: From Devil's to Multiple Advocacy. *Presidential Studies Quarterly*, 32(3): 484–508.

Gilpin, D. R. and Murphy, P. J. (2008). *Crisis Management in a Complex World*. Oxford: Oxford University Press.

Glad, B. (1980). *Jimmy Carter: In Search of the Great White House*. New York: W. W. Norton.

Gladwell, M. (2000). *The Tipping Point*. Boston: Little, Brown.

  (2005). *Blink: The Power of Thinking Without Thinking*. New York: Brown & Co.

Goldfinch, S. and 't Hart, P. (2003). Leadership and Institutional Reform: Engineering Macroeconomic Policy Change in Australia. *Governance*, 16(2): 235–70.

Goode, E. and Ben-Yehuda, N. (1994). *Moral Panics: The Social Construction of Deviance*. Oxford: Blackwell.

Graber, D. A., McQuail, D., and Norris, P. (1998). Introduction: Political Communication in a Democracy. In D. A. Graber, D. McQuail, and P. Norris, eds., *The Politics of News: The News of Politics*. Washington, DC: CQ Press, 1–16.

Griffin-Padgett, R. and Allison, D. (2010). Making a Case for Restorative Rhetoric: Mayor Rudolph Giuliani and Mayor Ray Nagin's Response to Disaster. *Communication Monographs*, 77(3): 376–92.

Grimm, S. and Schneider, S. (2011). Predicting Social Tipping Points: Current Research and the Way Forward. *Discussion Paper 8/2011*. Bonn: German Development Institute.

Grönvall, J. (2001). Mad Cow Disease: The Role of Experts and European Crisis Management. In U. Rosenthal, R. A. Boin, and L.K. Comfort, eds., *Managing Crises: Threats, Dilemmas, Opportunities*. Springfield, IL: Charles C. Thomas.

Gundel, S. (2005). Towards a New Typology of Crises. *Journal of Contingencies and Crisis Management*, 13(3): 106–15.

Haas, E. R. (1990). *When Knowledge Is Power: Three Models of Change in International Organizations*. Berkeley: University of California Press.

Hajer, M. (2009). *Authoritative Governance*. Oxford: Oxford University Press.

Haldeman, H. R. and Ambrose, S. E. (1994). *The Haldeman Diaries: Inside the Nixon White House*. New York: Putnam.

Hall, P. A. (1993). Policy Paradigms, Social Learning and the State: The Case of Economic Policy Making in Britain. *Comparative Politics*, 25(3): 275–96.

Halper, T. (1971). *Foreign Policy Crises: Appearance and Reality in Decision Making*. Columbus: Charles E. Merrill.

Hamilton, N. (2011). *Bill Clinton: An American Journey*. New York: Random House.

(2012). *Bill Clinton: Mastering the Presidency*. New York: Random House.

Hansén, D. and Stern, E. K. (2001). From Crisis to Trauma: The Palme Assassination Case. In U. Rosenthal, R. A. Boin, and L. C. Comfort, eds., *Managing Crises: Threats, Dilemmas, Opportunities*. Springfield, IL: Charles C. Thomas, 177–99.

Hargrove, E. C. (1994). *Prisoners of Myth: The Leadership of the Tennessee Valley Authority*. Princeton: Princeton University Press.

(1998). *The President as a Leader: Appealing to the Better Angels of Our Nature*. Lawrence: University of Kansas Press.

't Hart, P. (1993). Symbols, Rituals and Power: The Lost Dimensions of Crisis Management. *Journal of Contingencies and Crisis Management*, 1(1): 29–43.

(1994). *Groupthink in Government: A Study of Small Groups and Policy Failure*. Baltimore: Johns Hopkins University Press.

(2013). After Fukushima: Reflections on Risk and Institutional Learning in an Era of Mega-Crises. *Public Administration*, 91(1): 101–13.

(2014). *Understanding Public Leadership*. Houndmills: Palgrave.

't Hart, P. and Pijnenburg, B. (1988). *Het Heizeldrama: Rampzalig Organiseren en Kritieke Beslissingen*. Alphen aan de Rijn: Samsom.

't Hart, P. and Rijpma, J. (eds.) (1997). *Crises in het Nieuws: Samenspel en Tegenspel Tussen Overheid en Media*. Alphen aan den Rijn: Samsom.

't Hart, P., Stern, E. K. and Sundelius, B. (eds.) (1997). *Beyond Groupthink: Political Group Dynamics and Foreign Policy Making*. Ann Arbor: University of Michigan Press.

Hay, C. (2002). *Political Analysis: A Critical Introduction*. London: Palgrave Macmillan.

Hearit, K. M. (2006). *Crisis Management by Apology: Corporate Response to Allegations of Wrongdoing*. Mahwah, NJ: Lawrence Erlbaum.

Heath, R. L. (2004). Telling a Story: A Narrative Approach to Communication During Crisis. In D. P. Millar and R. L. Heath, eds., *Responding to Crisis*. Mahwah, NJ: Erlbaum, 167–87.

Heclo, H. (1974). *Modern Social Politics in Britain and Sweden*. New Haven: Yale University Press.

Heinzelman, J. and Waters, C. (2010). *Crowdsourcing Crisis Information in Disaster-Affected Haiti*. New York: U.S. Institute of Peace.

Henry, R. A. (2000). *You'd Better Have a Hose if You Want to Put Out the Fire*. Windsor: Gollywobbler Productions.

Herek, G. M., Janis, I. L., and Huth, P. (1987). Decision Making during International Crisis: Is Quality of Process Related to Outcome? *Journal of Conflict Resolution*, 31(2): 203–26.

Hermann, C. F. (1963). Some Consequences of Crisis Which Limit the Viability of Organizations. *Administrative Science Quarterly*, 8(1): 61–82.

(ed.) (1972). *International Crises: Insights from Behavioral Research*. New York: The Free Press.

Hermann, M. G. (1979). Indicators of Stress in Policy Makers during Foreign Policy Crises. *Political Psychology*, 1(1): 27–46.

Hermann, M. G. and Hagan, J. (1998). International Decision Making: Leadership Matters. *Foreign Policy*, 110, 124–37.

Helsloot, I., Boin, A., Jacobs, B., and Comfort, L. C. (eds.) (2012). *Mega-crises: Understanding the Prospects, Nature, Characteristics and Effects of Cataclysmic Events*. Springfield, IL: Charles C. Thomas.

Hilliard, M. (2000). *Public Crisis Management*. Lincoln: Writer's Club Press.

Holsti, O. R. (1972). *Crisis, Escalation and War*. Montreal: McGill-Queens University Press.

(1979). Theories of Crisis Decision-Making. In P. G. Lauren, ed., *Diplomacy: New Approaches in History, Theory, and Policy*. New York: The Free Press, 99–136.

Honig, J. W. (2001). Avoiding War, Inviting Defeat: The Srebrenica Crisis, July 1995. In U. Rosenthal, R. A. Boin, and L. K. Comfort, eds., *Managing Crises: Threats, Dilemmas, Opportunities*. Springfield: Charles C. Thomas, 61–73.

Honig, J. W. and Both, N. (1997). *Srebrenica: Record of a War Crime*. New York: Penguin.

Hood, C. (2011). *The Blame Game: Spin, Bureaucracy and Self-Preservation in Government*. Princeton: Princeton University Press.

Hood, C., Jennings, W., Hogwood, B., and Beeston, C. (2007). Fighting Fires in Testing Times: Exploring a Staged Response Hypothesis for Blame Management in Two Exam Fiasco Cases. *CARR Discussion Papers*, DP 42. London: Centre for Analysis of Risk and Regulation, London School of Economics and Political Science.

Hopkins, A, (ed.) (2009). *Learning from High Reliability Organisations*. Sydney: CCH Australia Ltd.

Houghton, D. P. (2001). *U.S. Foreign Policy and the Iran Hostage Crisis*. Cambridge: Cambridge University Press.

Howitt, A. M. and Leonard, H. B. (eds.) (2009). *Managing Crises: Responses to Large-Scale Emergencies*. New York: CQ Press.

Hoyt, P. D. and Garrison, J. A. (1997). Political Manipulation within the Small Group of Foreign Policy Advisers in the Carter Administration.

In P. 't Hart, E. K. Stern, and B. Sundelius, eds., *Beyond Group-Think: Political Group Dynamics and Foreign Policymaking*. Ann Arbor: University of Michigan Press, 249–74.

Independent Investigation Commission on the Fukushima Nuclear Accident (2014). *The Fukushima Daiichi Nuclear Power Station Disaster*. London: Routledge.

Information Resources Management Association (2014). *Crisis Management: Concepts, Methodologies, Tools, and Applications*. Hershey, PA: Information Science Reference.

Iyengar, S. (1996). Framing Responsibility For Political Issues. *The Annals of the American Academy of Political and Social Sciences*, 546: 59–70.

Jackall, R. (2009). *Moral Mazes: The World of Corporate Managers*. New York: Oxford University Press.

Jacobs, B. D. (1989). The Brixton Riots: London 1981. In U. Rosenthal, M. T. Charles, and P. 't Hart, eds., *Coping with Crises: The Management of Disasters, Riots and Terrorism*. Springfield, IL: Charles C Thomas, 340–66.

James, E. H., Wooten, L. P., and Dushek, K. (2011). Crisis Management: Informing a New Leadership Research Agenda. *The Academy of Management Annals*, 5(1): 455–93.

Janis, I. L. (1982). *Groupthink*. Boston: Houghton Mifflin.
    (1989). *Crucial Decisions: Leadership in Policymaking and Crisis Management*. New York: The Free Press.

Janis, I. L. and Mann, L. (1977). *Decision Making: A Psychological Analysis of Conflict, Choice and Commitment*. New York: The Free Press.

Jaques, T. (2014). *Issues and Crisis Management: Exploring Issues, Crises, Risk and Reputation*. Oxford: Oxford University Press.

Jenkin, G. L., Signal, L., and Thomson, G. (2011). Framing Obesity: The Framing Contest between Industry and Public Health at the New Zealand Inquiry into Obesity. *Obesity Reviews*, 12(12): 1022–30.

Jervis, R. (1976). *Perception and Misperception in International Politics*. Princeton: Princeton University Press.
    (1992). Political Implications of Loss Aversion. *Political Psychology*, 13(2): 187–204.

Jetten, J. and Hornsey, M. J. (eds.) (2011). *Rebels in Groups: Dissent, Deviance, Difference and Defiance*. UK: Wiley-Blackwell.

Johnson-Cartee, K. (2005). *News Narrative and News Framing: Constructing Political Reality*. Lanham: Rowman & Littlefield.

Johnston, E., Hicks, D., Nan, N., and Auer, J. (2011). Managing the Inclusion Process in Collaborative Governance. *Journal of Public Administration Research and Theory*, 21(4): 699–721.

Judah, B. (2014). *Fragile Empire: How Russia Fell in and out of Love with Vladimir Putin*. New Haven: Yale University Press.

Juergensemeyer, M. (2003). *Terrorism in the Mind of God*. Berkley: University of California Press.

Kaarbo, J. (2008). Coalition Cabinet Decision Making: Institutional and Personal Factors. *International Studies Review*, 10(1): 57–86.

(2012). *Coalition Politics and Cabinet Decision Making*. Ann Arbor: University of Michigan Press.

Kaase, M. and Newton, K. (1995). *Beliefs in Government*. Oxford: Oxford University Press.

Kahneman, D. (2011). *Thinking, Fast and Slow*. New York: Farrar, Straus and Giroux.

Kahneman, D. and Klein, G. (2009). Conditions for Intuitive Expertise: A Failure to Disagree. *American Psychologist*, 64(6): 515–26.

Kam, E. (1988). *Surprise Attack*. Cambridge, MA: Harvard University Press.

Kaplan, S. (2008). Framing Contests: Strategy Making Under Uncertainty. *Organization Science*, 19(5): 729–52.

Karyotis, G. and Gerodimos, R. (2015). *The Politics of Extreme Austerity: Greece in the Eurozone Crisis*. London: Palgrave.

Keane, J. (2009). *Life and Death of Democracy*. New York: Simon and Schuster.

Keeler, J. T. S. (1993). Opening the Window for Reform: Mandates, Crises and Extraordinary Policy Making. *Comparative Political Studies*, 25(4): 433–86.

Keen, D. (2008). *Complex Emergencies*. Malden, MA: Polity Press.

Keim, M. and Nojie, E. (2011). Emergent Use of Social Media: A New Age of Opportunity for Disaster Resilience. *American Journal of Disaster Medicine*, 6(1): 47–54.

Kendra, J. M. and Wachtendorf, T. (2003). Elements of Resilience in the World Trade Center Disaster: Reconstituting the Emergency Operations Center. *Disasters*, 27(1): 37–53.

Kertzer, D. I. (1988). *Ritual, Politics and Power*. New Haven: Yale University Press.

Kettl, D. F. (2003). Contingent Coordination: Practical and Theoretical Puzzles for Homeland Security. *American Review of Public Administration*, 33 (3): 253–77.

(2004). *System under Stress: Homeland Security and American Politics*. Washington, DC: CQ Press.

Key, V. O. (1961). *Public Opinion and American Democracy*. New York: Knopf.

(1966). *The Responsible Electorate: Rationality in Presidential Voting*. Cambridge, MA: Harvard University Press.

Kingdon, J. W. (1995). *Agendas, Alternatives, and Public Policies*. New York: HarperCollins.

Kirschenbaum, A. (2003). *Chaos Organization and Disaster Management*. New York: Marcel Dekker.

Klein, G. (1999). *Sources of Power*. Cambridge, MA: MIT Press.

(2001). *Sources of Power: How People Make Decisions*. 7th ed. London: The MIT Press.

(2009). *Streetlights and Shadows*. Cambridge, MA: MIT Press.

Klein, N. (2007). *The Shock Doctrine: The Rise of Disaster Capitalism*. New York: Metropolitan.

Klijn, E. H., Edelenbos, J., and Steijn, B. (2010). Trust in Governance Networks: Its Impact and Outcomes. *Administration and Society*, 42(2): 193–221.

Klinenberg, E. (2002). *Heat Wave: A Social Autopsy of Disaster in Chicago*. Chicago: University of Chicago Press.

Koliba, C., Zia, A., and Mills, R. (2011). Accountability in Governance Networks: An Assessment of Public, Private, and Nonprofit Emergency Management Practices Following Hurricane Katrina. *Public Administration Review*, 71(2): 210–20.

Koppenjan, J. and Klijn, E. (2004). *Managing Uncertainties in Networks*. London: Routledge.

Kott, A. (ed.) (2006). *Information Warfare and Organizational Decision Making*. New York: Artech House.

Kuipers, S. (2006). *The Crisis Imperative: Crisis Rhetoric and Welfare State Reform in Belgium and the Netherlands in the Early 1990s*. Amsterdam: Amsterdam University Press.

Kuipers, S. and 't Hart, P. (2014). Accounting for Crises. In M. Bovens, T. Schillemans, and R. Goodin, eds., *The Oxford Handbook of Public Accountability*. Oxford: Oxford University Press, 589–602.

Kurtz, R. S. and Browne, W. P. (2004). Crisis Management, Crisis Response: An Introduction to the Symposium. *Review of Policy Research*, 21(2): 141–43.

Kuypers, J. A., Cooper, S. D., and Althouse, M. T. (2012). George W. Bush, the American Press, and the Initial Framing of the War on Terror after 9/11. In E. R. Denton, ed., *The George W. Bush Presidency: A Rhetorical Perspective*. Lanham, MD: Lexington Books, 89–112.

LaFasto, F. and Larson, C. (2001). *When Teams Work Best*. London: Sage.

Lagadec, P. (1997). Learning Processes for Crisis Management in Complex Organizations. *Journal of Contingencies and Crisis Management*, 5(1): 24–31.

(2004). Understanding the French 2003 Heat Wave Experience: Beyond the Heat, a Multi-Layered Challenge. *Journal of Contingencies and Crisis Management*, 12(4): 160–69.

Lambright, K., Mischen, P., and Laramee, C. (2010). Building Trust in Public and Nonprofit Networks: Personal, Dyadic, and Third-Party Influences. *American Review of Public Administration*, 40(1): 64–82.

Lanzara, G. F. (1998). Self-Destructive Processes in Institution Building and Some Modest Countervailing Mechanisms. *European Journal of Political Research*, 33(1): 1–39.

LaPorte, T. R. (1996). High Reliability Organizations: Unlikely, Demanding, and At Risk. *Journal of Contingencies and Crisis Management*, 4(2): 60–71.

(August 6–10, 2003). Anticipating Rude Surprises: Reflections on 'Crisis Management' Without End. Paper presented at the Conference on Transatlantic Crisis Management. New York: Minnowbrook Conference Center.

Larsson, S., Olsson, E. K., and Ramberg, B. (eds.) (2005). *Crisis Decision Making in the European Union*. Stockholm: Swedish National Defence College.

Lazarus, R. S. (1966). *Psychological Stress and the Coping Process*. New York: McGraw-Hill.

Lebow, R. N. (1981). *Between Peace and War: The Nature of International Crisis*. Baltimore: Johns Hopkins University Press.

Lebow, R. N. and Stein, J. G. (1994). *We All Lost the Cold War*. Princeton: Princeton University Press.

Lee, S. (2006). *When the Levees Broke*. USA: HBO Home Video.

Leemans, A. F. (1976). *The Management of Change in Government*. The Hague: Martinus Nijhoff.

Leonard, H. B. and Howitt, A. M. (2013). Boston Marathon Bombing Response. *Crisis Response Journal*, 8(4): 18–21.

Leveson, N. (1995). *Safeware: System Safety and Computers*. Reading: Addison Wesley.

Lewis, D. (1997). *Hidden Agendas: Politics, Law and Disorder*. London: Hamish Hamilton.

Libertore, A. (1993). Chernobyl Comes to Italy: The Reciprocal Relationships of Radiation Experts, Government Policies, and the Media. In A. Barker and G. Peters, eds., *The Politics of Expert Advice: Creating, Using and Manipulating Scientific Knowledge for Public Policy*. Edinburgh: University of Edinburgh Press, 33–48.

Lindblom, C. E. (1979). Still Muddling, Not Yet Through. *Public Administration Review*, 39(6): 517–29.

Lindgren, K. (2003). *Vad Styr Ledaren? Om beslutsfattare och policyforandring i sakerhetspolitiska kriser*. PhD diss., Uppsala University.

Linwood, K. (2014). *Typhoons and Landslides: Risk Prediction, Crisis Management and Environmental Impacts*. Hauppauge: Nova Science.

Linz, J. J. and Stepan, A. C. (eds.) (1978). *The Breakdown of Democratic Regimes*. Baltimore: Johns Hopkins University Press.

Lipsky, M. (1980). *Street-Level Bureaucracy: Dilemmas of the Individual in Public Service*. New York: Russell Sage Foundation.

Lipsky, M. and Olson, D. J. (1977). *Commission Politics: The Processing of Racial Crisis in America*. New Brunswick: Transaction Books.

Littlefield, R., and Quenette, A. (2007). Crisis Leadership and Hurricane Katrina: The Portrayal of Authority by the Media in Natural Disasters. *Journal of Applied Communication Research*, 35(1): 26–47.

Lloyd, J. (2004). *What the Media are Doing to Our Politics*. London: Constable.

Lodge, M. and Wegrich, K. (eds.) (2012). *Executive Politics in Times of Crises*. Basingstoke: Palgrave.

Longley, J. and Pruitt, D. G. (1980). Groupthink: A Critique of Janis's Theory. *Review of Personality and Social Psychology*, 1: 74–93.

MacFarlane, R. and Leigh, M. (2014). Information Management and Shared Situational Awareness: Ideas, Tools and Good Practice in Multi-Agency Crisis and Emergency Management. *Emergency Planning College Occasional Papers*, 12. www.epcollege.com/EPC/media/MediaLibrary/Knowledge% 20Hub%20Documents/J%20Thinkpieces/Occ12-Paper.pdf (accessed May 12, 2015).

Mackiewicz, W. W. (2008). *Winning the War of Words: Selling the War on Terror from Afghanistan to Iraq*. Westport: Praeger.

Mackintosh, S. P. M. (2014). Crises and Paradigm Shift: A Response to Critics. *The Political Quarterly*, 86(1): 3–6.

Marais, K., Dulac, N., and Leveson, N. (March 28–31, 2004). *Beyond Normal Accidents and High Reliability Organizations: The Need for an Alternative Approach to Safety in Complex Systems*. Paper presented at the Engineering Systems Division Symposium. Cambridge, MA: MIT Press.

March, J. G. (2010). *The Ambiguities of Experience*. Ithaca: Cornell University Press.

(ed.) (1988). *Decisions and Organizations*. Oxford: Blackwell.

May, E. R. (1972). *"Lessons" of the Past*. New York: Oxford University Press.

McGuire, M., Brudney, J., and Gazley, B. (2010). The "New Emergency Management": Applying the Lessons from Collaborative Governance to Twenty-First-Century Emergency Planning. In R. O'Leary, D. Van Slyke, and S. Kim, eds., *The Future of Public Administration Around the World*. Washington DC: Georgetown University Press.

McGuire, M. and Silvia, C. (2010). The Effect of Problem Severity, Managerial and Organizational Capacity, and Agency Structure on Intergovernmental Collaboration: Evidence From Local Emergency Management. *Public Administration Review*, 70(2): 279–88.

Meijer, A. J. and Thaens, M. (2013). Social Media Strategies: Understanding the Differences Between North American Police Departments. *Government Information Quarterly*, 30(4): 343–50.

Meltsner, A. J. (1990). *Rules for Rulers: The Politics of Advice*. Philadelphia: Temple University Press.

Meyer, T. (2002). *Media Democracy: How the Media Colonize Politics*. Cambridge: Polity Press.

Miller, A. (2001). The Los Angeles Riots: A Study in Crisis Paralysis. In U. Rosenthal, R. A. Boin, and L. K. Comfort, eds., *Managing Crises: Threats, Dilemmas, Opportunities*. Springfield: Charles C. Thomas, 49–60.

Miller, A., Roberts, S., and LaPoe, V. (2014). *Oil & Water: Media Lessons from Hurricane Katrina and the Deepwater Horizon Disaster*. Jackson: University Press of Mississippi.

Mintz, A. and DeRouen, K. (2010). *Understanding Foreign Policy Decision-Making*. Cambridge: Cambridge University Press.

Mitroff, I. I. and Pauchant, T. C. (1990). *We're So Big and Powerful Nothing Bad Can Happen to Us*. New York: Carol Publishing Corporation.

Mitroff, I. I. and Silver, A. (2010). *Dirty Rotten Strategies: How We Trick Ourselves and Others Into Solving the Wrong Problems Precisely*. Stanford: Stanford University Press.

Moon, J. (1995). Innovative Leadership and Policy Change: Lessons from Thatcher. *Governance*, 8(1): 1–25.

Moore, J. (1998). *Hard Choices: Moral Dilemmas in Humanitarian Intervention*. Lanham: Rowman and Littlefield.

Moskowitz, H., Drnevich, P., Ersoy, O., Altinkemer, K., and Chaturvedi, A. (2011). Using Real-Time Decision Tools to Improve Distributed Decision-Making Capabilities in High-Magnitude Crisis Situations. *Decision Sciences*, 42(2): 477–93.

Moynihan, D. (2008). Learning under Uncertainty: Networks in Crisis Management. *Public Administration Review*, 68(2): 350–61.

(2009). The Network Governance of Crisis Response: Case Studies of Incident Command Systems. *Journal of Public Administration Research and Theory*, 19(4): 895–915.

(2012). A Theory of Culture-Switching: Leadership and Red Tape during Hurricane Katrina. *Public Administration*, 90(4): 851–68.

Mulgan, R. (2014). Accountability Deficits. In M. Bovens, R. E. Goodin, and T. Schillemans (eds.): *Oxford Handbook of Public Accountability*. Oxford: Oxford University Press, 545–59.

National Commission on the BP Deepwater Horizon Oil Spill and Offshore Drilling (2011). Deep Water: The Gulf Oil Disaster and the Future of Offshore Drilling. January 2011. Report to the President. www.gpo.gov/fdsys/pkg/GPO-OILCOMMISSION/pdf/GPO-OILCOMMISSION.pdf. (accessed June 10, 2015).

National Commission on Terrorist Attacks (2004). *The 9/11 Commission Report*. New York: W. W. Norton & Company.

Nemeth, C. and Goncalo, J. (2004). Influence and Persuasion in Small Groups. http://escholarship.org/uc/item/9n8060j4 (accessed July 3, 2015).

Neustadt, R. N. and May, E. R. (1986). *Thinking in Time: The Uses of History for Decision-Makers*. New York: The Free Press.

Nimmo, D. and Combs, J. E. (1985). *Nightly Horrors: Crisis Coverage in Television Network News*. Knoxville: University of Tennessee Press.

(1990). *Mediated Political Realities*. 2nd ed. New York: Longman.

Nisbett, R. and Ross, L. (1980). *Human Inference: Strategies and Shortcomings of Social Judgment*. Englewood Cliffs, NJ: Prentice-Hall.

Nixon, C. (2011). *Fair Cop*. Melbourne: Melbourne University Publishing.

Nobles, M. (2008). *The Politics of Official Apologies*. Cambridge: Cambridge University Press.

Nohrstedt, D. and Hansén, D. (2010). Converging under Pressure? Counterterrorism Policy Developments in the European Union Member States. *Public Administration*, 88(1): 190–210.

Nohrstedt, S. A. (1991). The Information Crisis in Sweden after Chernobyl. *Media, Culture and Society*, 13(4): 477–97.

Nudell, M. and Antokol, N. (1988). *The Handbook for Effective Emergency and Crisis Management*. Lexington, MD: Lexington Books.

OECD (2015). *The Changing Face of Strategic Crisis Management*. Paris: OECD Publishing.

Ohanian, R. (1991). The Impact of Celebrity Spokespersons' Perceived Image on Consumers' Intention to Purchase. *Journal of Advertising Research*, 31(1): 46–54.

Olmeda, J. (2008). A Reversal of Fortune: Blame Games and Framing Contests after the 3/11 Terrorist Attacks in Madrid. In R. A. Boin, A. McConnell, and P. 't Hart, eds., *Governing after Crisis: The Politics of Investigation, Accountability and Learning*. Cambridge: Cambridge University Press.

Olsen, J. P. (2014). Accountability and Ambiguity. In M. Bovens, T. Schillemans, and R. Goodin, eds., *Oxford Handbook of Public Accountability*. Oxford: Oxford University Press, 106–23.

Olsen, J. P. and Peters, B. G. (eds.) (1996). *Lessons from Experience: Experiential Learning in Administrative Reforms in Eight Democracies*. Oslo: Scandinavian University Press.

Olsson, E. K. (2009a). Rule Regimes in News Organization Decision-Making: Explaining Diversity in the Actions of News Organizations during Extraordinary Events. *Journalism*, 10(6): 758–77.

(2009b). Media Crisis Management in Traditional and Digital News Rooms. *Convergence: The International Journal of Research into New Media Technologies*, 15(4): 1–16.

(2014). Crisis Communication in Public Organisations: Dimensions of Crisis Communication Revisited. *Journal of Contingencies and Crisis Management*, 22(2): 113–25.

Olsson, E. K. and Nord, L. (2014). Paving the Way for Crisis Exploitation: The Role of Journalistic Styles and Standards. *Journalism*, 16(3): 341–58.

Olsson, E. K. and Xue, L. (eds.) (2012). *SARS: From East to West*. Lanham, MD: Lexington Books.

Paige, G. D. (1968). *The Korean Decision (June 24–30, 1950)*. New York: The Free Press.

Painter, M. and Peters, B.G. (eds.) (2010). *Tradition and Public Administration*. Basingstoke: Palgrave.

Parker, C. (2014). Complex Negative Events and the Diffusion of Crisis: Lessons from the 2010 and 2011 Icelandic Volcanic Ash Cloud Events. *Geografiska Annaler*, 97: 97–108.

Parker, C. and Dekker, S. (2008). September 11 and Postcrisis Investigation. In R. A. Boin, P. 't Hart, and A. McConnell, eds., *Governing after Crisis: The Politics of Investigation, Accountability and Learning*. Cambridge: Cambridge University Press, 255–84.

Parker, C. and Stern, E. K. (2002). Blindsided? September 11 and the Origins of Strategic Surprise. *Political Psychology*, 23(3): 601–30.

(2005). Bolt from the Blue or Avoidable Failure? Revisiting September 11 and the Origins of Strategic Surprise. *Foreign Policy Analysis*, 1(3): 301–33.

Parker, C., Stern, E., Paglia, E., and Brown, C. (2009). Preventable Catastrophe: The Hurricane Katrina Disaster. *Journal of Contingencies and Crisis Management*, 17(4): 206–20.

Patashnik, E. (2008). *Reforms at Risk*. Princeton: Princeton University Press.

Pauchant, T. C. and Mitroff, I. I. (1992). *Transforming the Crisis-Prone Organization: Preventing Individual, Organizational and Environmental Tragedies*. San Francisco: Jossey-Bass.

Pearce, T. and Fortune, J. (1995). Command and Control in Policing: A Systems Assessment of the Gold, Silver and Bronze Structure. *Journal of Contingencies and Crisis Management*, 3(3): 181–87.

Perrow, C. (1984). *Normal Accidents: Living with High-Risk Technologies*. New York: Basic Books.

(1994). The Limits of Safety: The Enhancement of a Theory of Accidents. *Journal of Contingencies and Crisis Management*, 2(4): 212–20.

(1999). *Normal Accidents: Living with High-Risk Technologies*. 2nd ed. Princeton: Princeton University Press.

Perrow, C. and Guillen, M. F. (1990). *The AIDS Disaster: The Failure of Organizations in New York and the Nation*. New Haven: Yale University Press.

Perry, J. W. and Quarantelli, E. L. (eds.) (2005). *What Is a Disaster? New Answers to Old Questions*. Philadelphia: Exlibris.

Petak, W. J. (ed.) (1985). Emergency Management: A Challenge for Public Administration. *Public Administration Review*, 45: 3–7.

Peters, B. G. and Pierre, J. (eds.) (2001). *Politicians, Bureaucrats, and Administrative Reform*. London: Routledge.

Peterson, R. S., Owens, P. D., Tetlock, P. E., Fan, E. T., and Martorana, P. (1998). Group Dynamics in Top Management Teams: Groupthink, Vigilance, and Alternative Models of Organizational Failure and Success. *Organizational Behavior and Human Decision Processes*, 73(2–3): 272–305.

Petroski, H. (1992). *To Engineer Is Human: The Role of Failure in Successful Design*. New York: Vintage Books.

Pfetsch, B. (1998). Government News Management. In D. Graber, D. McQuail, and P. Norris, eds., *The Politics of News: The News of Politics*. Washington, DC: CQ Press, 70–93.

Pidgeon, N. (1997). The Limits to Safety? Culture, Politics, Learning and Man-made Disasters. *Journal of Contingencies and Crisis Management*, 5(1): 1–14.

    (2010). Systems Thinking, Culture of Reliability and Safety. *Civil Engineering and Environmental Systems*, 27(3): 211–17.

Pierson, P. (2000). Increasing Returns, Path Dependence, and the Study of Politics. *American Political Science Review*, 94(2): 251–67.

Platt, A. (ed.) (1971). *The Politics of Riot Commissions, 1917–1970: A Collection of Official Reports and Critical Essays*. New York: Macmillan.

Pollitt, C. and Bouckaert, G. (2011). *Public Management Reform*. 3rd ed. Oxford: Oxford University Press.

Post, J. M. (1991). The Impact of Crisis-Induced Stress on Policy Makers. In A. George, ed., *Avoiding War: Problems of Crisis Management*. Boulder, CO: Westview Press, 471–94.

    (1993). *When Illness Strikes the Leader: The Dilemma of the Captive King*. New Haven, CT: Yale University Press.

Preston, T. (2001). *The President and His Inner Circle: Leadership Style and the Advisory Process in Foreign Affairs*. New York: Columbia University Press.

    (2008). Weathering the Politics of Responsibility and Blame: The Bush Administration and Its Response to Hurricane Katrina. In R. A. Boin, P. 't Hart, and A. McConnell, eds., *Governing after Crisis: The Politics of Investigation, Accountability and Learning*. Cambridge: Cambridge University Press, 33–61.

Preston, T. and 't Hart, P. (1999). Understanding and Evaluating Bureaucratic Politics: The Nexus Between Political Leaders and Advisory Systems. *Political Psychology*, 20(1): 49–98.

Quarantelli, E. L. (1954). The Nature and Conditions of Panic. *American Journal of Sociology*, 60(3): 267–75.

    (1996). The Future Is Not the Past Repeated: Projecting Disasters in the 21st Century from Present Trends. *Journal of Contingencies and Crisis Management*, 4(4): 228–40.

    (ed.) (1998). *What Is a Disaster? A Dozen Perspectives on the Question*. London: Routledge.

(2001). Sociology of Panic. In N. J. Smelser and P. B. Baltes, eds., *International Encyclopedia of the Social and Behavioral Sciences*. New York: Pergamon.

Rashid, F., Edmonson, A., and Leonard, H. (2013). Leadership Lessons from the Chilean Mine Rescue. *Harvard Business Review*, 91(7–8): 113–19.

Reason, J. (1990). *Human Error*. New York: Cambridge University Press.

Reese, S. and Lewis, S. (2009). Framing the War on Terror: The Internalization of Policy in the U.S. Press. *Journalism*, 10(6): 777–97.

Regester, M. and Larkin, J. (1997). *Risk Issues and Crisis Management: A Casebook of Best Practice*. London: Kogan Page.

Resodihardjo, S. L. (2006). *Institutional Crises and Reform: Constrained Opportunities*. PhD diss., Leiden University.

Ricks, T. E. (2006). *Fiasco: The American Military Adventure in Iraq*. London: Penguin.

Rijpma, J. A. (1997). Complexity, Tight-Coupling and Reliability: Connecting Normal Accidents Theory and High Reliability Theory. *Journal of Contingencies and Crisis Management*, 5(1): 15–23.

Roberts, J. M. (1988). *Decisionmaking During International Crises*. London: MacMillan.

Roberts, K. (ed.) (1993). *New Challenges to Understanding Organizations*. New York: MacMillan.

Rochlin, G. (ed.) (1996). New Directions in Reliable Organization Research. *Journal of Contingencies and Crisis Management*, 4(2): 55–112.

Rodriguez, H., Quarantelli, E. L., and Dynes, R. R. (eds.) (2006). *Handbook of Disaster Research*. New York: Springer.

Roe, E. and Schulman, P. R. (2008). *High Reliability Management: Operating on the Edge*. Stanford: Stanford University Press.

Rose, R. (1993). *Lesson-Drawing in Public Policy: A Guide to Learning Across Time and Space*. Chatham: Chatham House Publishers.

Rose, R. and Davies, P. L. (1994). *Inheritance in Public Policy: Change Without Choice in Britain*. New Haven: Yale University Press.

Rosenthal, U. (1998). Future disasters, Future Definitions. In E. Quarantelli, ed., *What Is a Disaster? A Dozen Perspectives on the Question*. London: Routledge, 146–60.

Rosenthal, U., Boin, R. A., and Bos, C. J. (2001). Shifting Identities: The Reconstructive Mode of the Bijlmer Plane Crash. In U. Rosenthal, R. A. Boin, and L. K. Comfort, eds., *Managing Crises: Threats, Dilemmas, Opportunities*. Springfield: Charles C. Thomas, 200–15.

Rosenthal, U., Boin, R. A., and Comfort, L. K. (eds.) (2001). *Managing Crises: Threats, Dilemmas, Opportunities*. Springfield, IL: Charles C. Thomas.

Rosenthal, U., Charles, M. T., 't Hart, P., Kouzmin, A., and Jarman, A. (1989). From Case Studies to Theory and Recommendations. In U. Rosenthal, M. T. Charles, and P. 't Hart, eds., *Coping with Crises: The Management of Disasters, Riots and Terrorism*. Springfield, IL: Charles C. Thomas, 466–67.

Rosenthal, U. and Kouzmin, A. (1997). Crises and Crisis Management: Towards Comprehensive Government Decision Making. *Journal of Public Administration Research and Theory*, 7(2): 277–304.

Rosenthal, U. and 't Hart, P. (1989). Managing Terrorism: The South Moluccan Hostage Takings. In U. Rosenthal, M. T. Charles, and P. 't Hart, eds., *Coping with Crises: The Management of Disasters, Riots and Terrorism.* Springfield, IL: Charles C. Thomas, 367–93.

Rosenthal, U., 't Hart, P., van Duin, M. J., Boin, R. A., Kroon, M. B. R., Otten, M. H. P., and Overdijk, W. I. E. (1994). *Complexity in Urban Crisis Management: Amsterdam's Response to the Bijlmer Air Disaster.* London: James & James.

Sabatier, P. A. (ed.) (1999). *Theories of the Policy Process.* Boulder, CO: Westview Press.

Sabatier, P. A. and Jenkins-Smith, H. (1993). *Policy Change and Learning: An Advocacy Coalition Approach.* Boulder, CO: Westview Press.

Sagan, S. D. (1993). *The Limits of Safety: Organizations, Accidents and Nuclear Weapons.* Princeton: Princeton University Press.

Scanlon, J. (1989). Toxic Chemicals and Emergency Management: The Evacuation of Mississauga, Ontario, Canada. In U. Rosenthal, M. T. Charles, and P. 't Hart, eds., *Coping with Crises: The Management of Disasters, Riots and Terrorism.* Springfield, IL: Charles C. Thomas, 303–21.

Schafer, M. and Crichlow, S. (2010). *Groupthink vs. High-Quality Decision Making in International Relations.* New York: Columbia University Press.

Schiffino, N., Taskin, L., Donis, C., and Raone, J. (eds) (2015). *Organizing after Crisis: The Challenge of Learning.* New York: Peter Lang.

Schmitt, C. (1985). *The Crisis of Parliamentary Democracy.* Cambridge, MA: MIT Press.

Schneider, S. K. (1993). *Flirting with Disaster: Public Management in Crisis Situations.* Armonk: Sharpe.

Schön, D. A. (1971). *Beyond the Stable State.* New York: Random House.

Schön, D. A. and Rein, M. (1994). *Frame Reflection: Toward the Resolution of Intractable Policy Controversies.* New York: Basic Books.

Schumpeter, J. A. (1943). *Capitalism, Socialism and Democracy.* London: Allen & Unwin.

Seeger, M. W., Sellnow, T. L., and Ulmer, R. R. (2003). *Communication and Organizational Crisis.* Westport: Praeger.

Seifert, C. (2007). Improving Disaster Management through Structured Flexibility among Frontline Responders. In D. E. Gibbons, ed., *Communicable Crises: Prevention, Response, and Recovery in the Global Arena.* New York: IAP, 83–116.

Sellnow, T. L. and Seeger M.W. (2013). *Theorizing Crisis Communication.* New York: Wiley.

Selznick, P. (1957). *Leadership in Administration: A Sociological Interpretation.* New York: Row-Peterson.

Senate Intelligence Committee (2004). *Report on the U.S. Intelligence Community's Prewar Intelligence Assessments on Iraq.* Washington, DC: U.S. Senate.

Shepsle, K. A. (2001). A Comment on Institutional Change. *Journal of Theoretical Politics,* 13(3): 321–25.

Shils, E. A. (1968). Ritual and Crisis. In D. R. Cutler, ed., *The Religious Situation.* Boston: Beacon Press, 730–40.

Shilts, R. (1987). *And the Band Played On: Politics, People and the AIDS Epidemic.* New York: St. Martin's Press.

Sick, G. G. (1985). *All Fall Down: America's Tragic Encounter with Iran.* New York: Random House.

Silverstein, A. M. (1981). *Pure Politics and Impure Science: The Swine Flu Affair.* Baltimore: Johns Hopkins University Press.

Simon, H. A. (1976). *Administrative Behavior: A Study of Decision Making Processes in Administrative Organization.* 3rd ed. New York: The Free Press.
  (1981). *The Sciences of the Artificial.* 2nd ed. Cambridge, MA: MIT Press.

Sinclair, T. (2012). Institutional Failure and the Global Financial Crisis. In W. Grant and G. K. Wilson, eds., *The Consequences of the Global Financial Crisis.* Cambridge: Cambridge University Press, 139–55.

Sitkin, S. B. (1992). Learning through Failure: The Strategy of Small Losses. *Research in Organizational Behavior,* 14: 231–66.

Skocpol, T. (1985). Bringing the State Back In: Strategies of Analysis in Current Research. In P. B. Evans, D. Rueschemeyer, and T. Skocpol, eds., *Bringing the State Back In.* Cambridge: Cambridge University Press, 3–37.

Smith, D. and Elliott, D. (2007). Exploring the Barriers to Learning from Crisis: Organizational Learning and Crisis. *Management Learning,* 38: 519–38.

Smith, H. (1989). *The Power Game: How Washington Works.* New York: Ballantine Books.

Solnit, R. (2009). *A Paradise Built in Hell: The Extraordinary Communities that Arise in Disaster.* New York: Viking.

Sondorp, E., Ansell, C., Stevens, R. H., and Denton, E. (2011). *Independent Evaluation of the Global Outbreak Alert and Response Network.* Geneva: World Health Organization.

Sorkin, A. R. (2010). *Too Big to Fail: The Inside Story of How Wall Street and Washington Fought to Save the Financial System – and Themselves.* New York: The Penguin Group.

Sparrow, M. (2000). *The Regulatory Craft.* Washington, DC: Brookings Institution.
  (2008). *The Character of Harms.* Cambridge: Cambridge University Press.

Staelraeve, S. and 't Hart, P. (2008). Dutroux and Dioxin: Crisis Investigations, Elite Accountability and Institutional Reform in Belgium. In R. A. Boin, A. McConnell, and P. 't Hart, eds., *Governing after Crisis: The Politics of Investigation, Accountability and Learning.* Cambridge: Cambridge University Press, 148–79.

Stallings, R. A. (1995). *Promoting Risk: Constructing the Earthquake Threat.* New York: Aldine De Gruyter.

Stark, A. (2010). Legislatures, Legitimacy and Crises. *Journal of Contingencies and Crisis Management,* 18(1): 2–13.
  (2011). The Tradition of Ministerial Responsibility and Its Role in the Bureaucratic Management of Crises. *Public Administration,* 89(3): 1148–63.

Staw, B. M. (2003). *Psychological Foundations of Organizational Behavior.* Englewood Cliffs, NJ: Prentice-Hall.

Staw, B. M., Sandelands, L. E., and Dutton J. E. (1981). Threat Rigidity Effects in Organizational Behaviour: A Multilevel Analysis. *Administrative Science Quarterly*, 26(4): 501–24.

Steinberg, T. (2000). *Acts of God: The Unnatural History of Natural Disaster in America*. New York: Oxford University Press.

Stephens, M. (1980). *Three Mile Island*. New York: Random House.

Stern, E. K. (1997a). Probing the Plausibility of Newsgroup Syndrome: Kennedy and the Bay of Pigs. In P. 't Hart, E. K. Stern, and B. Sundelius, eds., *Beyond Group-think: Political Group Dynamics and Foreign Policymaking*. Ann Arbor: University of Michigan Press, 153–89.

(1997b). Crisis and Learning: A Balance Sheet. *Journal of Contingencies and Crisis Management*, 5(2): 69–86.

(2003). Crisis Studies and Foreign Policy Analysis: Insights, Synergies, and Challenges. *International Studies Review*, 5(2): 183–202.

(2009). Crisis Navigation: Lessons from History for the Crisis Manager in Chief. *Governance*, 22, 189–202.

(2011). What the US Can Learn from the Two-Pronged Attack in Norway. www.emergencymgmt.com/safety/US-Learn-Two-Pronged-Attack-in-Norway.html (accessed September 26, 2011).

(2013). Preparing: The Sixth Task for Crisis Leadership. *Journal of Leadership Studies*, 7(3): 51–56.

(2014). *From Early Warning to Sensemaking: Identifying and Understanding Strategic Crises*. OECD High Level Risk Forum Working Paper. Paris: OECD.

(ed.) (2014). *Designing Crisis Management Research and Training for Strategic Leaders*. Stockholm: Swedish National Defence College.

Stern, E. K., Deverell, E., Fors, F., and Newlove-Eriksson, L. (2014). Post Mortem Crisis Analysis: Dissecting the London Bombings of July 2005. *Journal of Organizational Effectiveness: People and Performance*, 1: 402–22.

Stern, E. K. and Hansén, D. (eds.) (2000). *Crisis Management in a Transitional Society: The Latvian Experience*. Stockholm: Swedish National Defence College.

Stern, E. K. and Nohrstedt, D. (eds.) (1999). *Crisis Management in Estonia: Case Studies and Comparative Perspectives*. Stockholm: Swedish National Defence College.

Stern, E. K. and Sundelius, B. (1997). Sweden's Twin Monetary Crises of 1992: Rigidity and Learning in Crisis Decision Making. *Journal of Contingencies and Crisis Management*, 5(1): 32–48.

Stern, E. K., Sundelius, B., Nohrstedt, D., Hansén, D., Newlove, L., and 't Hart, P. (2002). Crisis Management in Transitional Democracies: The Baltic Experience. *Government and Opposition*, 37(4): 524–50.

Stevens, D. (2013). Redefining the Emergency Manager: A Proposal for Change. www.emergencymgmt.com/training/Redefining-the-Emergency-Manager.html (accessed June 13, 2013).

Suchman, M. C. (1995). Managing Legitimacy: Strategies and Institutional Approaches. *Academy of Management Review*, 20(3): 571–610.

Sulitzeanu-Kenan, R. (2010). Reflection in the Shadow of Blame: When Do Politicians Appoint Commissions of Inquiry? *British Journal of Political Science*, 40(2): 613–34.

Sunstein, C. and Hastie, R. (2014). *Wiser: Getting Beyond Groupthink to Make Groups Smarter*. Boston: Harvard Business School Publishing.

Svedin, L., Giacalone, R., and Jurkiewicz, C. (eds.) (2011). *Ethics and Crisis Management*. Charlotte: Information Age.

Sweeney, K. (2008). Crisis Decision Theory: Decisions in the Face of Negative Events. *Psychological Bulletin*, 134(1): 61–76.

Sylves, R. (2008). *Disaster Policy and Politics: Emergency Management and Homeland Security*. Washington, DC: CQ Press.

Sylves, R. and Cumming, W. R. (2004). FEMA's Path to Homeland Security: 1979–2003. *Journal of Homeland Security and Emergency Management*, 1(2): 1–21.

Taleb, N. N. (2007). *The Black Swan: The Impact of the Highly Improbable*. New York: Random House.

Tarrow, S. G. (1994). *Power in Movement: Social Movements, Collective Action and Politics*. Cambridge: Cambridge University Press.

Telford, J. and Cosgrave, J. (2007). The International Humanitarian System and the 2004 Indian Ocean Earthquake and Tsunamis. *Disasters*, 31(1): 1–28.

Terry, L. (1995). *Leadership of Public Bureaucracies: The Administrator as Conservator*. Thousand Oaks, CA: Sage Publications.

Tetlock, P. E. (2005). *Expert Political Judgement: How Good Is It? How Can We Know?* Princeton: Princeton University Press.

Tetlock, P. E. and Gardner, D. (2015). *Superforecasting: The Art and Science of Prediction*. New York: Crown.

Thomas, G. (1999). External Shocks, Conflict and Learning as Interactive Sources of Change in US Security Policy. *Journal of Public Policy*, 19(2): 209–31.

Thomas, W. and Thomas, D. (1928). *The Child in America: Behavior Problems and Programs*. New York: A. A. Knopf.

Thompson, J. D. (1967). *Organizations in Action: Social Science Bases of Administrative Theory*. New York: McGraw-Hill.

Thompson, P. (1999). *Persuading Aristotle*. Sydney: Allen and Unwin.

Tierney K., Lindell, M. K., and Perry, R. W. (2001). *Facing the Unexpected: Disaster Preparedness and Response in the United States*. Washington, DC: Joseph Henry Press.

Tilly, C. (2008). *Credit and Blame*. Princeton: Princeton University Press.

Tilly, C. and Stinchcombe, A. L. (1997). *Roads from Past to Future*. Lanham, MD: Rowman & Littlefield.

Torpey, J.C. (2006). *Making Whole What Has Been Smashed: On Reparations Politics*. Cambridge, MA: Harvard University Press.

Turner, B. A. (1976). The Organizational and Interorganizational Development of Disasters. *Administrative Science Quarterly*, 21(3): 378–97.

(1978). *Man-Made Disasters*. London: Wykeham.

Turner, B. A. and Pidgeon, N. (1997). *Man-Made Disasters*. 2nd ed. London: Butterworth Heinemann.

Ulmer, R. R., Seeger, T. L., and Sulnow, M. W. (2010) *Effective Crisis Communication: Moving From Crisis to Opportunity*. London: Sage.

Ulmer, R. R., Sellnow, T., and Seeger, M.W (eds.) (2015). *Effective Crisis Communication: Moving from Crisis to Opportunity*. London: Sage.

Van Duin, M. J. (1992). *Van Rampen Leren: Een Vergelijkend Onderzoek naar de Lessen uit Spoorwegongevallen, Hotelbranden en Industriële Ongelukken*. Phd diss., Leiden University.

Vaughan, D. (1996). *The Challenger Launch Decision: Risky Technology, Culture and Deviance at NASA*. Chicago: University of Chicago Press.

Verbeek, B. (2003). *Decision-Making in Great Britain During the Suez Crisis: Small Groups and a Persistent Leader*. Aldershot: Ashgate.

Vertzberger, Y. I. (1990). *The World in Their Minds: Information Processing, Cognition and Perception in Foreign Policy Decisionmaking*. Stanford: Stanford University Press.

Vizzard, W. J. (1997). *In the Crossfire: A Political History of the Bureau of Alcohol, Tobacco, and Firearms*. Boulder, CO: Lynne Rienner.

Wachtendorf, T. (2004). *Improvising 9/11: Organizational Improvisation Following the World Trade Center Disaster*. PhD diss. Delaware: University of Delaware.

Walker, S. (2015). Salutin' Putin: Inside a Russian Troll House. *The Guardian*. www.theguardian.com/world/2015/apr/02/putin-kremlin-inside-russian-troll-house (accessed April 2, 2015).

Walters, L. M., Wilkins, L., and Walters, T. (eds.) (1989). *Bad Tidings: Communication and Catastrophe*. Hillsdale, NJ: Lawrence Erlbaum Associates.

Warren, M.E. (2014). Accountability and Democracy. In M. Bovens, T. Schillemans, and R. Goodin, eds., *Oxford Handbook of Public Accountability*. Oxford: Oxford University Press, 39–54.

Waugh, W. L. (1990). *Terrorism and Emergency Management: Policy and Administration*. New York: Marcel Dekker.

(2009). Mechanisms for Collaboration in Emergency Management: ICS, NIMS and the Problem of Command and Control. In R. O'Leary and L. B. Bingham, eds., *The Collaborative Public Manager*. Washington, DC: Georgetown University Press, 157–76.

Weick, K. E. (1988). Enacted Sensemaking in Crisis Situations. *Journal of Management Studies*, 25(4): 305–17.

(1995). *Sense Making in Organizations*. Thousand Oaks, CA: Sage Publications.

(1998). Improvisation as a Mindset for Organizational Analysis. *Organization Science*, 9(5): 543–55.

Weick, K. E. and Sutcliffe, K. M. (2002). *Managing the Unexpected: Assuring High Performance in an Age of Complexity*. San Francisco: Jossey-Bass.

(2007). *Managing the Unexpected: Resilient Performance in an Age of Uncertainty*. New York: Wiley.

Weick, K. E., Sutcliffe, K. M., and Obstfeld, D. (1999). Organizing for High Reliability: Processes of Collective Mindfulness. In R. S. Sutton and B. M. Staw, eds., *Research in Organizational Behavior*, Vol. 1. Stanford: Jai Press, 81–123.

Wendling, C., J. Radisch, and S. Jacobzone (2013). The Use of Social Media in Risk and Crisis Communication. OECD Working Papers on Public Governance, No. 25. Paris: OECD Publishing.

White, R. K. (ed.) (1986). *Psychology and the Prevention of Nuclear War*. New York: New York University Press.

Wildavsky, A. B. (1984). *Speaking Truth to Power: The Art and Craft of Policy Analysis*. New Brunswick, NJ: Transaction.

(1995). *But Is It True? A Citizen's Guide to Environmental Health and Safety Issues*. Cambridge, MA: Harvard University Press.

Wildavsky, A. B. and Dake, K. (1991). Theories of Risk Perception: Who Fears What and Why? *Daedalus: Journal of the American Academy of Arts and Sciences*, 119(4): 41–59.

Wilensky, H. L. (1967). *Organizational Intelligence: Knowledge and Policy in Government and Industry*. New York: The Free Press.

Wilsford, D. (1994). Path-Dependency, or Why History Makes It Difficult, But Not Impossible to Reform Health Care Services in a Big Way. *Journal of Public Policy*, 14(3): 251–83.

Wilson, J. Q. (1989) *Bureaucracy*. New York: The Free Press.

Woodward, B. and Bernstein, C. (1994). *All the President's Men*. New York: Simon and Schuster.

Wukich, C. (2015). Social Media Use in Emergency Management. *Journal of Emergency Management*, 13(4): 281–94.

Zahariadis, N. (2014). Leading Reform Amidst Crises: Lessons From Greece. *Public Administration*, 91(3): 648–62.

Zelikow, P. and Rice, C. (1995). *Germany Unified and Europe Transformed: A Study of Statecraft*. Cambridge, MA: Harvard University Press.

Index